Mindful Eating from the Dialectical Perspective

Mindful Eating from the Dialectical Perspective is both a research reference and exhaustive guide to implementing a practice of mindful eating grounded in dialectical behavior therapy. This informative and timely new resource balances a presentation of empirical data with thorough and engaging instruction for hands-on application that features an innovative forbidden foods hierarchy construction. This invaluable guide makes the empirically supported approach accessible for therapists and anyone struggling with patterns of unbalanced eating.

Angela Klein, Ph.D., earned her doctorate in clinical psychology from the University of Missouri, Columbia, in 2009. Prior to this she began her study of eating disorders and psychology through the honors program at Kent State University, completing her B.A., with a minor in women's studies, as valedictorian, in 2002. As both a researcher and practitioner, Angela has had extensive experience delivering and conducting treatment trials emphasizing effectiveness in the real world, including her development and investigation of the mindful eating program presented in this book. She began specializing in dialectical behavior therapy (DBT) in 2004. She is also now actively engaged in radically open (RO) DBT, becoming one of the first intensively trained RO therapists in the U.S. in 2015. Her evidence-based approach retains perspectives from cognitive behavior therapy, balanced with Eastern wisdom. She has multiple journal publications in the field of eating disorders and has presented her research both nationally and internationally. She founded and directs her private practice, Centered Ground, providing individual therapy, family therapy, group skills training classes, and coaching support to adolescents and adults in the greater San Diego area, offering her expertise in DBT, RO, and mindful eating from the dialectical perspective.

Mindful Eating from the Dialectical Perspective
Research and Application

Angela Klein, Ph.D.

Routledge
Taylor & Francis Group

NEW YORK AND LONDON

First published 2017
by Routledge
711 Third Avenue, New York, NY 10017

and by Routledge
2 Park Square, Milton Park, Abingdon, Oxon, OX14 4RN

*Routledge is an imprint of the Taylor & Francis Group,
an informa business*

© 2017 Taylor & Francis

The right of Angela Klein to be identified as author of this work
has been asserted by her in accordance with sections 77 and 78 of
the Copyright, Designs and Patents Act 1988.

Library of Congress Cataloging in Publication Data
Names: Klein, Angela, 1981- author.
Title: Mindful eating from the dialectical perspective : research
and application / by Angela Klein.
Description: New York, NY : Routledge, 2016.
Includes bibliographical references and index.
Identifiers: LCCN 2016031777 | ISBN 9781138915909
(hbk : alk. paper) | ISBN 9781138915916 (pbk : alk. paper) |
ISBN 9781315689722 (ebk)
Subjects: | MESH: Feeding and Eating Disorders--therapy |
Mindfulness
Classification:
LCC RC552.E18
NLM WM 175
DDC 616.85/26--dc23
LC record available at https://lccn.loc.gov/2016031777

ISBN: 978-1-138-91590-9 (hbk)
ISBN: 978-1-138-91591-6 (pbk)
ISBN: 978-1-315-68972-2 (ebk)

Typeset in Sabon
by Saxon Graphics Ltd, Derby

Visit the eResources: www.routledge.com/9781138915909

This book is dedicated to my clients—past, present, and future, including the readers of these pages. I am forever grateful for the gift of being able to help guide you in your courageous journey. You have shaped this program and my own life in return. Thank you.

Contents

Preface

"Ah, interesting… Mindful eating… How do you define it? What is your approach? Do you talk about what foods to avoid, like gluten and dairy, or encourage focusing more on whole foods or organic? And why mindful eating? How did you come to this?"

I have grown used to this response over the process of writing this book when I have shared this with others. Likewise, it is a recurring line of questioning concerning my specialty in this area from new acquaintances and clients. In the pages ahead I will, of course, define my approach to mindful eating from the dialectical perspective and how it most certainly is not about what foods to avoid or what to focus on more. So, then, why and how did I come to this topic and book?

This question reminds me of when I ask clients what brings them to therapy when they present for a first intake session. This often prompts the question from them of "Where would you like me to start?" The answer can be very distal, if really traced to its roots, or more proximal, if limited to the more immediate context.

In my case, the chain of events perhaps originated more than 20 years ago. Growing up in a small town, I discovered a passion for writing. I wrote short stories and poems and dreamed of writing for the *New York Times* as an international correspondent. My front yard was a cornfield and the kitchen a cornucopia of home-cooked abundance.

Then I started middle school. A classmate noticeably started shrinking away and rumors were whispered that she had anorexia. The malady then surreptitiously seemed to spread to a male classmate and a slightly older male friend of my family. And then, on my fifteenth birthday, I found myself sitting in a therapist's office, my mother sobbing on one side of me, my dad stoic on the other, being told that my weight was dangerously low and reversing this was imperative through treatment that would include individual, group, and family therapy; medical monitoring; and meal planning under a dietician.

I was not exactly pleased by all of this and did not find it very helpful. I ultimately did want to move past the unbalanced eating patterns I had developed and yet, when I met with my therapists, they blocked me from talking about eating or food. Now that I am trained as a psychologist, I have a sense of the approach they were perhaps trying to take, and yet, on my side of the therapy room at the time, it was simply utterly frustrating and felt unsophisticated and invalidating.

And then I was literally fired by my physician. He said that my weight had plateaued and I was not cooperating, although I was medically stable at my persistently low weight. He said he could do nothing more to help me. With this, I discontinued all therapy. And while a large part of my teenage self relished being set free, with a sense of somehow winning against what was being imposed on me, another part of me recognized that I was not really free at all—that more than ever I needed to figure out how to find my own way out of my suffering, both with eating and the intertwined emotions.

By the end of my first year of college I took this even further and decided that I was being called to figure this out in such a way that I could help others. I changed my major from journalism to psychology and sought out Janis Crowther to begin studying disordered eating in the laboratory as an undergraduate honors student, my thesis topic investigating cognitions associated with forbidden and unforbidden foods in restrained and unrestrained eaters. I then progressed to graduate school, for my Ph.D. in clinical psychology, to focus on treatment research.

Along this journey, before leaving home for college, I spiraled into binge eating, classically drawn to the very foods I deemed forbidden: candy bars, cookies, and cartons of ice cream. When I was under extreme stress, this numbed the emotional pain, at least for a while, until the fog lifted and then the guilt and shame piled on top of the previous despair. Transition and relationship losses were especially triggering.

By the time I got to graduate school, I somehow had reached the conclusion that moving past my unbalanced eating would require facing every single food I judged and becoming O.K. with it. And I knew instinctually that I needed to do this in a gradual manner, taking it one food at a time, so that I would not feel overwhelmed and revert to binge eating. A budding scientist, I approached it systematically. And, of course, my life continued to unfold along the way, with many ups and downs and ample emotions to face. I continued to desensitize myself and learn new ways of coping, of taking care of myself, of relaxing and allowing myself to have some fun every now and then.

I found dialectical behavior therapy (DBT) through my first client. She was self-harming, suicidal, and struggling with binge eating, restricting, and self-induced vomiting. We began with traditional cognitive behavioral interventions. These helped reduce her eating disorder symptoms to a certain extent, but her self-harm and suicidality persisted and eating-related concerns still lingered. My supervisor at the time therefore suggested I join the new consultation team at my clinic for training in DBT to better address her self-harm and suicidality. I hesitated, given the extent of the commitment—to basically be on call for coaching 24/7—and given my judgment and skepticism, having walked away from my only DBT training experience thus far (a seminar that introduced mindfulness with a singing bowl I scoffed at) thinking "I will never do DBT." And now look at me!

Joining the DBT team at my training clinic, I was soon converted. Really learning the approach, and adopting it in my own life, truly changed my life and became how I lived. Its similar impact on that first client of mine and then the others who followed was undeniable.

While still working with my first client, mostly applying DBT to her self-harm and suicidality at the same time as continuing traditional cognitive behavior therapy (CBT) interventions for her continued eating disorder symptoms, I found myself sitting in a small workshop at one of the main international conferences on eating disorders. Lucene Wisniewski was presenting on DBT for eating disorders. Little did I know how that one talk would propel the course of my path. As she spoke about applying DBT specifically to eating disorders, I literally felt like I was going to cry. "These people get it. This is exactly what we need to be doing with eating disorders," I thought. The emphasis on validation, balanced with concrete strategies to foster change, and behavioral focus on eating behaviors as the main targets of treatment was a striking contrast to my own experience in therapy years earlier and also a contrast to the CBT approach for eating disorders that I had learned thus far in graduate school. Then and there I decided to further develop and research DBT adapted for eating disorders. This ultimately fully resolved my first client's eating disorder symptoms and became my dissertation, beginning with an uncontrolled trial and then a randomized trial design. The resulting program is the foundation of this book, fusing my own personal experience with rigorous research support.

Providing this program thereafter across a variety of settings, and now in my own clinic in private practice, I continue to refine and evolve its nuance. I have also expanded its delivery to varied presentations, including adolescents. With ongoing assessment to evaluate outcomes objectively, the impact it demonstrates on establishing new patterns of mindful eating remains consistent without wavering.

Receiving the invitation to write this book, I was ecstatic. Not only would I be able to finally write my first book but it would provide a vehicle to reach a much wider audience with this life-changing program, beyond my therapy office. In reviewing both the latest research supporting this approach and providing materials for practice, my intended audience includes academics, students, therapists, and anyone seeking a tested guide to foster greater balance with eating. The hands-on monitoring forms and worksheets are also available for download in a larger, printable format from www.routledge.com/9781138915916, provided to further support readers in applying this empirically reinforced approach.

Personally, I have left binge eating far in the past. I have fully completed my forbidden foods hierarchy and practice dialectical mindfulness not only as a way to eat, each and every day, but also as a way of life. I am still a work in progress when it comes to emotion. I believe we all are. And I use the tools in this book every day to continue in my journey.

I refused to give up on myself and consider it my duty to not give up on my clients. This includes you. If you are struggling, I urge you to not give up on yourself. Overcoming your patterns may feel impossible and I assure you it is not. Above all, be kind to yourself and compassionate. You are strong. You can overcome whatever is keeping you stuck. Keep going, even if you are crawling. Every moment is an opportunity to start again. And I am here with you to walk or crawl beside you. Please give yourself this gift—to create a new relationship with food and yourself, grounded in mindful nonjudgment, openness, and dialectical flexibility to truly nourish yourself, to honor what your emotion is trying to tell you, to live this life, your life, both in this moment and moving towards how you want it to be, for only then will your hunger truly be quenched.

1   The Open Table

All too often food is the target of judgment. It is, in perhaps its most basic definition, nourishment required to sustain life, and yet so often in modern times making decisions about food can feel like navigating a minefield. Of course, it makes sense that we are hardwired to evaluate what is "good" or "bad" to eat when it comes to deciphering what is edible and inedible. This would help us survive, for example, guiding us to nutritive options and protecting us from poisonous or spoiled intake. However, in modern times, food-related judgment is rarely about such imminently critical determinations. Instead, we often judge whether or not to eat certain foods based on our judgment of how they will impact our long-term health and mortality. More proximally, we make decisions based on our judgment of how they will impact our weight and appearance.

When I was growing up the devil was fat and anything low fat was heralded as the path to health and weight loss, with thinness revered as the symbolic embodiment of health and attractiveness. Consequently, carbohydrates, such as pasta, were considered a mainstay in dieting and items branded reduced fat or low fat were "safe." Margarine was certainly better than butter, and egg yolks were definitely off limits—egg whites only please! Then the tide turned with the Atkins craze, claiming that carbs were actually the problem and limitless quantities of bacon were much better. Somehow I could never really make the shift to that perspective. Nowadays I find myself being assaulted with more nuanced messages about the critical importance of high protein and organic, natural foods, with a mounting tide against the horrors of gluten, sugar, dairy, processed foods, and genetically modified organisms (GMOs).

All of the rules about what one should and should not eat can be paralyzing and leave consumers staring blankly at the wall of products in the grocery store aisle, unable to process the massive array of options, each calling for analysis to determine whether it passes the tests of acceptability. Even choosing where to shop can be daunting. Retailers heralded as organic and natural can be intimidating in their higher prices, again challenging more mainstream shoppers to divine the best choices within their budget. Deciphering nutrition labeling can be another rather disheartening quest. Of course, navigating this web of rules extends beyond the grocery store, to the many settings in which we eat, from myriad menus—extensive café boards offering just the right vehicles for responsible or indulgent caffeinating; hardbound restaurant menus that look more like novelettes, sometimes even illustrated; food truck line-ups; fast food displays with scratchy voices from a speaker taking our order—to potlucks at work, parties and gatherings, holiday feasts, and our own kitchen table.

Judgments about food can serve as rules. Rules provide a shorthand strategy for making decisions across situations more efficiently. For example, if one has a rule that gluten is forbidden, this quickly eliminates a number of items on most menus, narrowing down the choices to what is gluten-free. Similarly, if one has a rule that dairy is forbidden, this quite rapidly diminishes the options at any standard ice cream parlor. Basing decisions on such rules speeds up cognitive processing. This serves a purpose, since we usually have many other demands on our time beyond food and eating. However, when we use rules to make decisions, this takes us out of the present moment and the specific, unique context of that moment and, when it comes to eating especially, it can backfire.

On the Continuum: Restriction and Binge Eating

Research has suggested that there is a continuum of eating, ranging from balanced, unrestrained eating at one end to eating disorders at the other end (Butow, Beumont, & Touyz, 1993). The boundaries between pathology on this continuum are not necessarily entirely clear. At its most extreme, disordered eating can be categorized into anorexia nervosa (AN) and bulimia nervosa (BN), although the line between these disorders is not always straightforward. For example, restriction, binge eating, and purging, such as self-induced vomiting, diuretic and laxative abuse, and excessive exercise, can characterize both AN (binge/purge subtype) and BN. The American Psychiatric Association (APA) blurred the lines even further in 2013 by removing the classic distinguishing AN characteristics of emaciation (weight below certain thresholds, such as a body mass index of 17.5) and amenorrhea (the cessation of menses for at least three months) from the diagnostic criteria for AN. Furthermore, crossover between diagnoses is relatively common (e.g., Eddy et al., 2008; Peterson et al., 2011) and empirically derived classifications include alternative variants not necessarily captured in the current APA diagnostic system (e.g., Cain, Epler, Steinley, & Sher, 2010b; 2012; Crow et al., 2012; Dechartes et al., 2011; Peterson et al., 2011; Swanson et al., 2014; Wildes, Forbush, & Markon, 2013; for a summary see Wonderlich, Joiner, Keel, Williamson, & Crosby, 2007). Moreover, clinical presentations of disordered eating outside the defined categories of AN and BN comprise the greatest percentages of treatment seekers and have been repeatedly found to experience levels of detriment similar to diagnosable eating disorders (e.g., Andersen, Bowers, & Watson,

2001; Crow, Agras, Halmi, Mitchell, & Kraemer, 2002; Jorgensen, 1992; Le Grange et al., 2006; Martin, Williamson, & Thaw, 2000; Ricca et al., 2001; Striegel-Moore et al., 2000; Swanson, Crow, Le Grange, Swendsen, & Merikangas, 2011; Turner & Bryant-Waugh, 2004). This has driven an even greater movement towards conceptualizing disordered eating on a continuum, with many researchers and clinicians now adopting a transdiagnostic approach (Fairburn, Cooper, & Shafran, 2003).

All this having been said, somewhere between unrestrained eating and disordered eating is restrained eating. Restrained eating can be defined as purposely restricting food intake, typically due to weight or shape preoccupation. Restrained eating classically involves dividing food into the dichotomy of forbidden or unforbidden based on the perceived nutritional properties of the food, such as fat, sugar, and calories. For example, a candy bar, which is high in fat, sugar, and calories, may be judged to be forbidden, while lettuce, which is low in fat, sugar, and calories, may be judged to be unforbidden. From the continuum perspective, restrained eating can thus stand alone, while it can also be a symptom of greater pathology when crossing over into diagnosable eating disorders (combined with other symptoms to form a clinical constellation).

Binge eating is another pattern of eating that can stand alone as problematic or occur within diagnosable disorders, including AN, BN, and binge eating disorder (BED), officially included in the diagnostic nomenclature of the APA as of 2013. Binge eating can be either objective or subjective.

Objective binge eating can be defined as the consumption, in a limited period of time, such as two hours, of an amount of food that would be considered unusually large compared to what most individuals would consume in similar circumstances, along with at least several of the following characteristics: (a) eating much more rapidly than usual; (b) eating until feeling uncomfortably full; (c) eating large amounts of food when not physically hungry; (d) eating alone because of being embarrassed by what or how much one is eating; (e) feeling disgusted with oneself, depressed, or very guilty after overeating (Spitzer et al., 1993).

Given that the consumption of large amounts of food is so often a common thread woven into the modern social fabric, context is really critical for this definition. For example, according to this definition, it is possible to plow through multiple plates of food at the buffet and enjoy the bounty at holiday meals without the eating being a binge because in these situations, most or at least many people would consume a similar amount of food. Indeed, an all-you-can-eat buffet invites you to literally eat all you can, and when it comes to holidays, the centerpiece of celebrations is often the menu, from the parade of food at Thanksgiving, the turkey heralding the way like the opening of the Macy's Thanksgiving Day Parade, to the barbeques that are now seemingly synonymous with summer holidays, from Memorial Day to the Fourth of July to Labor Day, and the plethora of religious holidays, with their traditions of cherished dishes and desserts.

It is still possible to binge eat in such circumstances, but for objective binge eating this would require clearly exceeding cultural norms, along with the requisite additional characteristics outlined above.

Likewise, when large servings are presented or packaged in a manner that suggests individual consumption, such as an a la carte menu item at a restaurant or a container of ice cream that fits into your hand so easily, it is arguably within reason to enjoy the portion presented, even if it would be otherwise categorized as multiple servings by caloric or nutritional yardsticks. This means that it is possible to eat a pint of Ben and Jerry's or consume a massive entrée platter or serving bowl filled with a box of pasta when eating out and not be objectively binge eating.

In contrast, eating plate after plate of food at home on a regular weekday or more than a pint of ice cream would fall outside the definition of normative consumption in similar circumstances, meeting the criterion for an unusually large amount of food. At the same time, to be defined as binge eating, such behavior would still need to be accompanied by a sense of loss of control and several of the additional qualitative characteristics outlined above. Otherwise, the behavior may more accurately be termed overeating.

Subjective binge eating can be defined as eating an amount of food that would not be considered objectively large compared to what most individuals would consume in similar circumstances, but feeling out of control and experiencing several of the additional qualitative characteristics outlined above. In this case, cognitions—and, more specifically, judgments, are key. With subjective binge eating, someone can claim that they are binge eating when they are eating anything that is not within their definition of approval. For example, if sugar is considered forbidden, a binge could consist of one cookie or even a bite of a cookie; if only non-fat dressing is considered acceptable, eating a salad with a teaspoon of regular dressing could be a binge.

Grazing is another variant of overeating. Grazing refers to repetitive eating of unplanned, small amounts of food over a more extended period of time than a binge (for example, over the course of a day), accumulating to an objectively large amount of food, with a sense of loss of control (Carter & Jansen, 2012; Lane & Szabo, 2013; Saunders, 1999; 2004). For example, this could include a sense or pattern of eating more or less continuously throughout the day or during extended parts of the day (e.g., all afternoon; Lane & Szabo, 2013). While eating smaller portions throughout the day may be touted as a balanced form of eating to replace a more traditional pattern of three larger meals, grazing in this way, again, is accompanied by a sense of loss of control that distinguishes it as a more problematic pattern.

Theories of Restriction and Binge Eating

Several theories have been posited regarding the role of judgment in perpetuating restrained and disordered eating, including the Boundary

Model of Compensation (Polivy, Herman, Olmsted, & Jazwinski, 1984), Restraint theory (Harnden, McNally, & Jimerson, 1997), the Spiral Model (Heatherton & Polivy, 1992), and Vitousek and Hollon's (1990) Weight-Related Self-Schemata Model.

The Boundary Model of Compensation

The Boundary Model of Compensation suggests that restrained eaters regulate food consumption according to cognitive parameters, while unrestrained eaters predominantly use internal cues (Polivy et al., 1984). According to this model, unrestrained eaters essentially consume food when hungry and stop when sated. However, restrained eaters restrict their intake according to dietary rules, such as caloric limits. The maximum amount of food allowed determines the upper boundary of acceptable dietary consumption.

For restrained eaters, dietary disruptions then trigger eating more. This can be referred to as capitulating, which, defined colloquially, is the "screw it" factor or, more severely, the "fuck it" factor—basically thinking, "Well, I've already blown it, screw it, I might as well really go for it!" This is a form of imbalanced, all-or-nothing thinking.

Disruption can occur from consumption of a quantity of food perceived to be unacceptable; consumption of a forbidden food; stress; alcohol or other substance; or some other mechanism that overcomes cognitive inhibitions. The upper boundary of consumption for restrained eaters is then satiety. The upper boundary of consumption for individuals with eating disorders is nausea, physical inability to eat any more, or the termination of food availability (i.e., all the food is gone).

Restraint theory

Restraint theory emphasizes the role of cognition in eating as well (Harnden et al., 1997). According to Wegner, Schneider, Carter, & White (1987), suppression of a thought activates two opposing processes—Intentional Operating Process and Ironic Operating Process. Intentional Operating Process consciously searches for cognitive material unrelated to the suppressed thought, while Ironic Operating Process is consistently vigilant for the unwanted thought and ready to alert the individual if the thought occurs. As a result of the two processes contradicting each other, Intentional Operating Process falters, and, as a rebound effect, the individual experiences the thought even more frequently. According to this theory, suppressing thoughts about weight, food, and body shape actually increases such thoughts, leading to a preoccupation with weight, food, and body shape (Harnden et al., 1997). Furthermore, if an individual suppresses thoughts about their own weight and body shape, such thoughts will actually increase, leading to a preoccupation with his or her own weight and body shape. This preoccupation may motivate and sustain restrained eating. However, the continual bombardment of weight-, food-, and body-shape-related thoughts may cause breaks in willpower and thus lead to disinhibited eating.

The Spiral Model

Heatherton & Polivy's (1992) Spiral Model describes a spiral of increasingly damaged self-esteem with chronic dieting that can cascade into the development of eating disorders. This spiral is fueled by judgment, often starting when individuals compare their weight or shape to their perceived ideals, prompting restricted eating if there is a perceived deviation judged to be in need of change. In contrast, such comparison is less likely to trigger restricted eating if individuals perceive no deviance from their ideals, or if they determine any perceived deviation as not cause for change. According to the theory and supporting research, low self-esteem further heightens vulnerability to restricted eating.

Then, because dieting seldom results in significant or lasting weight loss, most individuals who begin dieting will experience dietary failure. If individuals attribute failure to internal deficits, such as lack of willpower or effort, they may continue to diet, increasing their efforts to succeed. Unfortunately, increased efficiency in metabolic response increases the difficulty in achieving and sustaining weight loss. Thus, successive attempts at dieting often lead to successive failures. These failures can then diminish self-esteem and increase negative affect.

Furthermore, through this process individuals can become increasingly reliant on cognitive guidelines and rules for eating rather than internal cues, such as hunger. This increases their vulnerability to external eating cues and may lead to overeating in response to such cues. Overeating then prompts more dieting.

Clearly this is a vicious hamster wheel that leads to nowhere productive. Moreover, this spiral can, at its most extreme, promote increasingly pathological behavior, including more extreme restriction, fasting, excessive exercising, and even purging—patterns that can ultimately develop into diagnosable eating disorders.

Weight-Related Self-Schemata Model

Vitousek and Hollon (1990) suggest that individuals with eating disorders have weight-related self-schemata. These schemata combine views of the self with information about weight. Weight and body shape serve as the predominant determinants of personal value. Dissatisfaction with the self is deflected onto the body. Cognitive representations take the form of rules that follow the format of "If I am fat (or thin), I am ... , I cannot (can) ..., and I will be revealed as ..." (p. 197). Fatness is associated with personal faults and flaws, and thinness is associated with self-control, virtue, beauty, and intelligence. According to this theory, in comparison with individuals who do not have eating disorders, individuals with eating disorders attach richer connotations to fatness, thinness, weight gain, and weight loss; construe themselves and others in more extreme terms; possess more detailed information about certain aspects of food and weight; possess more confidence about the correctness of their convictions about weight; view their beliefs about weight as particularly pertinent to the self; and assign a greater importance to weight-related domains and thus are more pleased by successes and distressed by failures related to these domains.

Psychological Consequences of Restriction: Research Findings

The White Bear effect

In a seminal study on thought suppression now known as the White Bear Experiment, Wegner and colleagues (1987) introduced a framework for understanding the impact of cognitive avoidance related to Intentional Operating Process and Ironic Operating Process. In this paradigm, participants in the experimental group were instructed to think about anything at all except a white bear and to indicate if they did think about a white bear by ringing a bell. They were also asked to share their thoughts aloud at the same time. What happened then was a fair amount of bell ringing and white bears showing up in the streams of verbalized thoughts (more than once per minute over the course of the five minutes of the task).

Participants were then told that they could think about anything at all and again, to verbalize their thoughts and indicate if they thought of a white bear by ringing a bell. Participants then verbalized more white bears and rang the bell more than participants who were not first instructed to not think about a white bear (the comparison group). In other words, there was a rebound effect from attempting to suppress the thoughts, such that the thoughts increased, compared to conditions without attempted suppression.

Subsequent studies suggest that the White Bear effect worsens with distraction (e.g., Arndt, Greenberg, Solomon, Pyszczynski, & Simon, 1997; Newman, Duff, & Baumeister, 1997; Page, Locke, & Trio, 2005, Wegner & Erber, 1992). For example, Wegner and Erber (1992) assigned participants to either suppress or focus on a particular target word; under each condition participants then engaged in a color-naming task (Stroop, 1935) while instructed to repeat either a nine-digit number (high cognitive load) or a one-digit number (low cognitive load). Stroop performance was worse, with more reporting of the target word, in the suppression condition with high cognitive load.

Relatedly, even earlier research similarly found that participants continued to report color associations when instructed to avoid making these associations. This suggested that they failed to cognitively block the associations, and the threat of being shocked for making the associations did not prevent this (McGranahan, 1940; Sears & Virshup, cited in Sears, 1943). Of course, paradoxically, perhaps the threat of shock made attempts at blocking even more difficult because then the cost of making the mistake was higher and so emotion was running higher, likely impairing efficiency.

Najmi and Wegner (2008) further demonstrated the White Bear effect in a cognitive accessibility paradigm. These researchers instructed participants to either suppress a thought or focus on it; under either condition participants then completed a task measuring reaction time influenced by priming. Participants in the thought suppression condition responded more quickly when primed with a word associated with the suppressed word. In contrast, priming with the suppressed thought did not increase reaction time for associated words. The researchers posited that these results reflect increased cognitive accessibility with movement towards the suppressed thought from associated words, while movement away from the suppressed thought to associated words is compromised. Again, the effect was most pronounced under high cognitive load (instructed repetition of a nine-digit number vs. a one-digit number (low cognitive load)).

The White Bear Experiment has been replicated and its implications supported across many investigations (e.g., see Abramowitz, Tolin, & Street, 2001; Beevers, Wenzlaff, Hayes, & Scott, 1999; Rassin, 2005; Shackelford, Wegner, & Schneider, 1987; Wenzlaff & Wegner, 2000), including electrophysiological corroboration for Ironic Processing (Giuliano & Wicha, 2010), and extended to eating-related concerns (Erskine & Georgiou, 2010; Soetens & Braet, 2006; Soetens, Braet, & Moens, 2008; Soetens, Braet, Van Vlierberghe, & Roets, 2008). For example, Soetens and Braet (2006) found a cognitive rebound effect for thoughts of food in clinically obese restrained eaters. This effect occurred after researchers instructed the participants to suppress their thoughts about food. In contrast, no rebound effect occurred when the researchers asked participants to simply monitor their thoughts.

Both laboratory studies and studies in the naturalistic environment have also compared the cognitions of restrained eaters, unrestrained eaters, and disordered eaters in content, valence, and frequency as measures of preoccupation with food, weight, and body shape. Interestingly, initial studies using thought monitoring and questionnaires found differences to be most pronounced with eating (Bonifazi & Crowther, 1996; Hickford, Ward, & Bulik, 1997; Lingswiler, Crowther, & Stephens, 1989; Zotter & Crowther, 1991), even when eating what would generally be considered ordinary foods (Kirkley, Burge, & Ammerman, 1988; Woody, Costanzo, Liefer, & Conger, 1981). That is, greater preoccupation with food, eating, weight, and body image characterized the cognitions of restrained eaters and disordered eaters, compared to unrestrained eaters, when they were eating or about to eat, but not necessarily when they were not eating. Interpreted along with the White Bear Experiment, this could be a result of a rebound effect. That is, if individuals are at least temporarily succeeding in their restriction by not eating at that time and avoiding cues related to food, eating, weight, and body image, it is possible that then when eating cues occur, they experience a rebound effect similar to the rebound of white bears, but instead related to food, eating, weight, and body image.

Indeed, Soetens, Braet, and Moens (2008) compared scores of thought suppression and intrusion in restrained and unrestrained eaters using the White Bear Suppression Inventory (WBSI; Wegner & Zanakos, 1994) and the Thought Control Questionnaire (TCQ; Wells & Davies, 1994). They further categorized the restrained eaters based on degree of dietary inhibition, forming groups of disinhibited restrained eaters, inhibited restrained eaters, and unrestrained eaters. The results showed meaningfully higher WBSI scores in disinhibited restrained eaters compared to the other groups overall and for thought suppression and intrusion. High WBSI scores were also associated with high TCQ scores for the subscales of distraction, worry, and punishment.

Research also points to neural correlates of thought suppression (Mitchell et al., 2007; Wyland, Kelley, Macrae, Gordon, & Heatherton, 2003), linking thought suppression to the dorsolateral prefrontal cortex (PFC) and the occurrence of unwanted thoughts to activation in the anterior cingulate cortex (ACC). Interestingly, results indicate more diffuse activation, including the insular cortex, when participants received instructions to suppress all thoughts versus a particular thought (Wyland et al., 2003). Of note, the gray matter volume of the ACC has been shown to be reduced in AN compared to healthy controls, even after weight restoration (Freiderich et al., 2012; Muhlau et al., 2007) and multiple studies have found hypoactivation in the ACC with AN (Zastrow et al., 2009). In contrast, studies have found hyperactivation in the ACC with BN for both non-food and food-related cues (Lock, Garrett, Beenhakker, & Reiss, 2011; Schienle, Schafer, Hermann, & Vaitl, 2009). Further research is needed to elucidate the impact of this related to thought suppression in BED, BN, and AN, both acutely and in weight recovery.

The Pendulum between Famine and Feast

Research supports theories linking restriction and excessive consumption, such as binge eating. Franklin, Schiele, Brozek, and Keys (1948) provide one of the earliest reports of diet-induced binge eating. These researchers conducted a study of dieting in young men who were conscientious objectors to World War II and deemed to be normal (i.e., mentally, physically, and socially "healthy") according to extensive screening. They restricted the participants' intake on a reduced-calorie diet until they weighed 74 percent of their initial weight. They then permitted the men to resume unrestrained eating and weight restore. The men then exhibited the tendency of objective binge eating at meals when exposed to readily available food that had been previously restricted. The researchers described the men's binge eating after resumption of unrestricted eating and weight restoration as "attempts to avoid wasting even a particle... in the face of unlimited supplies of immediately available food. An irrational fear that food would not be available or that the opportunity to eat would somehow be taken away from them was present" (Polivy et al., 1984, p. 115). Consequently, they "ate more food than they were prepared to cope with," making themselves sick (p. 115).

The physiological effects of restricted eating arguably influence overeating and binge eating in restrained eating and eating disorders. For example, restrained eaters have been found to salivate more than unrestrained eaters in response to attractive food cues, and levels of motilin, which causes gastric emptying and thus reduces bloating, have also been found to increase in restrained eaters before and after eating (Brunstrom, Yates, & Witcomb, 2004; Polivy & Herman, 1985). Interestingly, increased salivation seems linked with the variable dieting associated with binge eating and BN rather than the unrelenting dieting in restricting AN (LeGoff, Leichner, & Spigelman, 1988).

Physiological influences on lowered inhibitions to eating and heightened internal pressures to eat are also not necessarily predictive of the amount of food eaten on any given occasion. For example, Klajner, Herman, Polivy, and Chhanbra (1981) found that despite their heightened salivary response to the cues of freshly baked pizza and chocolate chip cookies, restrained eaters did not overeat either the pizza or cookies. It is possible that this is due to lack of specificity in the food presented—that is, that if individuals are presented with a food item they have specifically been working on restricting, rather than general restraint, they would overeat. This hypothesis is supported by findings from Polivy, Coleman, and Herman (2005) that participants assigned to deprive themselves of chocolate for a week then ate more chocolate in a taste test than participants not assigned to restrict chocolate the preceding week. Similarly, there is evidence linking the combination of restraint and disinhibition with the greatest consumption after restriction of a favorite food item followed by presentation of the food item (Soetens, Braet, Van Vlierberghe, & Roets, 2008).

Research suggests that cognitive factors play a greater role than physiological factors in determining intake on a given occasion (e.g., Polivy et al., 1984). In particular, the counterregulation of restrained eaters seems to be mediated by cognitions. Counterregulation refers to the increase in food intake following consumption of food perceived to be high in calories. This differs from regulation, or the decrease in food intake following consumption of food that is perceived to be high in calories. Researchers have investigated this by administering a preload—an initial food prior to further consumption—to restrained and unrestrained eaters, then measuring their subsequent consumption (Polivy, 1976; Spencer & Fremouw, 1979; Woody et al., 1981). Results indicated that restrained eaters ate little after the preload if they believed they had ingested relatively few calories, but more if they believed they had consumed a high number of calories. Unrestrained eaters exhibited the opposite effect, eating only slightly after a preload that was labeled as high in calories and more if a preload was labeled lower in calories.

Lingswiler and colleagues' (1989) study comparing individuals with BN, binge eaters, and unrestrained eaters linked dichotomous cognitions about food (e.g., all-or-nothing, black-and-white judgments or rules about food being good or bad) to binge eating. Participants recorded detailed information about the antecedents to their eating and what and how much they ate at each sitting. Individuals with BN were found to have more dichotomous thinking than unrestrained eaters prior to eating in general (whether or not binge eating), and this effect was also found when comparing the thinking of binge eaters to unrestrained eaters prior to bingeing and eating (but not bingeing), respectively. Likewise, the most dichotomous thinking preceded binge eating, distinguished from cognitions prior to eating but not bingeing, for both individuals with BN and binge eaters. These findings are consistent with a continuum model of eating, with increasingly pervasive and unbalanced thinking with increasingly disordered eating.

In a more direct demonstration of a link between thought suppression and eating, Erskine and Georgiou (2010) examined the effects of three different conditions on subsequent consumption of chocolate under the guise of a taste test. The researchers assigned the participants to one of the three conditions. In the first condition the researchers asked participants to suppress thoughts about chocolate, in the second, participants were asked to think about chocolate, and in the third, participants were told to think about anything they desired. All participants then proceeded to a taste test that was presented as a separate study, but their intake was actually monitored. What happened was that restrained eaters who had been asked to suppress thoughts about chocolate consumed significantly more chocolate than restrained eaters in the other conditions. In contrast, no difference in consumption emerged across conditions among participants low in restraint. Participants with higher WBSI scores on thought suppression also reported more chocolate cravings.

Research examining associations between dieting and either objective or subjective binge eating further suggest that it is cognitive factors rather than physiological that account for dieting lapses triggering increased consumption, with findings that this consumption may not be to a degree that would be considered objectively large (Kerzhnerman & Lowe, 2002). Indeed the very definition of subjective binge eating suggests that cognitions do not inevitably trigger consumption of large amounts of food, as in objective binge eating—and yet, the psychological impact can be just as damaging or worse (Birgegard, Clinton, & Norring, 2013; Brownstone et al., 2012; Dalle Grave, Calugi, & Marchesini, 2012; Kerzhnerman & Lowe, 2002; Shomaker et al., 2010). This has been demonstrated in both adult (Birgegard et al., 2013; Brownstone et al., 2012; Dalle Grave et al.,

2012; Kerzhnerman & Lowe, 2002) and pediatric samples (Dalle Grave et al., 2012; Shomaker et al., 2010) with outcomes suggesting similar rates with objective binge eating and subjective binge eating for disordered eating attitudes, emotional eating, eating in the absence of hunger, depressive and anxiety symptoms, adiposity, and low self-directedness, and similar treatment outcomes. Furthermore, the labeling of an incident of eating as a binge is a stronger predictor of purging behavior than whether consumption can be labeled an objective binge, consisting of an objectively large amount of food (Gleaves, Williamson, & Baker, 1993). Further research in this area is needed to better understand the nuanced role of cognition across the continuum of eating, with data especially lacking regarding grazing.

Dialectical Mindfulness

Mindfulness can be defined as being in the present moment in a nonjudgmental way. This requires letting go of evaluation and instead just noticing, not reacting to push away the content of the present moment and not getting stuck in thoughts or emotions about the past or future. At the same time, when thoughts or emotions about the past or future arise, as they naturally will, mindfulness is observing these thoughts and emotions and letting them pass without attaching to them.

Mindful eating is, quite simply, applying the practice of mindfulness to food and the process of eating—observing with all five senses, without judgment of the food as good or bad based on pre-existing rules, without judgment of the virtue of eating or not eating the food, with, quite simply, an openness and curiosity towards the object as if never encountered previously, without distraction. The act of observing from an unbiased, new perspective can be referred to as **beginner's mind**.

Dialectics refers to the acknowledgment and balancing of polarities, fostering a middle ground. For example, we can completely accept ourselves in this moment as we are and we can work on moving forward in valued directions. Indeed, acceptance is the first step to change, and only with acceptance can we change. For example, if we do not accept that we have a rash, we will never apply lotion or seek medical treatment to heal it. If we do not accept that our light bulb has burnt out, we will never replace it and, as a result, be left in darkness. Thus these seeming opposites of acceptance and change can both be true at the same time and, moreover, cannot exist in isolation.

Dialectics mitigate dichotomies. For example, dividing food into good or bad, forbidden or unforbidden, based on its perceived impact on health or weight, creates two extremes of judgment. Dividing food into healthy or unhealthy does the same. With this black-and-white thinking, any consumption of a food deemed bad, forbidden, or unhealthy is an unacceptable violation. In contrast, dialectical thinking lets go of judgment, to permit a more flexible stance, not rejecting valid information and yet not getting rigidly fixed in it to the extent that the current context is lost. From a dialectical perspective it is thus possible and, moreover, necessary to consider the context of potential consumption to determine the most effective course of action for the circumstances. From a dialectical stance, there are no good or bad foods, forbidden or unforbidden, or even healthy or unhealthy—everything is relative.

For example, consider the case of an emaciated patient with cancer. Arguably, heavy cream, high carbohydrates, and desserts would be "healthy" for this patient to counter weight loss and malnourishment, while a diet high in fat-free items would be "unhealthy." Perhaps this example seems extreme, and at the same time, the point it intends to make is that any food can be more or less desirable for consumption in any given moment, based on the needs and function of eating the food in the context at hand.

At the same time, dialectics does not blindly equate foods or eating patterns, dismissing that foods and eating styles can be more or less advantageous for certain outcomes over time. Rather, dialectics balances both short-term and long-term considerations. That is, for example, a dialectical perspective does not assert that a piece of candy has the same nutritional value as a piece of kale. That would be rejecting important facts and thus not grounded in reality. And at the same time, a dialectical perspective is open to the possibility that sometimes we may just need to eat a piece of candy, for various reasons, and if we do so with awareness, it can be an effective choice.

Similarly, dialectics lets go of rules to permit behavior that is adaptive in the current situation rather than based on an imposed structure that may or may not apply. For example, we may have a rule that we are not supposed to eat right before going to sleep for the night, and yet sometimes we may find ourselves getting home close to bedtime without having yet eaten dinner. If we followed our rule, even if we were ravenous, we could then struggle to fall asleep or wake up excessively early and in any case may sacrifice our own self-care because of a cognitive boundary we have imposed, when instead, from a dialectical perspective we could hold true at the same time that there can be benefits to not eating right before bed and there can also be benefits to not going to bed hungry and thus permit ourselves to nourish ourselves adequately regardless of the time. Such rules can be challenged for a variety of reasons. For example, imagine that your partner surprises you with a fancy dessert before bed as an expression of love. Rigid adherence to a rule about not eating before bed could deprive you of a meaningful, intimate connection. We have many reasons for eating and need to be able to flexibly navigate them to truly be balanced.

Mindfulness from a dialectical perspective balances internal and external observation to permit effectiveness in the current situation. Thus we can be alternately mindful of our internal thoughts, emotions, urges, and physical sensations and of our external surroundings. At any given moment in time, effectiveness may call for more or less of either focus. For example, mindfulness of anxiety from a dialectical perspective would balance making space for the emotion, validating it, and listening to the information being provided by it (acceptance) with utilizing strategies to manage it if needed to achieve objectives in a given context (e.g., using grounding and breathing to avert a panic attack when giving a speech). Likewise, mindfulness from a dialectical perspective encourages graded exposure, moving through increasingly distressing triggers, building mastery to face each next step, and permits refocusing to distress tolerance depending on the situation.

Applying mindfulness from a dialectical perspective to eating allows us to move beyond the plate in front of us to see the entire space around us, as well as our internal urges, motivations, emotions, and thoughts, to help us most effectively nourish ourselves. It nonjudgmentally observes food and the process of eating with beginner's mind while at the same time not dismissing history and desired goals. It encourages graded exposure, moving through increasingly distressing eating-related triggers, building mastery to face each next step, and calls upon distress tolerance for effectiveness depending on the situation. We can thus walk the middle path between eating to live and living to eat, not depriving ourselves of the joys that food can provide and also taking care of our own unique needs, physical and emotional, to ultimately sustain a meaningful, resilient life.

Impact of Mindfulness: Research Findings

Mindful eating has been researched most with binge eating and related disorders (Klein, Skinner, & Hawley, 2012; 2013; Kristeller, Wolever, & Sheets, 2014; Proulx, 2008; Woolhouse, Knowles, & Crafti, 2012), with more limited, but encouraging, investigations of mindful eating with restrictive AN variants thus far (Albers, 2010; Hepworth, 2010). It has also been most researched with adults. Consequently, further research is needed to bolster evidence for the efficacy of mindful eating with restrictive eating disorders and adolescents.

The investigations provide a range of models, typically delivering mindful eating within more comprehensive approaches of mindfulness (e.g., mindfulness-based stress reduction; Proulx, 2008), cognitive behavior therapy, (CBT; Woolhouse et al., 2012), or dialectical behavior therapy (DBT; Klein et al., 2012; 2013). Study designs include case study (Albers, 2010), uncontrolled (Hepworth, 2010; Klein et al., 2012; Proulx, 2008; Woolhouse et al., 2012), and randomized controlled trials (Klein et al., 2013; Kristeller et al., 2014). Findings indicate high rates of diagnostic remission to sub-threshold levels (e.g., 100%, Klein et al., 2013; 95%, Kristeller et al., 2014), abstinence from binge eating by the end of treatment (e.g., 100%, Klein et al., 2013), and statistically significant improvement in measures of eating disorder psychopathology and related emotional distress, including the Eating Disorder Examination (Fairburn & Wilson, 1993), the Binge Eating Scale (Gormally, Black, Daston, & Rardin, 1982), Emotional Overeating Questionnaire (Masheb & Grilo, 2006), the Power of Food Scale (Lowe et al., 2009), the Eating Self-Efficacy Scale (Glynn & Ruderman, 1986), Eating Disorder Inventory scales (e.g., Bulimia, Drive for Thinness, and Interoceptive Awareness; Garner, Olmsted, & Polivy, 1983), the Bulimic Automatic Thoughts Test (Franko & Zuroff, 1992), the Multifactorial Assessment of Eating Disorders Scale (Anderson, Williamson, Duchmann, Gleaves, & Barbin, 1999), the Dutch Eating Behavior Questionnaire (van Strien, Fritgers, Bergers, & Defares, 1986), the Ben-Tovim Walker Body Attitudes Questionnaire (Ben-Tovim & Walker, 1991), the Cognitive and Affective Mindfulness Scale–Revised (Feldman, Hayes, Kumar, Greeson, & Laurenceau, 2007), the Beck Depression Inventory (Beck, Steer, & Brown, 1996), and the Rosenberg Self-Esteem Scale (Rosenberg, 1979). Of note, findings link more practice of mindfulness with greater reductions in binge eating (Kristeller et al., 2014).

Available data suggests that outcomes persist at least through one month post-treatment (Kristeller et al., 2014). Further follow-up research is needed to elucidate maintenance of change. Additional dismantling and randomized trials with active comparison treatments are also needed to bolster understanding of the incremental efficacy of mindful eating beyond existing traditional treatments.

Chapter Summary

In summary, judgment of food and eating is pervasive. At the same time, there is now ample evidence indicating that dietary restriction, behaviorally and cognitively, sets up conditions for increased attention to the very foods labeled for restriction; this can backfire into overeating and binge eating, followed by regret, guilt, and remorse (and not uncommonly a variety of other unpleasant emotions!), further attempts at restriction, further violations of restraint—and on, and on. Mindful eating offers an alternative to dieting that has been shown to break this cycle. Paradoxically, it seems that only through nonjudgmental openness to all foods can balanced eating be achieved. Thus, if one's goal is to ultimately eat a particular "healthy" or "clean" diet, the research suggests that, to actually effectively reach this goal, one must not promulgate such rules about forbidden foods. In particular, within the context of adapted DBT, mindful eating is now supported by both open and randomized trials, for disorders characterized by binge eating, including BED and BN. From a dialectical perspective, mindfulness encompasses awareness of effectiveness and a place for distress tolerance. It is thus arguably possible and completely appropriate for mindful eating to be a universal approach to food and eating. Welcome to the table.

2   Orientation

So, before we continue, let us take a look at the menu ahead of us. Mindful eating from the dialectical perspective can be a challenging, complex undertaking. It calls for you to nourish your body from the wisdom of the current moment rather than the dictates of dogma or popular belief about health. It asks you to consider the possibility that sometimes eating a Twinkie is precisely what you need to do—and that actually by doing so you can reach a place of balance that paradoxically may just match that dogma anyway.

As outlined further in the chapters ahead, the research-based protocol for this practice emphasizes approaching foods that you may think you need to avoid or that you currently are avoiding or trying to avoid, more or less successfully. This can be anxiety-provoking at the least and sometimes even downright terrifying, especially if you struggle with purging behavior. For example, you will be asked to eat the very foods that your body may now automatically want to reject, that may trigger painful memories of previous incidents of binge eating and purging, and that may feel truly physically torturous to sit with in your stomach.

This will also challenge any zealous alignment with not eating certain types of foods, such as gluten, dairy, sugar, or processed foods. This can be confusing, countering strong messages pervading society, including guidance from other practitioners and dieticians. With this program the expectation, unless there are truly imminently, medically compromising contraindications like a peanut allergy, is to have at least a bite of whatever is presented in the forbidden foods hierarchy, which will probably include gluten, dairy, and sugar at least at some point. It is possible that your body will react to this. For example, there was a period of time when I did not eat pork. Then one night, I was at a gathering with the family of my boyfriend at the time and they were serving barbequed pork. It looked tasty and I wanted to join the experience as part of getting to know them. So I ate a pork sandwich. And my stomach was not happy, let us just say that! But I was not in true mortal danger. Our bodies are incredibly resilient. Do not underestimate this and fragilize yourself! My stomach just needed to get used to this food again. So I ate pork again after that.

And I adapted. And I can now eat pork without any physical reaction. My clients have had similar experiences when reintroducing gluten, dairy, processed foods, and meat. And yet they have all worked through it in their own ways to cultivate a more compassionate relationship with food.

All of this takes courage, strength, and commitment. So why would you want to do this? Well, let us look at the pros and cons.

To break this down you can use a matrix such as provided here (see Handout 2.1). If this is not enough space, feel free to use additional paper. Note that all handouts are also available in a larger, printable format from www.routledge.com/9781138915916. For professionals working with clients, often this is best outlined on a whiteboard or with extra-large notebook paper. The figure is thus provided primarily as a guide for the general format.

First, let us start with the pros of mindless eating. Sometimes, when I say that to clients they raise their eyebrows and look at me like I have two heads, saying, "There are no pros." And yet, if there were no pros, why would people mindlessly eat? As human beings, we do not engage in behavior without reason. It is doing something for us. So, first, we need to look at this, acknowledge it, and validate it. We can then look at how we may be able to meet those needs in other ways.

Also, let us start with the short-term pros. These may differ from the long-term configuration.

After the short-term pros, fill in the long-term pros of mindless eating. If you cannot think of many, that is O.K. Just try to write down at least one or two.

Then move to the short-term cons of mindless eating, then the long-term cons of mindless eating.

After you have thoroughly completed the pros and cons of mindless eating move onto the cons of mindful eating, short-term and long-term. Then finish the matrix with the pros of mindful eating, short-term and long-term.

Complete this matrix, as best you can, before reading further, so it reflects your own experience first, before we discuss common pros and cons that clients share.

O.K., so how was that process for you? What did you notice? What stood out? What do you take away from it?

When considering the pros and cons, it is important to note that completing them from a centered place will be most effective. If you complete the pros and cons when you are experiencing high emotion or urges, the pros of acting on your urges for mindless eating will likely appear greater than the cons. This is because that is how we are hardwired— to focus on what will get us to the next moment in time to satisfy our current needs—not what will get us most effectively to where we ultimately would like to be in our lifetime or even the next day. To help with this, give yourself time for various pros and cons to surface into your awareness. Perhaps check in on this daily for a week or so and see what arises.

Handout 2.1 Pros and Cons of Mindful Eating

Mindless eating		Short-term	Long-term
	Pros		
	Cons		

Mindful eating		Short-term	Long-term
	Pros		
	Cons		

Usually what emerges is that mindless eating is serving an emotion regulation function, particularly in the short term. It is a way of escaping from painful emotion that you do not want to experience—ranging from boredom to severe memories of trauma. Basically, it can be an escape from anything that you do not want to be feeling, at least for a few moments in time, be that sadness, anxiety, fear, anger, or even happiness. Sometimes happiness can provoke feelings of discomfort because of a sense of unfamiliarity, unworthiness, or thoughts of it being transitory and inevitably doomed to ending. Whatever the experience, mindless eating can serve as an escape.

The function of mindless eating as an escape from emotion is supported by neurobiology. The very act of chewing activates the social safety system, which is associated with loving feelings. This may be especially soothing if the emotion you are trying to evade is loneliness (Shiba, Nitta, Hirono, Sugita, & Iwassa, 2002). Furthermore, consuming certain foods that are typically avoided, such as carbohydrates, can increase dopamine and serotonin, to counter states of depression (e.g., Avena, Rada, & Hoebel, 2007; Avena, Rada, Moise, & Hoebel, 2006; Goldfield, Adamo, Rutherford, & Legg, 2008; Mathes, Brownley, Mo, & Bulik, 2009; Rada, Avena, & Hoebel, 2005).

From a behavioral perspective the function of mindless eating as an escape from emotion also makes sense. Think of all the positive associations we make with food: cake for birthdays, feasts for holidays, going out to eat as an occasion for celebration or a romantic night. By eating certain foods and in certain ways we trigger associations that can generate desired emotions, to shift our emotion from the less pleasant emotions we do not want to be feeling.

And yet, when you are mindlessly eating, are you really fully permitting yourself to reap the potential benefits of eating, such as countering loneliness or generating desired emotions? And are there other ways to fill these needs that would not produce the undesired consequences you listed? With mindless eating we are plowing through food without full awareness of it—what it looks like, smells like, feels like, tastes like, and even sounds like—so we are, by definition, depriving ourselves of the full power of positivity it could offer. In one kernel of popcorn exists a landscape of nuance that is uniquely its own that we utterly miss when we are shoveling in handfuls in a dark theater. Likewise, in each spoonful, forkful and morsel of anything there exists such a gift that we can choose to observe or ignore and arguably only by being fully present with these moments can we fully enjoy their benefits. When we instead judge what we are eating and judge ourselves for eating it, we are not really soothing ourselves or being kind to ourselves. We may temporarily escape from the undesired emotions we feel before eating, but then pile on top of that original emotion other uncomfortable feelings such as guilt and shame.

And even if we bring our full attention to the food in front of us and mindfully self-soothe through it, we may only temporarily feel better—because eating to address underlying emotions such as sadness and loneliness is never going to have a sustained effect given that you are not addressing the information that the emotion is providing—the message it is sending you—that you are experiencing a loss and therefore have a need to fulfill in ways that, usually, have nothing to do with food, such as connecting with other people in meaningful ways. Moreover, mindless eating, in particular binge eating, often occurs alone and can be isolating, not just in the act itself but also from the resulting shame and the often associated weight gain. In this way, the solution really perpetuates the problem, so to speak.

The challenge is thus often turning away from at least partial short-term gratification towards more long-term resolution, while also not judging short-term self-soothing. If in the moment you truly want to eat a piece of cake, then eat a piece of cake—but do so mindfully, recognizing that if you are trying to not feel sadness, there is not enough cake in the world to fill the hole of loss and that you will also need to put your fork down and move towards resolving grief and further cultivating relationships that will ultimately nourish your need for connection. Likewise with anger and any emotion—you can temporarily take a vacation from it through eating with full awareness, and yet to be truly mindful requires you to recognize that you also need to address those emotions beyond the plate, to validate, honor, and resolve the source of the emotion, be it conflict, threat, or desire.

Other cons of mindless eating can include its cost, in monetary terms and time. Think of all the money you would save if you did not end up eating large quantities of food. How would you spend it instead? And how would you spend the time you would save? Of course you would still need to spend money on food—and yet the surplus of money you would save from eating in a more balanced way could almost certainly fund other more valued directions. Do the math. Take a look at your receipts or bank account. Add up how much money you spend each week on food that you eat in an unbalanced way. If you add up what you spend for a month or even a year, then average this you can get a sense of how much money each week is going towards unbalanced eating. Could you fund a vacation with the money you would save eating in a more balanced way over the course of a year? Or buy a long-desired item (e.g., to enjoy as a pastime, perhaps a musical instrument, art supplies, or sports equipment; or to create a kinder environment at home, perhaps some new furniture; or to create a kinder closet, perhaps some fabulous new shoes or new clothes from that store you just love that costs a little bit more)? Or maybe you could actually put the money you save towards your savings account or retirement fund. Oftentimes, the savings would really add up and, if spent otherwise, more fully enhance your quality of life.

When it comes to saving time, it may be less obvious. Certainly, we can sometimes perceive mindless eating as a timesaver. For example, if we are working under a deadline we may eat while typing, or if we want to get started on a movie at home, we may eat dinner while the movie plays. And uncoupling these activities may result in a time cost. For example, my friend and I have developed a consistent pattern of not finishing movies when we plan evenings to catch up over dinner and then watch a movie. When we first began this pairing my friend asked me if I wanted to eat while we watched the movie and I expressed my preference to eat first, then watch the movie. The result was definitely a longer evening and since then we have either not finished the movie because my friend has gotten too tired or, most recently, not even gotten to the movie! And if the cost of connecting further over our meal and conversation is not finishing a movie, I much prefer the connection, which is more truly nourishing. So mindful eating may take more time.

And yet oftentimes eating in an unbalanced way, especially when isolated and binge eating, can steal so much more time. And the time cost can extend far beyond the actual incident of eating, to the food preoccupation and craving that can infiltrate our thoughts in a persistent soundtrack. Again, reflect on this. Estimate how much time you are really spending, in terms of both your actions and thoughts, on eating in an unbalanced way and consider how you might instead fill this time. You may well find that you have a massive amount of extra time freed. And this may be scary, especially if you have been engaging in unbalanced eating for a long time. And yet it can be liberating. Give yourself some time to sit with this.

Another theme that often arises with the consequences of mindless eating is health. Eating disordered behavior can certainly have a serious impact on this, including a markedly elevated risk of mortality, across the spectrum of disordered eating (e.g., Crow et al., 2012; Emborg, 1999; Hoek, 2006; Jorgensen, 1992; Neumarker, 2000; Nielsen et al., 1998; Thomas, Vartanian, & Brownell, 2009). Across domains of health functioning, lower functioning has been linked to BN and BED (Baiano et al., 2014; Bulik & Reichborn-Kjennerud, 2003; Johnson, Spitzer, & Williams, 2001). In a sample of 4,651 female patients from eight primary care facilities, this finding persisted after controlling for somatic symptoms and alcohol, anxiety, and mood disorders, and included a threefold increased likelihood of reporting sleep difficulties, a higher likelihood of endorsing health problems as very or extremely difficult, and, for BED specifically, an elevated likelihood of reporting impaired health status to the extent of preventing usual activities (Johnson et al., 2001). Likewise, in a sample of 2,163 female twins, women with obesity and binge eating reported greater health dissatisfaction and elevated rates of major medical disorders (Bulik, Sullivan, & Kendler, 2002). BED and BN have also demonstrated elevated rates of joint pain, headaches, gastrointestinal concerns, shortness of breath, chest pain, and Type II diabetes compared to patients without eating disorders (Johnson et al., 2001; Reichborn-Kjennerud, Bulik, Sullivan, Tambs, & Harris, 2004), and menstrual issues have been found to be pervasive across eating disorder types (Johnson et al., 2001; Pinhiero et al., 2007). In addition to cross-sectional self-report findings, longitudinal research points to a role in hypertension onset with BN and BED (Stein et al., 2014). Taken together, there is a multitude of evidence suggesting that binge eating and eating disordered behavior can have debilitating and dire health outcomes.

After completing this practice over time, what do you take away from the pros and cons? Do the pros of mindful eating outweigh the cons? Are the cons of mindless eating more costly than the pros? Are you ready to embark on moving more towards mindful eating? If so, what will that entail?

The mindful eating program outlined further in the chapters ahead includes several key components. The program can stand alone or be combined with individual sessions. Individual sessions may be recommended if comorbidity is present or eating disordered behaviors are occurring frequently (e.g., more than a few times/week).

When delivered as a group-based treatment, based on my research and clinical experience, this orientation material is discussed in an orientation and commitment session prior to beginning the group. Earlier models of DBT-based mindful eating incorporated aspects of orientation into the first group session. The risk of this is clients beginning without full commitment, then dropping out, impacting group dynamics and feasibility with a reduced census. In both models, orientation follows screening for diagnostic symptoms and treatment information to determine appropriate fit. For screening, formal measures are recommended to provide the most valid information, including a structured diagnostic interview and questionnaires (e.g., the Eating Disorder Inventory, see Garner et al., 1983; forbidden vs. unforbidden foods ratings, see Klein et al., 2012).

Material

Diary Card

One of the core components, an essential foundational tool, for developing mindful eating in the DBT-based program we are embarking upon is diary card self-monitoring. The diary card is a daily practice in adopting a reasonable, nonjudgmental stance. It consists of tracking daily urges, emotions, and actions, as well as daily skills use (see Handout 2.2 for an example with both binge eating and purging). Decades of research supports such self-monitoring alone as an effective tool for change (e.g., Aittasalo, Miilunpalo, Kukkonen-Harjula, & Pasanen, 2006; Baker & Kirschenbaum, 1993; Boutelle, Kirschenbaum, Baker, & Mitchell, 1999; Conn, Valentine, & Cooper, 2002; Diabetes Prevention

Program Research Group, 2004; Gormally & Rardin, 1981; Jeffrey, Vender, & Wing, 1978; Leermakers, Auglin, & Wing, 1998; Madsen et al., 1993; Sperduto, Thompson, & O'Brien, 1986). Likewise, recommendations for trying to manage eating behavior include self-monitoring (Foreyt & Goodrick, 1991; Foreyt & Poston, 1998). The process of self-monitoring heightens self-awareness, provides the information necessary for establishing realistic goals, permits evaluation of progress, facilitates insight into potential causes of difficulty, and promotes behavior changes consistent with goals (Burke & Dunbar-Jacob, 1995; Febbraro & Clum, 1998; Foreyt & Poston, 1998; Kirschenbaum & Wittrock, 1984). When self-monitoring documents progress, it can be reinforcing (Burke & Dunbar-Jacob, 1995) and boost self-efficacy, instilling confidence for achieving goals. In addition, this diary card specifically has evidence for its effectiveness, along with therapist support (Klein et al., 2012), with outcomes for a 15-session package indicating statistically significant improvement in binge eating, bulimic symptoms, and interoceptive awareness.

The diary card differs from CBT intake monitoring, which focuses on all food and liquid consumed, whether it is a binge or not, with the associated circumstances, emotions, and cognitions (see p. 58, Fairburn, 2008). Across client populations, including borderline personality disorder (BPD), substance use disorders, and eating disorders, DBT utilizes diary cards as a central and essential treatment component, collected and reviewed at each session. This DBT component alone may disrupt key eating disorder mechanisms, including low interoceptive awareness (e.g., Garner, Olmsted, & Polivy, 1983; Lilenfeld, Wonderlich, Riso, Crosby, & Mitchell, 2006) and feelings of ineffectiveness (e.g., Cooley & Toray, 1996; 2001), by specifically increasing emotional awareness and thus improving coping.

The diary card is thus not just a piece of paper or busywork. And I can validate that it may be the last thing you want to see or fill out, especially when you are really overwhelmed or not wanting to face your own behavior. As a DBT therapist, as part of my training, I have myself filled out many diary cards and it can be incredible how insurmountable that one sheet of paper can seem (note: if you are a therapist new to DBT, I would ask that you complete your own diary cards as well, along with the other practices for this program, to permit you to best learn the tools and thus better be able to teach them from a radically genuine stance). And yet it can be extremely beneficial, so if it is not completed, this is therapy-interfering behavior and needs to be addressed and problem solved by therapists and group leaders in the group-based program.

Handout 2.2 Diary Card and Instructions

Diary Card

Name: _____

How often did you fill out this diary card? ___ Daily ___ 4–6x ___ 2–3x ___ Once

Day and date	Restriction Urge (0–5)	Binge eating #	Binge eating Urge (0–5)	Urge to purge #	Urge to purge (0–5)	Self-induced vomiting #	Laxatives # of times/# taken	Diuretics # of times/# taken	Fasting Hrs & mins	Exercise[2] Hrs & mins	Mindless eating #	Apparently irrelevant behavior[3] Circle one	Capitulating (0–5)	Food craving (0–5)	Food preoccupation (0–5)	Anger (0–5)	Sadness (0–5)	Fear (0–5)	Shame (0–5)	Pride (0–5)	Happiness (0–5)	Joy (0–5)
Mon												yes/no										
Tues												yes/no										
Wed												yes/no										
Thurs												yes/no										
Fri												yes/no										
Sat												yes/no										
Sun												yes/no										

Urge to quit therapy (0–5): Before group session: ___ After group session: ___

[2] Describe exercise:

[3] Describe apparently irrelevant behavior:

Notes—Mon:

Notes—Tues:

Notes—Wed:

Notes—Thurs:

Notes—Fri:

Notes—Sat:

Notes—Sun:

DBT Skills Used

0) Not thought about or used
1) Thought about, not used, didn't want to
2) Thought about, not used, wanted to
3) Tried, but could not use them
4) Tried, could use them, but did not help
5) Tried, could use them, helped
6) Didn't try, used them, didn't help
7) Didn't try, used them, helped

How often did you fill out this side? ___ Daily ___ 4–6x ___ 2–3x ___ Once

	Skill	M	T	W	T	F	S	S
Core mindfulness	Wise Mind: Accessed wisdom and truth. Being centered and calm. Balancing Emotion Mind and Reasonable Mind.							
	Observe: Just noticing the experience. "Teflon mind". Controlling your attention. Experience what is happening.							
	Describe: Putting experiences into words. Describing to yourself what is happening. Putting words on the experience.							
	Participate: Entering into the experience. Acting intuitively from Wise Mind.							
	Nonjudgmental Stance: Seeing but not evaluating. Ungluing your opinions. Accepting each moment.							
	One-Mindfully: Being in the moment. Doing one thing at a time. Concentrating your mind on the task at hand.							
	Effectiveness: Focusing on what works. Playing by the rules. Acting skillfully. Letting go of vengeance and useless anger.							
	Mindful eating: Applying mindfulness to eating.							
	Urge Surfing: Observing urges without acting on them, riding them like a wave. You cannot stop the waves, but you can learn to surf.							
Emotion regulation	Accumulating Positive Experience in the short term: Doing pleasurable things that you can do now.							
	Accumulating Positive Experiences in the long term: Making choices that match morals and values.							
	Building Mastery: Trying to do one hard or challenging thing a day to make yourself feel confident and in control.							
	Coping Ahead: Rehearsing a plan ahead of time so you are more prepared to cope skillfully with emotional situations.							
	PLEASE: Reducing vulnerability to Emotion Mind: Treating Physical Illness, Balancing Eating, Avoiding Drugs and Alcohol, Balancing Sleep, Balancing Exercise.							
	Opposite to Emotion Action: Changing emotions by acting in the opposite way, e.g., approaching rather than avoiding.							
	Pros and cons: Thinking about the +/– aspects of tolerating the distress and the +/– aspects of not tolerating the distress.							
Distress tolerance	Distract with ACCEPTS: Activities, Contributing, Comparisons, Opposite Emotions, Pushing Away, Other Thoughts, Strong Sensations.							
	Self-Soothe with the five senses: Enjoying sights, sounds, smells, tastes and touch. Being mindful of soothing sensations.							
	IMPROVE the moment: Imagery, Meaning, Prayer, Relaxation, One Thing in the Moment, Vacation, and Encouragement.							
	Diaphragmatic breathing: Belly breathing, recommended pace of six breaths/minute.							
	Half-Smile: If you cannot change your feelings, change your face.							
	Alternate Rebellion: Acting in ways that feel rebellious but have no potential negative consequences.							
	Radical Acceptance: Choosing to recognize and accept reality (not approval) from suffering for freedom from suffering (not approval) from deep within.							
	Turning the Mind: Choosing over and over again to accept even though Emotion Mind wants to reject reality.							
	Willingness: Choosing to do what is needed in each situation.							
	Burning bridges: Letting go of options for turning back.							
	Skill use level							

Instructions for Completing Your Diary Card

Completing your diary card on a daily basis is an essential component of treatment. *Mindful* completion of the diary card (i.e., paying attention *without* judging) increases awareness of what is going on for you. Therefore, completing the diary card is a skillful behavior. You will derive the greatest benefit if you complete the diary card on a daily basis. We suggest you complete it at the end of each day or the beginning of the day for the previous day, but if another time is more convenient for you, that is fine. Here is how you complete the card:

How often did you fill out this diary card?: Place a check mark to indicate how frequently you filled in the diary card during the past week.

Day and date: Write in the calendar date (month/day/year) under each day of the week.

Urge to restrict: 0 = no urge; 5 = the most intense. Please rate the most intense of the day.

Restriction: Write the number of times you restricted each day. Restriction is dieting or otherwise limiting your food intake based on categorizations of food and/or food's nutritional content, e.g., fat, calories, carbohydrates, when consumption would otherwise be appropriate. This is not the same as choosing foods based on taste preference, values, cost, or balanced eating. This is also not refraining from overeating or binge eating. Rather, this is refraining from balanced eating and/or denying certain foods because of judgments about them and/or the consequences of eating them.

Urge to binge eat: 0 = no urge; 5 = the most intense. Please rate the most intense of the day.

Binge eating: Write the number of times you binged each day. A binge refers to eating an objectively large amount of food with a feeling of loss of control (i.e., feeling you cannot stop). Record the food consumed during each binge on a **Binge Record Sheet**.

Urge to purge: 0 = no urge; 5 = the most intense. Please rate the most intense of the day.

Self-induced vomiting (SIV): Write the number of times you made yourself throw up to purge each day.

Laxatives: Write the number of times you used laxatives to purge each day and the number of laxatives you took each time. For example, if you took laxatives three times in one day and took two pills the first time, three the second, and four the third, record this as 3/2, 3, 4.

Diuretics: Write the number of times you used diuretics to purge each day and the number of diuretics you took each time. For example, if you took diuretics three times in one day and took two pills the first time, three the second, and four the third, record this as 3/2, 3, 4.

Exercise: Write how long you exercised each day and what you did.

Fasting: Write how long you fasted to purge each day. Fasting is skipping a meal or going for an extended period of time (e.g., eight waking hours) without eating for the purpose of influencing your weight or shape or counteracting the effects of eating.

Mindless eating: Write the number of mindless eating episodes that you had each day. Mindless eating is eating while not paying attention to what you are eating. A typical example of mindless eating would be sitting in front of the TV and eating a bag of microwave popcorn without any awareness of the eating (i.e., somehow, the popcorn was gone and you were only vaguely aware of having eaten it). *If you count an eating episode as a binge, do **not** count it again as mindless eating and vice versa.*

Apparently irrelevant behaviors (AIB): Circle either "yes" or "no" depending on whether you did or did not have any AIBs that day. If you did, briefly describe the AIB in the place provided or on another sheet of paper. An AIB refers to behaviors that, upon first glance, do not seem relevant to eating disordered behavior but which actually are important in the behavior chain leading to these behaviors. You may convince yourself that the behavior does not matter or really will not affect your goal to stop eating disordered behavior when, in fact, the behavior matters a great deal. A typical AIB might be buying several boxes of your favorite Girl Scout cookies because you wanted to help out a neighbor's daughter (when you could buy the cookies and donate them to the neighbor).

Capitulating: 0 = no urge; 5 = the most intense. Please rate the most intense of the day.

The key characteristics to consider when making your rating are intensity (strength of the capitulating) and duration (how long it lasted). Capitulating refers to giving up on your goals to stop binge eating and to skillfully cope with emotions. Instead, you capitulate or surrender to binge eating, acting as if there is no other option or way to cope than with food.

Food craving: 0 = no urge; 5 = the most intense. Please rate the most intense of the day.

Food craving refers to an intense desire for a particular food or taste. The experience often involves sensations such as your mouth watering for the taste of chocolate. For example, you may desire a particular ice cream so much that other sweets do not seem capable of quenching the desire.

Food preoccupation: 0 = no urge; 5 = the most intense. Please rate the most intense of the day.

Food preoccupation refers to your thoughts or attention being absorbed or focused on food. For example, your thoughts of a dinner party and the presence of your favorite foods may absorb your attention so much that you have trouble concentrating at work.

Emotion columns: 0 = no urge; 5 = the most intense. Please rate the most intense of the day.

Urge to quit therapy: 0 = no urge; 5 = the most intense. Please indicate your urge to quit therapy each week before and after your individual or group session or if you are completing this program from a self-guided approach, before and after your weekly review time. It is best to make both of these ratings as soon as possible following that day's session or review time.

Guide to the Diary Card Emotion Categories

Anger Words

anger
aggravation
agitation
annoyance
bitterness
contempt
cruelty
destructiveness

disgust
dislike
envy
exasperation
ferocity
frustration
fury
grouchiness

grumpiness
hate
hostility
irritation
jealousy
loathing
mean-spiritedness
outrage

rage
resentment
revulsion
scorn
spite
torment
vengefulness
wrath

Sadness Words

sadness
agony
alienation
anguish
crushed
defeat
dejection
depressing

despair
disappointment
discontentment
dismay
displeasure
distraught
gloom
glumness

grief
homesickness
hopelessness
hurt
insecurity
isolation
loneliness
melancholy

misery
neglect
pity
rejection
sorrow
suffering
unhappiness
woe

Fear Words

fear
apprehension
anxiety
distress
dread

edginess
fright
horror
hysteria
jumpiness

nervousness
overwhelmed
panic
shock

tenseness
terror
uneasiness
worry

Shame Words

shame
contrition
culpability

discomposure
embarrassment
guilt

humiliation
insult
invalidation

mortification
regret
remorse

Joy Words

joy
amusement
bliss
cheerfulness
contentment
delight
eagerness
ecstasy
elation

enjoyment
enthrallment
enthusiasm
euphoria
excitement
exhilaration
gaiety
gladness
glee

happiness
hope
jolliness
joviality
jubilation
optimism
pleasure
pride
rapture

relief
satisfaction
thrill
triumph
zaniness
zeal
zest

For each diary card, monitoring begins the day of session, then continues through the day before the next session. Each diary card then typically captures a week of data (if sessions are weekly). With this time frame, the diary card is definitely most effective and helpful if it is completed daily. Try to remember for a moment what you wore each day for the past week. If you are like me, you may need to pause to let the outfits seep back into your awareness. If just this one example of attempting to recall experience can be so elusive, now imagine trying to fill in all the specifics required on the diary card for the past week. This will likely be a strain or even verge on the impossible, diluting more fine-grained accuracy into very broad strokes. Even trying to recapture a few days ago can be a stretch. Moreover, not completing the diary card daily deprives you of the daily practice in nonjudgmental awareness of your patterns and skills. I thus urge program participants to follow through on regular, ideally daily, frequency.

This includes the back of the diary card (the DBT skills monitoring). Often this gets neglected. In part I contribute to this with my clients, initially primarily reinforcing their completion of the front by my focus on it, but usually less frequently reviewing the back, due to the need to first target the behaviors noted on the front. Then inevitably, at some point in our therapy together, when eating-related behaviors are stabilizing and we have more time in session, I turn the diary card over and nearly invariably, it is blank! When I express concern about this my clients often respond that they did not think it was as important, in part, at times, because of my not attending to it. Yet, it is very important for solidifying skills learning, to increase accessibility, especially when compromised by high emotion. The more you interact with the skills, the more you will learn them and the more quickly you will learn them. This stands even if I have shaped the behavior of diary card skills monitoring otherwise. All this said, given that it is a not uncommon pattern to complete the front of the diary card more than the back, note that there is a section to record frequency of completion for the front and back of the diary card.

There are several different approaches to daily completion that can be taken. One popular approach is to fill it out at night, at the end of the day, reflecting on the day that has passed. Another time that can work well is to fill it out at the beginning of the day, reflecting on the preceding day. And others find it works best for them to carry it with them throughout the day, to take notes as events occur. Whatever works for you is fine. Find what is most effective for you. I have tried all of these approaches and found them helpful at different times. I found carrying the diary card with me to be especially effective as I also was working on being more on time. I then used the idle moments when I was early to a meeting or event to fill in my diary card, quenching my sometimes anxious and restless nature and drive for productivity.

And if you do not fill it in daily, because life happens, and maybe you forget or you are avoiding and just do not want to fill it out at times, be sure to complete it at least once per week, summarizing the preceding week. This will be less accurate than daily completion but will still be more useful than no data and can serve as an effective consequence for not completing it more frequently because it almost definitely takes more time and effort and is not as helpful for learning. Completing the diary card at least once per week in this way is required. This means that if you are a professional seeing a client for individual sessions, you cannot continue with the session until the client completes the diary card; in group settings, due to needing to keep the group session moving, usually the consequence is a behavior chain and solution analysis (see the next section on this), then potentially also the requirement to complete the diary card on break (although be careful of this functioning as a way to avoid eating snacks on break; if you suspect or observe this you can try other contingencies like the client staying after group to finish their diary card or assigning an additional behavior chain and solution analysis of homework).

Note also that the time taken to complete the diary card is considered session time. Thus if someone arrives on time but takes 30 minutes to complete their diary card and their individual session is scheduled for an hour, then the rest of their session is only 30 minutes. Especially in private practice settings where clients are paying out of their own pocket, this is a high price to pay, a rather costly way to fill out the piece of paper and usually not how the client wants to spend their time and money!

Time and time again I have oriented clients to this and yet they have still arrived to their next individual session after orientation without their diary card completed. Perhaps they do not think I am serious about holding them accountable or they do not fully process all of the requirements with orientation or they simply run into barriers. For professionals guiding clients through this process it is imperative when this occurs to reiterate the requirement and importance of diary card monitoring. Oftentimes, to balance this with maintaining initial therapeutic alliance, I give clients one pass the first time they arrive with their diary card not completed, asking them to at least verbally report on only the main behavioral treatment targets, such as binge eating, and warning them that the next time it happens I will literally have them complete the full diary card before proceeding with session. Then clients typically either offer to go ahead and complete it that session still, or they express appreciation and show up the next session with it at least partially completed. Then, moving forward, holding this requirement firmly is imperative.

With teens especially, this can result in very interesting individual sessions, spent in a great deal of silence, while the teen pouts or otherwise protests against filling out the diary card. As a therapist, you need to not attend to this, to not reinforce the behavior, thereby promoting it to cease (see Chapter 3 for more on behavioral principles such as reinforcement). You can sit silently and read, reviewing your notes or other material, avoiding eye contact, working on other administrative tasks, or checking your phone.

Whatever it is, the key is to not engage with the client in a way that would be reinforcing. It can be quite a standoff, but this consistently shapes behavior in the desired directions, eventually with the client, perhaps with a very deep sigh, picking up the piece of paper and completing it. Then you can celebrate the completion and move forward. You can also shape the behavior, accepting partial completion at first then increasing the bar of expectation.

If you are completing this program on your own, I would strongly encourage you to hold yourself to the same standard for diary card completion turned in weekly. That is, have a time once a week that you check in with yourself; if you have not yet completed your diary card, do so at that time before reviewing or moving forward with further material.

In addition to the consequence of accountability and completion before proceeding, it can be helpful to make the diary card more rewarding to increase motivation for completion. After all, reinforcement is usually more effective than punishment. You can do this by printing the diary card on bright, colorful, inviting paper; changing the font to fun lettering; pairing the diary card with a soothing ritual, like drinking a cup of tea; or giving yourself small tangible rewards, like stickers or change towards a desired larger item (e.g., perhaps a quarter/day, adding up to a Redbox movie at the end of the week or a larger reward at the end of the month or program). These ideas come from my clients, adolescent and adult, and have been effective.

It can also be important to determine where you will keep the diary card. Clients often keep it by their bed or in their mindful eating skills training binder. This can facilitate completion but may interfere with bringing the diary card completed to session if the diary card or binder is then left at home. In such cases, the diary card is still due, so the consequence of completing it still remains, which can be especially frustrating for clients. In problem solving this, establishing a routine is usually important. For example, to facilitate coming to sessions prepared, clients have often developed the pattern of putting their diary card or binder in their car or backpack the night before session. It can also be helpful to set reminders (e.g., by phone alarms) for completing and bringing the diary card to session. With reminders, problem solve barriers to actually following through, determining the most effective time for the reminders and confirming a commitment to responding to the alarm rather than continuing to procrastinate, snoozing or ignoring the alarm.

Extra copies of the diary card can also be important. For example, clients sometimes stash blank copies in their car, backpack, or binder so, if they forget their diary card, they can still complete it before session, on their car ride to session (e.g., if they are a teen being driven by their parent) or in the lobby. I also email clients electronic copies of their diary card so they can print out copies if they lose their paper copies. Of course, then printers can become a barrier but can be problem solved.

Regarding electronic copies, clients sometimes also like to complete their diary cards electronically and email them to me before session. There are also apps available for general DBT diary cards. Whatever works is fine, as long as the copies are accessible when they are needed for review.

So basically, the diary card is important and not negotiable. If you struggle with it, problem solve it and use **Opposite to Emotion Action** to get it done anyway (take the action opposite to the urge associated with the emotion; see Chapter 9)! Again, I can validate that this can be extremely challenging—and you will benefit most from this program if you consistently do your diary card. As we are just beginning this process, think about what might get in the way for you and preemptively outline how you will work through this (see also downloadable Handout 2.3).

Handout 2.3 Plan for Diary Card Completion

I will complete my diary card at this time daily:

_____

I will keep my diary card in this location: _____

If I am participating in this program through sessions with a professional, I will follow these steps to ensure that I bring my diary card to session:

_____

_____

_____

_____

_____

If I am completing this program from a self-guided approach, I will check in with myself at this time each week, holding myself accountable for completing the previous week's diary card at that time if I have not already done so:

_____

I anticipate these barriers to completing my diary card and will address them in the following ways:

_____

_____

_____

_____

_____

_____

_____

If I am participating in this program through sessions with a professional, I anticipate these barriers to bringing my diary card to session and will address them in the following ways:

_____

_____

_____

_____

_____

_____

_____

If I am completing this program from a self-guided approach, I anticipate these barriers to holding myself accountable weekly to diary card completion and will address them in the following ways:

_____

_____

_____

_____

_____

_____

_____

Binge Record Sheets

In addition to noting any binges on the diary card, monitoring of binges includes recording the details of the items consumed on a Binge Record Sheet (see Handout 2.4). As the instructions on the Binge Record Sheet outline, when recording consumption it is important to include as much detail as possible to the extent that someone could use the sheet to literally recreate what was consumed exactly (e.g., including brand names and exact quantities). As with the diary card, the rationale for this originates in self-monitoring as an empirically supported tool for change (e.g., Aittasalo et al., 2006; Baker & Kirschenbaum, 1993; Boutelle et al., 1999; Conn et al., 2002; Diabetes Prevention Program Research Group, 2004; Foreyt & Goodrick, 1991; Foreyt & Poston, 1998; Gormally & Rardin, 1981; Jeffrey et al., 1978; Leermakers et al., 1998; Madsen et al., 1993; Sperduto et al., 1986).

Handout 2.4 Binge Record Sheet

Binge Record Sheet

Name: _____

Date: ____/____/_____

Time: from _____ a.m./p.m. (circle) to _____ a.m./p.m. (circle)

Total number of minutes: _____

Food consumed:
Be specific! Include brand or restaurant name and quantity. Also include any liquid drank. (E.g., pint of Ben and Jerry's Chunky Monkey ice cream; ½ homemade butterscotch pie; box of White Cheddar Cheez-Its; 8 ounces Kraft mild cheddar cheese; sleeve of Ritz crackers; ½ liter Diet Coke.)

_____

_____

_____

_____

_____

_____

_____

_____

_____

_____

_____

_____

_____

_____

_____

_____

_____

_____

This particular form of self-monitoring is also, in part, consistent with intake monitoring in CBT for eating disorders, but focuses on binges only rather than CBT intake monitoring of all food and liquid consumed (see p. 58, Fairburn, 2008). Thus the Binge Record Sheet offers a middle ground for bringing attention to consumption when it is arguably most problematic (compared to balanced meals or less severe overeating) but not inadvertently promoting hypervigilance to intake. This may seem counterintuitive, given the goal of mindful awareness across consumption— and yet, remember, with mindful eating from the dialectical perspective, the goal is balance and moving away from food preoccupation, or overly attending to food, to the exclusion of other experience, and clinically, clients often report feeling overwhelmed or further dysregulated by CBT food intake monitoring—that it makes their food preoccupation worse. If the latter occurs, it may be an opportunity for working through the emotion from an exposure perspective—and the timing may be important. Especially if clients are prone to elevated anxiety, a more gradual exposure process may better match their clinical presentation and temperament, so simply focusing on the exact details of consumption on the Binge Record Sheet as a place to start, rather than their entire consumption, is consistent with a graded exposure approach.

Clinically, the Binge Record Sheet is also a consequence that can preemptively curtail binges. Writing down every detail of a binge can bring shame and other difficult emotions, with the urge to hide. Clients have thus reported that before a potential binge they thought of the Binge Record Sheet and decided to not binge because they did not want me to see what they ate. Perfect! That is precisely one of the ways that the Binge Record Sheet can be helpful. Then the learning can be that the urge to binge can be survived without acting on it and instead managed in other ways.

The Binge Record Sheet is also a consequence if a binge occurs, requiring acknowledgment rather than dismissal of its occurrence. This can also be a form of exposure to the emotional consequences of binge eating, such as guilt and shame. This can be helpful for preventing future binges. At the same time, it is a balance. It is usually most effective to record the details as close to the binge as possible for accuracy but, to prevent it from being overly dysregulating, after enough time has passed to permit perspective and reduce vulnerability to further spiraling of emotion and compensatory behavior such as purging.

If you do not complete Binge Record Sheets this is also therapy-interfering behavior and thus a target for completion and problem solving before proceeding with sessions, as outlined above for diary cards. As we are just beginning this process, think about what might get in the way for you and preemptively outline how you will work through this (see also downloadable Handout 2.5).

Handout 2.5 Plan for Binge Record Sheet Completion

I will complete my Binge Record Sheets at this time daily: _____

_____

I will keep my Binge Record Sheet copies in this location: _____

_____

If I am participating in this program through sessions with a professional, I will follow these steps to ensure that I bring my Binge Record Sheets to session:

_____

_____

_____

_____

_____

If I am completing this program from a self-guided approach, I will check in with myself at this time each week, holding myself accountable for completing the previous week's Binge Record Sheets at that time if I have not already done so: _____

I anticipate these barriers to completing my Binge Record Sheets and will address them in the following ways: _____

_____

_____

_____

_____

_____

_____

_____

If I am participating in this program through sessions with a professional, I anticipate these barriers to bringing my Binge Record Sheets to session and will address them in the following ways: _____

_____

_____

_____

_____

_____

_____

If I am completing this program from a self-guided approach, I anticipate these barriers to holding myself accountable weekly to Binge Record Sheet completion and will address them in the following ways:

_____

_____

_____

_____

_____

_____

_____

_____

Skills Assignments

This program covers skills in mindfulness (see Chapters 4, 5, 7, and 8), emotion regulation (see Chapters 5, 6, and 9), and distress tolerance (see Chapter 6). Following the research-based protocol, covering these skills is packaged into fifteen weeks (four weeks of core mindfulness; six weeks of Emotion Regulation; five weeks of Distress Tolerance; see Klein et al., 2012; 2013). Thereafter continuing and deepening these skills can continue for a lifetime.

Note that although the forbidden foods hierarchy is outlined in Chapter 7, after Emotion Regulation and Distress Tolerance, in the group setting this is initiated after completing core mindfulness (Chapter 4) and the seven hungers (Chapter 5), with the start of Emotion Regulation. The current placement after Emotion Regulation and Distress Tolerance proposes a structure for self-guided practice, to permit a more solid foundation of skills before embarking on the triggering process of the forbidden foods hierarchy. To follow the research-based protocol, individuals can likewise initiate the forbidden foods hierarchy beginning alongside Emotion Regulation. In doing so, be mindful of how you are coping and pace yourself accordingly, returning to skills acquisition more independently of mindful eating challenges if you find yourself getting overwhelmed in embarking on the forbidden foods hierarchy.

Each skills discussion includes assignments to practice the skills in real life, in the face of the urges, feelings, thoughts, and situations associated with mindless eating, beyond the pages of this book. Insight from reading this book will go only so far. Making changes takes practice—and practicing again, and again, and again to counter the patterns that have otherwise been established over time, from perhaps years and even decades or a lifetime of acting in another way. This will not be easy and it is imperative to consistently bring awareness to this process to benefit the most from this program.

At the same time, the assignments will not require all-nighters or hours at the library. Again, the point is to be practicing the skills in your life, so the assignments typically focus on trying out the approaches discussed in the lesson and recording notes on this. In the group-based program these assignments are discussed during the group, with therapist feedback.

Again, not completing skills assignments is therapy-interfering behavior and a target for completion and problem solving consistent with the process outlined for the diary card and Binge Record Sheets, so as we are just beginning this process, think about what might get in the way for you and preemptively outline how you will work through this (see also downloadable Handout 2.6).

Handout 2.6 Plan for Completion of Skills Assignments

I will complete my skills assignments at this time daily: _____

_____

I will keep my book and skills assignments in this location: _____

_____

If I am participating in this program through sessions with a professional, I will follow these steps to ensure that I bring my skills assignments to session:

_____

_____

_____

_____

If I am completing this program from a self-guided approach, I will check in with myself at this time each week, holding myself accountable for completing skills assignments at that time if I have not already done so:

_____

I anticipate these barriers to completing my skills assignments and will address them in the following ways: _____

_____

_____

_____

_____

_____

_____

_____

If I am participating in this program through sessions with a professional, I anticipate these barriers to bringing my skills assignments to session and will address them in the following ways: _____

_____

_____

_____

_____

_____

If I am completing this program from a self-guided approach, I anticipate these barriers to holding myself accountable weekly to skills assignment completion and will address them in the following ways:

_____

_____

_____

_____

_____

_____

_____

Behavior Chain and Solution Analysis

Behavior chain and solution analysis is another key practice in this program. The process outlines, in great detail, moment by moment, the precursors of a target behavior or urge, including feelings, thoughts, bodily sensations, and actions; its consequences; and opportunities for skillful alternatives. This is recorded on worksheets as a standing weekly assignment (at least one set of chain worksheets/week) in addition to the diary card and skills assignments (see Handouts 2.7–2.11, which comprise instructions, a set of blank worksheets, and examples). In the group-based program, behavior chain and solution analysis also occurs during the group, retracing the chain of events beyond the worksheets, together, with group feedback.

Behavior chain and solution analysis is an integral part of DBT and, moreover, clients have consistently shared finding this one of the most helpful parts of the group-based program. There are many potential benefits from this process. The detailed retracing permits more accurate awareness of the influences on behavior and feelings, thoughts, and bodily sensations and thus more effective generation of alternative solutions. It can also uncover and reinforce skillful behavior that is occurring. In any chain of events there is skillful behavior to acknowledge and build upon. Like the diary card, the process also promotes a reasonable stance which can counter elevated emotion surrounding behavior. The process can also be at least mildly aversive and serve as a consequence for targeted behavior, promoting movement towards more skillful patterns, although it is usually most effective to approach the process with a nonjudgmental stance of curiosity, using the behavior chain and solution analysis as a learning tool for increased awareness and problem solving. Behavior chain and solution analysis can also be helpful for not just mindless eating patterns but also therapy-interfering behavior (see Handout 2.10). In addition, behavior chain and solution analysis need not be reserved only for the occurrence of problem behavior. This practice can also be a tool for understanding what went well, for skillful behavior and not acting on urges (see Handout 2.11).

Behavior Chain Analysis of Problem Behavior: Page 1

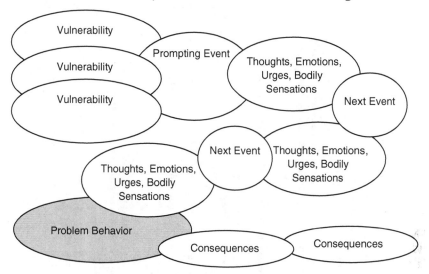

What Exactly Is the Problem Behavior That I Am Analyzing?

Identify the specific problem behavior, e.g., restricting, binge eating, purging, mindless eating, missing a group session, not calling for coaching and then acting on an urge, not doing homework, not fully completing the diary card.

What Things in Myself and My Environment Made Me Vulnerable?

Start day: _____

Describe vulnerability factors happening before the prompting event. What factors or events made you more vulnerable to a problematic chain? Describe:
1. Factors in *you*, e.g., physical illness, hunger, sleep deprivation, emotions (anger, fear, etc.), behaviors (inactivity, procrastination, etc.).
2. Factors in *the environment*, e.g., tempting foods, increased demands at home or work.

What Prompting Event Started Me on the Chain to My Problem Behavior?

Start day: _____

Describe in detail the specific prompting event that started the chain reaction, even if it does not seem like that the event "caused" the problem behavior. What happened first or started the problem behavior? Describe:
1. Factors in *you*: What you were doing, thinking, imagining, feeling.
2. Factors in *the environment*: Exactly what was happening.

Behavior Chain Analysis of Problem Behavior: Page ___

Actual (Not Skillful?)

Skillful Alternatives

Use this sheet to fill in, step by step, what happened. Include what you were feeling (emotions and bodily sensations) and thinking, along with what happened. Include enough detail that someone could recreate the experience precisely as if from a script. First, fill in the chain of experience on the left side of the paper, then continue onto the next page. Then, when you are completing your solution analysis, go back and look at each link in the chain and generate any skillful alternatives that may have been helpful to result in a more effective outcome, not leading to eating disordered behavior.

The bubbles on the edge with number signs are meant to simply be a visual for each link in the chain. Most chains will require multiple copies of this middle sheet, so do not be shy! Use as many sheets as you need to adequately capture the details of the event. Remember, we want to be able to recreate what happened just by reading these papers. Also, the more information you include, the more you will generate insight and opportunities for other skillful alternatives.

1. Imagine that your problem behavior is chained to the prompting event.

2. Write out all the links in the chain between the prompting events and the problem behavior. Detail each and every link, using as many sheets as needed. Be very specific—as if you were writing a script for a play or a chapter in a novel.

3. Describe the links in the sequence they occurred. Notice what came first—the sensation, the feeling, or the thought? Then what thought, feeling, action, sensation, or event followed? Then what followed that, etc., etc.?

4. After completing your behavior chain analysis (when you have reached the occurrence of the problem behavior and then completed the box entitled "What were the consequences of my behavior?" on the last page), in your solution analysis, describe in detail what you could have done differently at each link in the chain of events to avoid the problem behavior. Describe the specific skills you could have used to replace the links and avoid the problem behavior.

\#

\#

\#

\#

\#

\#

Behavior Chain Analysis of Problem Behavior: Last Page

Day: _____   Date filled out: _____

What Were the Consequences of My Behavior?

1. Describe the consequences of the problem behavior.
2. Specifically, describe the consequences that reinforce the problem behavior, i.e., that make it more likely to happen again, e.g., temporary decreases in emotional intensity, increased sense of power over others.
3. Describe the consequences:
   a. In *you*: how you felt, what you thought, what you did.
   b. In *the environment*: effects on the environment and others' reactions.

Ways to Reduce My Vulnerability in the Future

Describe in detail ways you can prevent the chain of events from starting by reducing your vulnerability to the chain, e.g., improving sleep habits, not purchasing large quantities of tempting foods, balancing work with relaxation.

Ways to Prevent the Precipitating Event from Happening Again

Describe in detail things you can do to prevent the prompting event from happening again, e.g., make an agreement with your partner/boyfriend/girlfriend/spouse/roommate to take a time out before an argument escalates and then follow through on the agreement.

Plans to Repair, Correct, and Overcorrect Harm Caused

Describe in detail what you will do to repair what you have damaged with the problem behavior. What will you do to correct, for example, the blow to your self-confidence or the interference in relationships that the problem behavior caused? Be sure to use your Wise Mind here!

Reflections to Share

Spend some time observing your thoughts and feelings about this chain of events and problem behavior. Write down those thoughts and feelings that you want to share in group.

Behavior Chain Analysis of Problem Behavior: Page 1

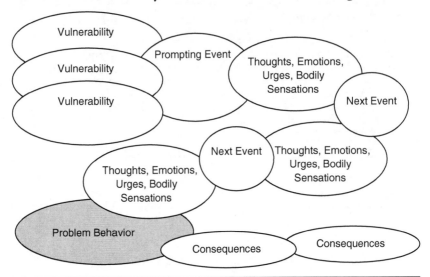

What Exactly Is the Problem Behavior That I Am Analyzing?

What Things in Myself and My Environment Made Me Vulnerable?

Start day: _____

What Prompting Event Started Me on the Chain to My Problem Behavior?

Start day: _____

Behavior Chain Analysis of Problem Behavior: Page _

Skillful Alternatives

Actual (Not Skillful?)

#

#

#

#

#

#

Behavior Chain Analysis of Problem Behavior: Last Page

Day: _____ Date filled out: _____

What Were the Consequences of My Behavior?

Ways to Reduce My Vulnerability in the Future

Ways to Prevent the Precipitating Event from Happening Again

Plans to Repair, Correct, and Overcorrect Harm Caused

Reflections to Share

Behavior Chain Analysis of Problem Behavior: Page 1

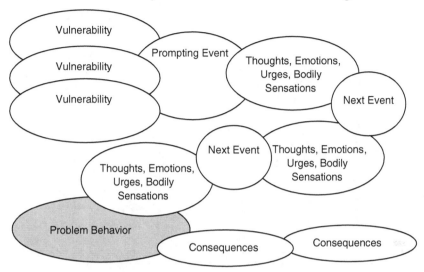

What Exactly Is the Problem Behavior That I Am Analyzing?

Binge Eating

What Things in Myself and My Environment Made Me Vulnerable?

Start day: _____*Saturday*_____

Stressful week
Up late night before, so tired, 7 hours of sleep instead of 8
2 glasses of wine night before
Need to get groceries, so not many balanced choices in the house
No exercise since Thursday

What Prompting Event Started Me on the Chain to My Problem Behavior?

Start day: _____*Saturday, evening*_____

Home alone, trying to work, memory thoughts of ex-.

Behavior Chain Analysis of Problem Behavior: Page _2_

Actual (Not Skillful?)	Skillful Alternatives
#1 Opened refrigerator, looking for something to eat; hunger 2/5, heavy muscles 2/5	Mindfulness of emotion → reach out to friend
#2 Saw shelves bare, just fruit in bin; tortillas in drawer, condiments, salad dressings, and beverages in the door; sighed; thought "When am I going to go to the store? I don't have time," hunger 4/5, bitter 4/5, heavy muscles 3/5	Mindfulness of thought, labeling thought "I don't have time" as a thought; evaluate evidence for and against self-validation Self-soothing by self-massage of sore muscles
#3 Opened freezer; saw frozen meat, vegetables; bread, cheese, and desserts—container of cake, two batches of cookies, and ice cream; sighed; sadness 3/5, heavy muscles 3/5, thought of ex- out at a bar with other women, hunger 4/5	Mindfulness of emotion → reach out to friend Self-Soothing by self-massage of sore muscles Mindfulness of thought, labeling as thought
#4 Pushed away thought; opened cupboard; saw crackers, pasta, and old box of Valentine's candy; thoughts of ex- giving candy, sadness and anger 4.5/5, shoulder muscles tightened 4/5, jaw tightened 4/5, hot 3/5	Mindfulness of thought, labeling as thought self-validation Opposite to Emotion Action to walk away from cupboard; express anger effectively, play piano angrily
#5 Capitulated 5/5; grabbed candy; crying; started eating the candy; sadness and anger 5/5, shaking	Self-validation; Opposite to Emotion Action
#6 Ate entire box of candy, then sleeve of Ritz crackers; crying; numb 3/5, no thoughts	Throw away the candy!! Opposite to Emotion Action

Behavior Chain Analysis of Problem Behavior: Last Page

Day filled out: __Sunday_____

What Were the Consequences of My Behavior?

Felt disgusted with myself 4/5;
told myself "It's no wonder your ex- left;"
felt fat 4/5;
urge to overexercise 4/5;
urge to go to bed and stay in bed all day the next day 4/5.

Ways to Reduce My Vulnerability in the Future

Address stress more with ABC PLEASE, in particular:
(1) Yoga, also for Self-Soothing and finding Wise Mind; Cope Ahead
by finding class schedules and special events of interest; find a
night option for after work; (2) Get back into music more;
(3) Be more mindful of drinking while still vulnerable from the
break-up, limit as needed; (4) Cool room at night with fan;
(5) Purchase groceries more in advance for more balanced options.

Ways to Prevent the Precipitating Event from Happening Again

Make plans with friends so not home alone on Saturday nights or
treat self to a more enjoyable night, e.g., go shopping, go to the
movies, get a massage—work can wait and you will probably be
more productive at another time anyway, especially if you permit
yourself ample self-care.

Plans to Repair, Correct, and Overcorrect Harm Caused

Radical Acceptance for self-forgiveness; this solution analysis!

Reflections to Share

I need to continue to work on finding more balance and
radically accepting that at least for right now, while I am
recovering from this break-up, I may need to take more time away
from work and that is not necessarily ineffective avoidance.

Behavior Chain Analysis of Problem Behavior: Page 1

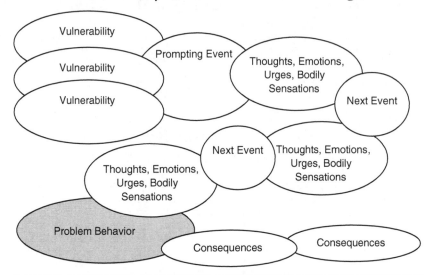

What Exactly Is the Problem Behavior That I Am Analyzing?

Not completing my diary card yesterday

What Things in Myself and My Environment Made Me Vulnerable?

Start day: ___*Yesterday, Monday*_____

Didn't sleep well, got about 6 hours of sleep
Did not go on morning run because trying to get more sleep, snoozing alarm

---

What Prompting Event Started Me on the Chain to My Problem Behavior?

Start day: __*Sunday*_____

Stayed up late, replaying weekend in my head, regretting actions

---

Behavior Chain Analysis of Problem Behavior: Page _2_

Actual (Not Skillful?)	Skillful Alternatives
# 1 Thoughts: "I'm so stupid. Why did I do that?", shame 4/5, muscles tense 3/5	Nonjudgmental Stance; Radical Acceptance
# 2 Try to just notice the thoughts and let them go, shame 3/5, muscles tense 3/5	Journal to describe more effectively
# 3 Watch a movie, thoughts of the weekend, shame 1/5, muscles tense 3/5	Read instead so no stimulating screen
# 4 1 a.m., movie ends, shame 1/5, muscles tired 3/5, thought, "I need to try to get at least 6 hours of sleep. It's going to be a long day tomorrow," set alarm for an hour later than usual, 7 a.m., turn off light	Nonjudgmental Stance; Radical Acceptance Cheerleading
# 5 Alarm goes off, 7 a.m., think "I do not want to get up," hit snooze, feeling of dread 1/5, heavy muscles 3/5	Mindful noticing thought and letting it go Cheerleading Opposite to Emotion Action to get out of bed
# 6 Snoozed alarm goes off, 7:10 a.m., think "I do not want to get up," hit snooze, feeling of dread 1/5, heavy muscles 3/5	Mindful noticing thought and letting it go Cheerleading Opposite to Emotion Action to get out of bed
# 7 Snoozed alarm goes off, 7:20 a.m., think "I do not want to get up, but I have to," use Opposite to Emotion Action to turn off alarm and get out of bed, feeling of dread 1/5, heavy muscles 2/5	Cheerleading, maybe with music especially! **Repeat Opposite to Emotion Action!

Behavior Chain Analysis of Problem Behavior: Page _3_

Actual (Not Skillful?)	Skillful Alternatives

 # 8 — Go to the bathroom, feeling of dread 1/5, tired 3/5, heavy muscles 2/5

Cheerleading, maybe with music especially!

 # 9 — Wash my hands, look in the mirror, checking thighs, think "Ugh, you are getting so flabby," disgust 1/5, tense shoulders 3/5

Mindful noticing thought and letting it go
Comparisons

 # 10 — Look at the time, 7:25 a.m., debate if I have time to run, anxiety 3/5, tense shoulders 3/5

Pros and cons

 # 11 — Decide I don't have time to run and I need to get in the shower, anxiety 3/5, disappointment 3/5, tense shoulders 3/5

Radical Acceptance
Comparisons, reminding myself that I ran 2 days ago and for a while I wasn't running at all

 # 12 — Go to the kitchen, make coffee, choose my favorite kind, hold mug, take first sip, feeling grateful 3/5, tense shoulders 2/5

**Do this again—Self-Soothing and mindfulness
Maybe also self-soothe by rubbing shoulders

 # 13 — Look at the time, 7:35 a.m., think "Oh, shoot, I don't have time to eat breakfast. I'm going to have to eat a granola bar in the car," anxiety 3/5, frustration 3/5, tense shoulders 3/5

Radical Acceptance
Effectiveness

 # 14 — Undress quickly for the shower, notice naked body, think, "Ugh, I'm so fat," disgust 2/5, try to notice the thought and let it go and get into the shower as quickly as possible, heavy muscles 3/5

Mindful noticing thought and letting it go
Cheerleading

Behavior Chain Analysis of Problem Behavior: Page _4_

	Actual (Not Skillful?)	**Skillful Alternatives**
# 15	In the shower, try to focus on the water, bath wash, shampoo, and conditioner One-Mindfully, disgust 1/5, sadness 1/5, anxiety 2/5, tired 2/5, heavy muscles 2/5	**Do this again—One-Mindfully! Mindful noticing emotion and letting it go
# 16	Get out of the shower, see flabby legs, try to just notice the thoughts and let them go, disgust 1/5, tired 2/5, heavy muscles 2/5	**Do this again—Mindful noticing thought and letting it go
# 17	Look at the time, 7:55 a.m., think "I'm gonna be late," anxiety 4/5, tense shoulders 4/5	Cheerleading, maybe with music especially!
# 18	Go to my closet, stare at my clothes, considering what to wear, anxiety 4/5, tense shoulders 4/5	Cheerleading, maybe with music especially!
# 19	Think "I need to do laundry," pick out dress I like, anxiety 2/5, tense shoulders 2/5	Effectiveness; **Do this again—Self-Soothing with dress I like
# 20	Look at the time, 8:02 a.m., think "Hurry up," anxiety 4/5, tense shoulders 4/5	Cheerleading, maybe with music especially!
# 21	Get dressed, trying to be one-mindful, anxiety 3/5, tense shoulders 3/5	**Do this again, One-Mindfully

Behavior Chain Analysis of Problem Behavior: Page _5_

Actual (Not Skillful?)

 # 22 — Do my hair and make-up quickly, think "Ugh, it is so hot in here," turn on fan, anxiety 3/5, tense shoulders 3/5

 # 23 — Grab shoes, lunch, and bags and get into car, start driving to work, think "I'm going to be late again," anxiety 3/5, tense shoulders 3/5

 # 24 — Turn on the radio, start channel surfing, trying to find a decent song, anxiety and irritability 3/5, tense shoulders 3/5

 # 25 — Find a song I decide will work, relief 3/5, anxiety 2/5, tense shoulders 2/5

 # 26 — Think back over the morning, realize I did not complete my diary card, think "I did it again," disappointment 3/5, frustration 3/5

#

#

Skillful Alternatives

**Turn on fan again but sooner for self-soothing Cheerleading, maybe with music especially!

Effectiveness, Radical Acceptance

Radical Acceptance

Participate with song, singing along

Radical Acceptance

© Taylor & Francis 2017, Angela Klein, *Mindful Eating from the Dialectical Perspective*

Behavior Chain Analysis of Problem Behavior: Last Page

Day filled out: ___Tuesday_____

What Were the Consequences of My Behavior?

Disappointment 3/5; frustration 3/5; this behavior chain!

Ways to Reduce My Vulnerability in the Future

Radical Acceptance, Opposite to Emotion Action, and cheerleading, especially with music, to get out of bed for run; Cope Ahead night before by putting running clothes and shoes by bed; read instead of watching a movie to get sleepy, to fall asleep earlier.

Ways to Prevent the Precipitating Event from Happening Again

Complete behavior chain and solution analysis of event triggering shame.

Plans to Repair, Correct, and Overcorrect Harm Caused

This behavior chain and solution analysis!; completing diary card the next day for the day missed.

Reflections to Share

I need to continue working on finding balance in work and pleasant events, not making everything more complicated by behaviors that provide only short-term relief but then generate shame. I need to work on sitting with boredom, restlessness, and sadness instead of staying so busy and engaging in short-term coping, instead keeping in mind as a greater priority long-term goals and values.

Behavior Chain Analysis of Problem Behavior: Page 1

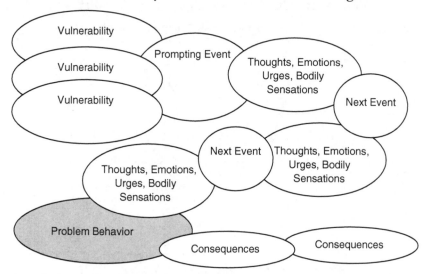

What Exactly Is the Problem Behavior That I Am Analyzing?

Not acting on urges to binge eat

What Things in Myself and My Environment Made Me Vulnerable?

Start day: ___Wednesday_____

Stressful week
Not enough sleep the night before, 7 hours instead of 8, and restless/interrupted
No morning snack
Drank more caffeine than usual, chai tea latte in addition to usual coffee

---

What Prompting Event Started Me on the Chain to My Problem Behavior?

Start day: ___Wednesday_____

Lunch with friend; ordered pizza and size was massive, like two feet in diameter, a foot wide; ate half; took rest in to-go box back to work

---

Behavior Chain Analysis of Problem Behavior: Page _1_

	Actual (Not Skillful?)	**Skillful Alternatives**
# 1	Get into my car to drive back to the office to continue the work day, sadness 3/5, because no plans to see friend again until probably a month, thought "I'm still hungry," urge to binge by finishing pizza 3/5, no bodily sensations noted	Mindfulness of current emotion, e.g., text friend to thank her for lunch and let know looking forward to next time meet up; text other friends to make plans in the meantime Consider whether hunger is actually sadness
# 2	Think "It's really not that much anyway, the crust is so thin," urge to binge by finishing pizza 3/5, no awareness of emotions or bodily sensations	Mindfulness of thought; label as thought from Emotion Mind; remember Wise Mind Mindfulness of bodily sensations, body scan
# 3	Think "I'll just finish this one half a slice," anxiety 2/5, tense muscles 2/5	I think this was fine—just be sure being honest
# 4	Open pizza box, smell pizza smell, think "Mmm," happiness 1/5, anxiety 1/5, tense muscles 1/5	I think this was fine—just be sure being honest
# 5	Mindfully observe piece—its temperature in the summer sun, its limp crust, its flavor, happiness 3/5, no anxiety, relaxed muscles	I think this was fine—just be sure being honest
# 6	Think, "O.K., back to work," urge to keep eating/binge 1/5, contentment 2/5, relaxed muscles	I think this was fine—just be sure being honest

Behavior Chain Analysis of Problem Behavior: Last Page

Day filled out: __Sunday_____

What Were the Consequences of My Behavior?

Pride 3/5, contentment 3/5, gratitude 3/5; leftover pizza enjoyed the next day for lunch!

Ways to Reduce My Vulnerability in the Future

Continue working on balance—commit to physical activity at least 3 times/week; radically accept fatigue if less than 8 hours of sleep to prevent overcaffeinating.

Ways to Prevent the Precipitating Event from Happening Again

Ask how big pizza is in terms of dimensions (we asked about number of slices and clearly got an underestimate!); suggest splitting pizza with friend (I thought about this but dismissed it because I secretly wanted the whole pizza to myself!).

Plans to Repair, Correct, and Overcorrect Harm Caused

No need to repair—I resisted the urge to binge eat and mindfully found a middle ground.

Reflections to Share

Thought: I wonder if I was also vulnerable because the pizza reminded me of my ex-, so my sadness may have been compounded. Overall, I am proud of myself for finding a middle ground with not harshly restricting and also not plowing through the rest of the pizza!

Again, not completing behavior chain and solution analysis is therapy-interfering behavior and a target for completion and problem solving consistent with the process outlined for the diary card, Binge Record Sheets, and skills assignments, so again, as we are just beginning this process, think about what might get in the way for you and preemptively outline how you will work through this (see also downloadable Handout 2.12).

Handout 2.12 Plan for Completion of Behavior Chain and Solution Analysis Worksheets

I will complete my behavior chain and solution analysis worksheets at this time weekly:

_____

I will keep my behavior chain and solution analysis worksheets in this location:

_____

If I am participating in this program through sessions with a professional, I will follow these steps to ensure that I bring my behavior chain and solution analysis worksheets to session:

_____

_____

_____

_____

If I am completing this program from a self-guided approach, I will check in with myself at this time each week, holding myself accountable for completing the previous week's behavior chain and solution analysis worksheets at that time if I have not already done so:

_____

I anticipate these barriers to completing my behavior chain and solution analysis worksheets and will address them in the following ways:

_____

_____

_____

_____

_____

_____

If I am participating in this program through sessions with a professional, I anticipate these barriers to bringing my behavior chain and solution analysis worksheets to session and will address them in the following ways:

_____

_____

_____

_____

_____

_____

If I am completing this program from a self-guided approach, I anticipate these barriers to holding myself accountable weekly to behavior chain and solution analysis completion and will address them in the following ways:

_____

_____

_____

_____

_____

_____

_____

Coaching Calls

When delivered in a therapeutic context (as researched within a group-based setting or adapted for individual sessions), the mindful eating program outlined in the following chapters includes coaching calls (Klein et al., 2012; 2013). Coaching calls consist of texts or calls to facilitators between sessions for skills guidance to address urges or challenging situations. Thus facilitators are able to help clients access skills when experiencing high emotion that can interfere with their ability to do so more independently. This helps foster skills generalization when the opportunity for learning is arguably greatest, when urges and emotions are arising in vivo, in the naturalistic environment, and differs from therapies that are constrained to sessions in the office. Including coaching calls is consistent with standard DBT and more comprehensive than Telch and colleagues' (2000; 2001) protocol, which omitted coaching calls.

Coaching calls are not meant to be extended, additional therapy, but rather brief (e.g., 5–10 minutes) and focused on skills support. While there can be a shaping process, permitting longer contact when first beginning the program, then tapering to shorter contact (and coaches set their own boundaries, so more extended calls may be included accordingly, if clinically indicated), it is imperative that coaches mindfully monitor whether skillful coaching outcomes are resulting from the client using skills or from simply talking with them and receiving that connection, validation, and cheerleading. Ultimately, coaching is intended, in time, to help clients learn how to access skills on their own, to no longer need the coaching. For example, after some time working with me on coaching, clients will tell me, "I didn't contact you because I knew what you were going to say." Similarly, clients will say "I heard your voice telling me how to be skillful," or "I feel like you are part of my inner dialogue now."

The structure of coaching consists of first getting a sense of the situation, including the client specifying the urges they are having and rating them 0–5. In addition to urge ratings, the coach can ask for emotion ratings, thoughts, and bodily sensations, consistent with behavior chain and solution analysis as outlined above. Then the coach would ask the client what skills they have tried, since it is not efficient and can be frustrating for the client if the coach is suggesting skills that they have already tried and not found helpful. Then the coach would recommend other skills for the client to try, ask if there are any barriers to these skills (since they may be the most wonderful skills in the world, but if the client is not willing or able to try them, then they are rather useless!), problem solve any barriers, such as lack of motivation, and then ask the client to implement the skills and let the coach know how they work and if further coaching is needed. Also, to monitor the degree to which skillful outcomes are resulting from the skills implementation or rather the connection to the coach, the coach would ask the client to rate their urges at the end of the call as well. Ideally the urges would decrease slightly but not markedly, since marked decrease before any skills implementation would suggest that the decrease in distress was simply occurring from the contact with the coach.

Coaching was traditionally a phone conversation and can still occur in this format, although texting has become common in practice, in my experience and those of my fellow colleagues over the recent years. Texting seems to work well, especially with younger clients, when it is so much the norm now, and when social anxiety may be a barrier to even making phone calls, let alone having them. At the same time, if social anxiety is a barrier, working up to phone conversations could be part of a treatment plan to overcome this gradually, if indicated. In addition, it remains at the discretion of the coach whether a phone conversation is needed when texting is instead initiated. This can be the case in particular with crisis situations (e.g., potentially imminent suicidal behavior) in which time is of the essence and texting is just not going to permit this adequately.

Again, using coaching will help extend learning beyond the context of group or regular individual sessions, so using it is important; not using it can be considered therapy-interfering behavior. Addressing this can include behavior chain and solution analysis, and assignment of check-ins to increase comfort. This may begin with just check-ins about topics unrelated to eating, for example, just saying hello or sending a picture of a skillful, fun activity being done (e.g., a pedicure, a day at a festival), then progress to assigned coaching to address urges a certain number of times per week. To increase comfort, check-ins can be at scheduled times or open, with a specific number of times assigned (e.g., just text the coach once the first week about anything, then increase this to twice the next week). Ultimately, clients are asked to initiate the coaching as needed when experiencing urges for eating disordered behavior that they are targeting for change with the program.

For coaches, this requirement places you on call basically 24/7, within reasonable limits. You thus need to be open to and willing to accept this responsibility and availability in your nights and weekends. To help maintain this, you reserve the right to not answer calls or texts if it is not a good time for you, unless it is a crisis situation that requires you to extend your limits. You thus need to be aware of your self-care limits. Part of this is a process. You will know when they are crossed by the emotional energy that follows. Examples of self-care limits can include postponing coaching responses until after other sessions, after social events, and until the morning. Group leaders are able to set their own limits. For example, through the years I have slept with my phone by my bed and answered calls in the night, although I ask clients to call during the night only if it is truly a situation that cannot wait until morning, since I will function better for them as a coach if I get a full night's sleep. Other therapists turn their phone on silent and advise clients that they are not available during the hours they reserve for sleep. Whatever your limits are, it is essential to honor them to prevent burning yourself out. This is especially important working with eating patterns, given the likelihood for issues to arise at least several times per day, for example, with breakfast, lunch, and dinner.

It is also important to call before acting on urges to maintain access to coaching calls. If clients instead call after acting on disordered eating-related urges (e.g., binge eating or purging), then coaching is actually not available for a period of time under what is referred to as the Next Meal/Next Snack Rule. For example, if a client binge eats at breakfast and then calls for coaching, the next opening for coaching under the Next Meal/Next Snack Rule would actually be the next time approximated for morning snacking according to the coach. To roughly calculate this, the day is divided into three meal times (breakfast, lunch, and dinner) and then three snack times after each meal (mid-morning, mid-afternoon, and later in the evening). These times are times when it would make sense to eat according to this overall framework, not necessarily times that the client is eating. Also, this is not to say that this is an eating structure recommended by the program. Rather, it is intended as a guideline to balance reasonable resumption of access to coaching throughout the day, with meals and snacks, on the one hand, with minimization of positive reinforcement of disordered eating-related behavior on the other hand (see Chapter 3 for further discussion of positive reinforcement). That is, hopefully clients value their connection to their coach and find it helpful, so according to the principles of positive reinforcement, if this support followed disordered eating-related behavior, it would, even if inadvertently, increase the likelihood of the behavior occurring again in the future due to the pairing with the desired support. Blocking contact for a period of time under the Next Meal/Next Snack Rule attempts to minimize this outcome, in the interest of ultimately supporting movement past disordered eating-related behavior. Like the consequence of Binge Record Sheets, keeping in mind the Next Meal/Next Snack Rule can also motivate clients to not act on urges in order to not lose access to coaching calls. This is a modification of DBT's 24-hour rule, which blocks coaching for 24 hours if clients engage in self-harm or suicidality and then call for coaching (Linehan, 1993). The reduction from 24 hours intends to not strand clients struggling with disordered eating-related concerns to face an entire day of triggering meals and snacks.

Of note, comorbidity calls upon coaches to integrate the different DBT coaching rules. For example, if a client self-harms and then calls for coaching, the 24-hour rule would trump the Next Meal/Next Snack Rule according to the DBT treatment hierarchy of first addressing life-threatening behavior, above therapy-interfering behavior (Linehan, 1993). Likewise, an exception to the Next Meal/Next Snack Rule could be when clients report self-harm urges or suicidal urges after engaging in disordered eating-related behavior. Coaches can then choose to provide coaching to divert life-threatening actions, while still minimizing discussion of previous disordered eating-related behavior, only permitting details of this as related to the current life-threatening urges, still deferring any further discussion until the next designated meal or snack time. For additional adjustments to consider with presentations including alcohol or substance use see descriptions by Dimeff (Dimeff & Linehan, 2008; McMain, Sayrs, Dimeff, & Linehan, 2007).

Treatment Hierarchy

As noted above, life-threatening behavior is the number one target in standard DBT. This includes self-harm behavior, as well as suicidality, because you cannot do any treatment if the client is not alive. Self-harm behavior is included not because it is necessarily imminently life-threatening but rather because it can escalate to a life-threatening scale, even if this is unintentional. Indeed, clients sometimes conceptualize self-harm as a way to stay alive and not act on suicidal urges, a way to feel something or numb their emotions, and yet, due to increasing tolerance to the physical pain, what originally "worked" as a temporary coping strategy usually stops working, so the severity of self-harm increases. Self-harm also statistically increases the risk of ultimately committing suicide to such an extent that it is taken just as seriously (Cooper et al., 2005; Owens, Horrocks, & House, 2002). Life-threatening behavior is explicitly designated under this treatment hierarchy in DBT given its origin as a treatment model for chronic suicidality and self-harm in BPD. In DBT adapted for eating disorders, medical monitoring informs whether eating disordered-related behavior rises to this category of life-threatening behavior (Wisniewski & Kelly, 2003). Likewise, any concern about possible medical complications from eating disordered-related behavior calls for swift attention throughout the course of the mindful eating program being outlined, with screening (e.g., electrolyte testing) before embarking on the program and thereafter as indicated. Stabilization is especially critical in medically compromised presentations needing weight restoration.

As referenced throughout this chapter, DBT also gives attention to therapy-interfering behavior (e.g., incompletion of the diary card, Binge Record Sheets, skills assignments, behavior chain and solution analysis, and coaching calls; tardiness to sessions). This is the second target in the DBT treatment hierarchy. This is prioritized over any further targets (after life-threatening behavior and before other disordered eating-related behavior) because clients cannot benefit from treatment if they are not doing the treatment. Likewise, if professionals are not adherent in providing the program, clients will not benefit fully. Therefore, feedback is invited from clients and problem solving to overcome any barriers is essential.

Finally, after life-threatening behavior and therapy-interfering behavior, DBT delineates the third target of treatment as quality-of-life-interfering behavior—anything that is getting in the way of a life worth living. Disordered eating-related behavior typically falls under this level in standard DBT (except when it rises to the level of life-threatening behavior). Given its emphasis on this quality-of-life-interfering behavior, it is a prerequisite to first resolve any self-harm or suicidality concerns before beginning the mindful eating program being outlined (especially when delivered in the group-based format) and to immediately address any lapses with indicated clinical measures (e.g., adding individual DBT sessions or setting contingencies to enable continued participation).

Commitment

Commitment can be a scary word. It can seem absolute and final, not just closing doors but barricading them shut with no keys to open them. This can generate so much anxiety that it destroys relationships before or after the walk down the aisle and at the very least can prompt us to pause before proceeding into any venture. For the mindful eating program further outlined in the upcoming chapters, commitment is required. Commitment to this program calls for full participation and a pledge of abstinence from eating disordered behavior.

You may wonder how this is possible. After all, if stopping eating disordered behavior were as simple as pledging to no longer engage in the behavior, this book could stop now and programs would be extremely brief. Of course, it is not that easy. Moving away from the behavior requires full commitment to fully succeed, cognitively eliminating the behavior as an option, and then when lapses occur—as they can be expected to, when trying to change any behavior—the commitment is to fully examine the lapses, learn from them, and recommit to abstinence. This is thus a commitment to what is called dialectical abstinence—full commitment to abstinence on the one hand and full commitment to learning from lapses on the other hand. Using the metaphor of marriage, the commitment would be fully pledging to love and honor your spouse and when unloving feelings and difficulties arise, to work through them, learn from them, and recommit to continue fully loving that partner. Likewise, as we have discussed, the commitment to this program includes addressing therapy-interfering behavior, working through any issues that interfere with participation, such as not completing diary cards, not completing behavior chain and solution analysis worksheets, and not fully completing assignments and practices.

As with marriage, the commitment to abstinence from eating disordered behavior is ideally for a lifetime. And for the sake of this program material, as noted above, the time commitment is 15 weeks. For group-based delivery, this requires consistent attendance. The commitment is for attendance weekly. And if this is not possible (e.g., due to illness, travel, or just choosing not to attend a certain week), then absences need to be minimized or you may be asked to step out of the program until another group begins. This is considered a therapy vacation, which may sound fun and exciting (I like vacations and I am imagining you do as well!), but means that no therapy with the therapy team is permitted until resumption of the program—no individual or group sessions or coaching calls—so this can be a major consequence that disrupts connection to helpful support. It is thus extremely important that a commitment to this program is not made lightly and instead is given due consideration because you will then be held to this commitment. Thus, technically, once you begin the program, you cannot quit. If you choose to not continue, you will still be considered to be part of the group-based program until the therapy team dismisses you and places you on a vacation. If you return from a vacation and then are dismissed again, the therapy team will need to consider if you will be eligible to return to the program in the future.

For group-based programs, the therapists also make the commitment to the program, to be present each week or otherwise provide ample notification and repair any absences. For example, when I have missed sessions for vacation I return with souvenirs for the group. This is intended to demonstrate that I have kept the group in mind while I have been away and reaffirms my commitment to the clients.

To formalize the commitments, the group-based protocol includes both clients and therapists signing contracts (see Handout 2.13). Modified versions of the contracts are included here, as well, for readers embarking on this journey independently (see Handout 2.14). I would ask you to sign the contract before continuing if you intend to participate fully in working through the skills and mindful eating practices and not just read the book to gather knowledge, for example, academically. As with the pros and cons exercise, do not rush through this process. Consider it fully before continuing. And, when you are ready, sign. You will see that I have signed my contract to you in return.

Chapter Summary

We have now considered possible benefits and costs of continuing your patterns of eating or moving to greater balance, both short-term and long-term, and walked through the key components of the current mindful eating program from a dialectical perspective. To review, commitment to this program includes completing daily diary cards turned in weekly, Binge Record Sheets, skills assignments, behavior chain and solution analysis, and, for participants working with professionals, coaching calls. We will cover skills in mindfulness, emotion regulation, and distress tolerance and specifically apply mindfulness to eating once we have established a foundation in core mindfulness.

Thank you for investing your time and energy in this journey. You are moving into a way of not only relating to food but also relating ultimately to life that many choose to continue to fully or partially avoid, instead persisting in unending allegiance to rules about eating and food. You are choosing to open yourself up entirely to the emotional experience of life and effectiveness within this emotion rather than closing yourself off from the experience. Instead of simply settling for managing your patterns or avoiding triggers, you are striking out on a path to face them head on, to ultimately set you free. Once you have made this commitment, it can truly be life-changing. I wholeheartedly commend you for this. Let us continue!

Mindful Eating Group Participant Contract

Group Member Agreements

1 I agree to commit to abstinence from eating disordered behaviors and to work on other problematic eating behaviors, such as mindless eating.
2 I agree to stay in the group program for the entire 15-session curriculum, attending all sessions and arriving on time and staying for the entire two and a half hours.
3 I agree to abide by the expectations for group members.
4 I agree to work on any problems that interfere with my progress, such as not attending group sessions, not fully completing my diary card, not completing homework, and not completing behavior chain analysis worksheets of incidents.
5 I give consent for data obtained about me through assessment and treatment to be used for the purposes of program evaluation.

_____   _____

Group Member Signature   Date

Mindful Eating Group Leader Contract

Group Leader Agreements

1 I agree to practice mindful eating in my daily life.
2 I agree to attend all group sessions, arriving on time and staying for the entire two and a half hours. If I cannot attend a group session or need to leave early, I agree to let the class know in advance and bring a repair to the next group session.
3 I agree to work on therapy-interfering behavior which may include any behavior which makes the therapy unbalanced such as being too accepting or pushing too hard for change, being too flexible or being too rigid, being too irreverent or behaving in a disrespectful manner.
4 I agree to make every reasonable effort to conduct competent and effective therapy, including obtaining consultation when I need it.
5 I agree to obey the Code of Ethics of my profession, including the guidelines for research.

_____   _____

Group Leader Signature   Date

Expectations for Group Members

1 Group members are not to come to sessions under the influence of drugs or alcohol.
2 Information obtained during group about other group members, including the fact that they attend the group, must remain confidential.
3 Group members who are going to be late or miss a session need to notify the group leader.
4 Group members who miss group are responsible for obtaining and completing the missed homework assignments by the next group meeting attended.
5 Diary cards, Binge Record Sheets, behavior chain and solution analysis worksheets, and homework assignments are due at the beginning of each group session.
6 Group members may not form private relationships outside of skills training sessions.
7 Sexual partners may not be in skills training together.
8 Food brought to group is to be consumed only during break.
9 Food provided by group is to be consumed only during corresponding group practices or break.
10 Group members can miss no more than two group meetings in a row.
11 Group members are to work on willingness.

Mindful Eating Book Participant Contract

Active Reader Agreements

1   I agree to commit to abstinence from eating disordered behaviors and to work on other problematic eating behaviors, such as mindless eating.
2   I agree to stay in the program for the entire curriculum, reading the material fully and completing all assignments and practices.
3   I agree to abide by the expectations for self-guided participants.
4   I agree to work on any problems that interfere with my progress, such as not fully reading material, not fully completing my diary card, not completing assignments and practices, and not completing behavior chain and solution analysis worksheets of incidents.

_____   _____

Book Participant Signature   Date

Mindful Eating Author Contract

Author Agreements

1   I agree to practice mindful eating in my daily life.
2   I agree to work on therapy-interfering behavior which may include any behavior which makes the therapy unbalanced such as being too accepting or pushing too hard for change, being too flexible or being too rigid, being too irreverent or behaving in a disrespectful manner.
3   I agree to make every reasonable effort to conduct competent and effective therapy, including obtaining consultation when I need it.
4   I agree to obey the Code of Ethics of my profession.

___*Angela S. Klein, Ph.D.*___   __ *July 13, 2016* __
Author Signature   Date

Expectations for Self-Guided Participants

1　Participants are not to come to review times under the influence of drugs or alcohol.
2　Diary cards, Binge Record Sheets, behavior chain and solution analysis worksheets, and homework assignments are due at the beginning of each review time.
3　During review times food is to be consumed only during corresponding practices or break.
4　Participants are to work on willingness.

3 Roots

Mindful eating from the dialectical perspective is an emerging descendent of the rich therapy tradition of behaviorism and CBT. It expands behavior therapy (BT) and CBT to incorporate a balance between acceptance and mindfulness, then cognitive and behavioral strategies for change. Such mindfulness-based CBT has been referred to as Third Wave Behaviorism.

Behaviorism and BT

Researchers first began studying learning from a behavioral perspective in the early twentieth century, with Pavlov and his dogs, and through the 1940s, with B.F. Skinner. In this era, research built upon Pavlov's discovery that a neutral stimulus (i.e., a stimulus that does not naturally provoke a certain response, e.g., a bell) could be conditioned to produce a conditioned response (i.e., a learned response, e.g., salivating) paralleling an unconditioned response (i.e., a naturally occurring response, e.g., salivating) after pairing the neutral stimulus (e.g., a bell) with an unconditioned stimulus (i.e., a stimulus that naturally prompts a certain response, e.g., food). In other words, the pairing of an initially neutral stimulus with an unconditioned stimulus produced an unconditioned response to the unconditioned stimulus which then became associated with the neutral stimulus (making it a conditioned stimulus), eliciting the same response, as a conditioned response. This process is known as **classical conditioning**.

Operant conditioning is the process by which behavior is shaped by consequences. When behavior increases, it is governed by what is known as reinforcement; when it decreases, it is governed by punishment. In both cases, there are two different forms of consequences: positive and negative. This can be confusing because positive is often associated with what is desired or liked and negative is often associated with what is undesired or disliked. In this context, positive means simply addition, or adding, and negative means simply subtraction, or taking away. Depending on whether the behavior is increasing (and reinforcement is thus operating) or decreasing (and punishment is thus occurring), what is given or taken away is either desired or undesired. That is, in the case of **positive reinforcement,** behavior is increased by the addition of a desired outcome; in **negative reinforcement,** behavior is increased by removal of what is undesired; in **positive punishment,** behavior is decreased by the addition of an undesired outcome; in **negative punishment,** behavior is decreased by the removal of what is desired. For example, if a parent is trying to motivate their child to increase the behavior of completing chores, they may implement positive reinforcement by paying an allowance (a desired outcome) if chores are completed and negative reinforcement by withdrawing nagging (an undesired outcome) if chores are completed. Concomitantly, to decrease the behavior of chore avoidance, a parent may employ positive punishment by nagging (an undesired outcome) and negative punishment by taking away the child's phone (a desired object) if chores are not completed (and thus chore avoidance is occurring, e.g., through procrastination).

Experiments studied fear induction and then how to basically reverse the effect. For example, John B. Watson (1920) conditioned Little Albert, a baby, to fear furry objects by pairing the unconditioned stimulus of a loud, clanging noise (i.e., a stimulus observed to naturally produce a fear reaction in infants) with the neutral stimulus of furry objects (which are not inherently threatening, like Santa Claus' beard, and when presented initially alone, triggered no distress or fear response). The unconditioned stimulus would trigger an unconditioned fear response, with crying. The neutral stimulus then became a conditioned stimulus that could elicit a conditioned fear response of crying and trying to move away from the furry objects when presented independently of the noise. This is an example of classical conditioning. In the case of such a phobia, escape behavior is then maintained by negative reinforcement through the removal of distress (i.e., by leaving a situation triggering fear, the fear goes away, increasing the likelihood of escaping again in the future).

In studying how to reverse such effects, researchers discovered the powerful impact of sustained exposure to the feared stimulus, while blocking escape responses. This uncoupled the classical conditioning, permitting new learning, and interrupted operant conditioning of negative reinforcement from escape behavior. For example, to decondition Baby Albert (which, unfortunately, did not actually occur), the process uncovered by the research would be to repeat exposure to the furry objects without the loud noises and prevent escape, until the habituation of distress and relearning that the furry objects are harmless and can be endured occurs.

Proponents of BT then began applying the principles of behaviorism to the treatment of psychological disorders, such as phobias, in the 1950s. Of particular relevance for mindful eating from the dialectical perspective, research support grew for exposure and response prevention (e.g., Page, 1955; Page & Hall, 1953; Solomon, Kamin, & Wynne, 1953) and Joseph

Wolpe (1958) developed the treatment approach of systematic desensitization, for phobias and other anxiety disorders. Systematic desensitization is based on reciprocal inhibition, which is the principle that you cannot be simultaneously relaxed and in a state of threat at the same time. Thus, by pairing a feared object that is not inherently dangerous with a relaxed state (e.g., induced by progressive muscle relaxation and slow, deep breathing), learning that the object is safe results. The consequence is again habituation. In other words, the emotional distress associated with the feared object diminishes, producing desensitization to the cue as a trigger for fear.

The process is systematic because it is gradual. For example, to desensitize a phobia of rabbits, a first step may be simply looking at pictures of rabbits. Then a next step could be watching TV shows with images of rabbits. Then a next step might be going to a petting zoo with rabbits but just looking at them, not touching them. Then a next step might be petting a rabbit while someone else holds it or it remains on the ground of its habitat. Then a next step might by holding a rabbit, then petting it while holding it. Then a final step may be holding and ultimately petting multiple rabbits. This contrasts with flooding, which would be jumping straight to the final step of holding and petting multiple rabbits.

Research suggests that flooding may be just as effective as systematic desensitization, if not more effective. Similarly, the pairing of exposure with relaxation as in systematic desensitization may not be needed above and beyond simply graded or graduated exposure without relaxation strategies, and relaxation strategies may even disrupt the full experience of emotion and resulting habituation that is lasting. In other words, relaxation strategies may perpetuate escape conditioning at some level, setting up vulnerability to relapse of the fear, in particular, if relaxation strategies are not employed. However, compared to flooding, willingness to participate or continue to participate in treatment can be higher if the exposure is graded or graduated and supported by relaxation, as packaged in systematic desensitization (Spiegler & Guevremont, 2015). This makes sense. Flooding is intense and overwhelming. Systematic desensitization is also intense but permits time to acclimate and build a sense of mastery for each next step. This can be like getting into a pool gradually, first dipping your toe in, then submerging your calf, then gradually, your legs, then walking slowly into the deeper water, letting it rise to your neck, then putting your head under (systematic desensitization to the cold water) versus jumping off a diving board into the deep end (flooding). Of course, flooding may be faster but risks reinforcing the fear if it prompts escape rather than sustained exposure to the feared object. For example, if the flooding with the rabbits is not tolerated and the client flees, escaping the fear that the flooding elicited, they have just reinforced the idea that rabbits are scary and escaping or avoiding them will permit relief from distress.

Interestingly, when eating disorders started gaining more attention in the psychiatric nomenclature, behavioral approaches competed with psychoanalytic, systemic, and feminist conceptualizations among therapists and researchers (e.g., Wachtel, 1976; for an exception see Price, 1974). Then CBT, with a strong emphasis on cognitive therapy (CT), rather than BT, emerged as the predominant force in the field. Yet, ironically behaviorism began with dogs salivating over food. Surely behavioral principles deserved application to eating disorders, as well, with consideration of reinforcement principles maintaining the behavior. This realization finally gained greater recognition with Third Wave Behaviorism.

Cognitive Theory, CT, and CBT

With cognitive theory, the relationship between stimulus and response was expanded to include thinking as a mediator. For example, returning to Baby Albert, cognitive theory would posit that the link between the stimulus of a white furry object and Albert's distress response would be an interpretive thought about the white furry object being threatening (e.g., "That is dangerous."). Following from this, according to cognitive theory, if Albert instead interpreted the white furry object as safe, he would not be distressed, or his distress would be diminished over time, once he learned that he could trust this thought as true.

This theory largely emerged from Aaron Beck's research in the 1960s, in which he observed the thoughts of individuals with depression to be characterized by markedly negative thoughts about themselves, the world, and the future (e.g., Beck, 1963; 1964). From his clinical work and studies he further developed the theory to include levels of thinking and beliefs. CT then grew out of cognitive theory, teaching clients to examine the evidence for and against their thoughts to foster more realistic thinking and thus reduce their distress (e.g., Beck, 1970; 1993).

CBT then integrated CT and BT. CT and CBT can also be considered BT emphasizing the specific behavior of thinking. That is, thinking can be conceptualized as a behavior—a stimulus or a response—within the behavioral framework—simply internal rather than external.

Cognitive theory and associated understanding of CT have also now been expanded to integrate neurobiology (Clark & Beck, 2010). Key areas implicated include the amygdala and hippocampus, shown to decrease activity connected to "negative" emotion with CT, and frontal regions, shown to increase activity connected to cognitive control of "negative" emotion with CT. In other words, neurobiological research is now supporting a conceptualization of cognitive theory and CT as a top down approach to emotion regulation, exerting its effect on emotion after it occurs (differing from a bottom up approach, curtailing emotions before they occur).

More broadly, the evidence for CBT is now exponential, extending across disorders (e.g., for a review of meta-analyses see Hofmann, Asnaani, Vonk, Sawyer, & Fang, 2012). In the field of eating disorders, this approach gained increasing attention beginning in the 1980s, with a wealth of research from Christopher Fairburn in particular (e.g., Fairburn, 1981; 1983; Fairburn et al., 1995; 2009; 2015), and now has a large following in both research and clinical service. This approach targets distorted thoughts (e.g., related to feeling fat; perfectionism; low self-esteem; feared consequences of eating) through psychoeducation, exposure, and cognitive reframing (examining evidence for and against thoughts and beliefs both within and outside of session, with homework assignments and self-monitoring), emphasizing the elimination of restriction, replaced by regular, adequate consumption.

Yet, even with the advancement of CBT, not all benefit and other approaches are needed. Rates for abstinence from bulimic symptoms following CBT have ranged markedly, from as low as 8 percent to as high as 80 percent (Mitchell et al., 2002), and even when individuals have achieved abstinence by the end of CBT, symptoms have been found to recur (e.g., for 44 percent; Halmi et al., 2002). Attrition rates also call into question how amenable CBT is to those who present for treatment and how to reach those who self-select out of CBT, with average drop-out rates around 28 percent (Mitchell et al., 2002). Fairburn's latest iteration of the treatment, labeled to be an enhanced version of CBT (CBT-E), has begun to recognize such areas for growth, in particular extending the model across the transdiagnostic spectrum of disordered eating and further attending to emotion regulation, as well as comorbidity, such as personality disorders.

Third Wave Behaviorism and CBT

Arising out of the previous two major traditions of behaviorism and CT/CBT, Third Wave Behaviorism and Third Wave CBT call into question the belief that cognitive reframing is essential for change. This rethinking of the role of thinking gained momentum from research comparing traditional BT with CBT and finding limited or no incremental benefit for cognitive strategies above and beyond the behavioral interventions (Longmore & Worrell, 2007). Similarly, research has not necessarily found changes in cognitions to actually significantly statistically mediate changes in outcomes (Longmore & Worrell, 2007). In other words, evidence seems to fall short in attributing changes in outcomes to changes in cognitions. A new evolution emphasizing mindfulness and acceptance thus emerged, drawing upon long-standing Eastern wisdom.

From the perspective of Third Wave Behaviorism and CBT, the act of thinking rather than the content of thinking is perhaps more of the issue. That is, our thoughts are just thoughts. They may or may not be true. We can evaluate the accuracy of them and that may be helpful. At the same time, it may instead be sufficient to step back from the thoughts and let them pass without getting attached to them. By simply labeling the thoughts as thoughts we reduce their power and can more fluidly choose how to direct our behavior based on our core values and ultimate goals rather than our various thoughts.

DBT and mindful eating from the dialectical perspective are Third Wave treatments. A dialectical perspective retains an appreciation for the potential utility of cognitive reframing while also embracing the approach of first mindfully noticing the thoughts and potentially simply letting them go in any given moment. A dialectical perspective also acknowledges that thoughts may emerge from learning, having been reinforced in the past, so we can both consider this history and untangle it from the present moment to inform the most effective response in the present moment. Applied to eating disorders, this approach emphasizes mindful detachment from thoughts more than the classic cognitive reframing that is intimately characteristic of traditional CBT for eating disorders. There is also a greater emphasis on emotion regulation and the role of listening to the information being provided by emotions.

In the most cutting edge adaptation of DBT currently available for weight stabilized restrictive disorders, such as AN, radically open DBT (RO DBT) shifts the emphasis even further to neurobiology and social signaling (Lynch et al., 2013), with the conceptualization that those with overcontrolled presentations associated with restrictive disorders need to most critically learn how to connect socially to overcome their emotional difficulties given their temperamental elevations in harm avoidance and threat sensitivity. Interestingly, this temperament is inherently characterized by rigidity and hypervigilance, with an often chronic judgmental stance, social comparisons, critical nature, and attachment to rules. Theoretically, mindfulness would thus arguably be imperative for moving to a more effective nonjudgmental stance in general and towards food specifically, while at the same time this would be inherently challenged by the hardwiring of temperament. However, given its roots in primarily treating overeating, binge eating, and emotional eating rather than sustained restrictive disorders such as restricting AN, mindful eating from the dialectical perspective is thus currently grounded in standard DBT, rather than RO DBT, and most indicated for individuals caught in the cycle of judgment towards food that perpetuates vacillating between extremes of eating, with overeating and binge eating predominating.

Future research on the integration of mindful eating from the dialectical perspective and RO DBT would be invaluable for potentially expanding the efficacy of these two approaches across the spectrum of disordered eating. If you thus find yourself more on the overcontrolled, restricting end of the spectrum or you are a professional working with clients who have this presentation, stay tuned for further research to enhance the approach of mindful eating for you or your clients and recognize that adopting a nonjudgmental stance may be more challenging and take more time given the powerful influence of temperament. However, along with overcontrolled presentations is a tenacity and strength in persistence that will serve you or your clients well on a more extended journey with this approach.

Research on neurobiology also points to a role for reward sensitivity in eating disorders, with heightened reward sensitivity linked to binge eating and BN and mixed findings for restrictive AN presentations (Schienle, Schafer, Hermann, & Vaitl, 2009; Wierenga et al., 2014). Interestingly, this may depend on genotype involving the dopamine D2 receptor (Davis et al., 2008). The degree to which reward sensitivity impacts behavioral learning in eating disorders warrants further investigation.

Chapter Summary

In summary, mindful eating from the dialectical perspective grows out of a rich heritage in behaviorism, cognitive theory and therapy, and Eastern philosophy grounded in acceptance and detachment. The practice rests upon both a strong foundation in rigorous methods of study and wisdom that has informed a mindful approach to life across centuries. With this grounding in research and history, all are welcome at the table of mindful eating, so I hope you will continue to join us. The table is now set, so pull up a chair.

4 Basic Ingredients

In DBT and mindful eating from the dialectical perspective, the path to more balanced living begins with foundational elements of mindfulness training. As we have discussed, mindfulness can be defined as being in the present moment in a nonjudgmental way, bringing awareness to what is happening, internally or externally. Looking inward we can notice our thoughts, our emotions, our physical sensations, and our urges. Looking outward we can notice our environment, using our five senses. For example, we may notice,

> I am having the thought "I have a lot of work to do," I am having the emotion of anxiety, I am feeling a physical sensation of my stomach slightly churning, I am having an urge to scratch an itch on my ankle, I am noticing the feeling of air moving on my arm from the fan (touch), I am noticing the whirring sound of the fan (sound), I am noticing the scent (smell) and taste of my coffee, sipping it slowly, I am noticing the sight of the words I am typing (sight).

This chapter will further outline specific core mindfulness skills from DBT, adapted for eating-related concerns. If you are a professional, you can use this material to teach and assign homework to clients for practice.

States of Mind

The first core mindfulness skills teaching from DBT proposes three states of mind: **Emotion Mind, Reasonable Mind,** and **Wise Mind** (see Linehan, 1993; 2014a; 2014b). Emotion Mind refers to the state of emotion being in control, Reasonable Mind refers to the state of logic being in control, and Wise Mind is the integration of Emotion Mind and Reasonable Mind, extracting the wisdom from both perspectives to guide our actions most effectively. For more information, handouts, and homework, please see Linehan's texts (1993; 2014a; 2014b).

Emotion Mind

Emotion Mind can be considered the fight/flight/freeze response, distributed across the sympathetic nervous system. In a neurobiological framework, focusing on the brain, key areas of this consist of our limbic system, or "mammal brain," in particular, the amygdala, which signals our brain stem, or "lizard brain," to activate a cascade of effects intended to facilitate necessary action, for example increasing heart rate and breathing to pump more oxygen into our muscles to help us run. This is the part of us that relates to short-term survival, designed to keep us safe. For example, if a tiger were suddenly to charge into the safe space where you are reading this book (hopefully you are reading in a safe space!), your Emotion Mind would hopefully kick in immediately, triggering fear that would prompt you to either flee the scene as quickly as possible, fight (if you feel equipped to win!), or freeze, if you are overwhelmed, so maybe the tiger will just think you are a benign part of the scenery rather than food. From Emotion Mind comes our full range of emotions: anxiety, fear, panic, melancholy, sadness, despair, irritation, anger, rage, guilt, shame, embarrassment, happiness, pride, joy, and love. Emotion Mind motivates our empathy and connection to others. It fuels our creativity and brings us fun. Emotion Mind is our protector and party instigator. So thank goodness we have Emotion Mind.

However, hopefully in present time we are not encountering many tigers unless we are safely distanced from them in a controlled environment! And yet how many times do we feel anxiety and fear? Often this happens when we are entirely safe. So our Emotion Mind can misfire and send us faulty signals; if we act on this information by just doing what our urges tell us to do (e.g., running away when we are afraid, attacking when we are angry, isolating and withdrawing when we are sad), then we will reinforce the message as if it were accurate and stay stuck in the emotion. Consequently, it is essential that we also developed Reasonable Mind to help us evaluate the accuracy of the messages our emotions are providing.

Reasonable Mind

Reasonable Mind can be considered our frontal lobe and, in particular, the PFC, the seat of executive function, analytical thinking, and planning. This part of our brain developed to help us move towards not just the short-term next minute of time (which our Emotion Mind helps us reach) but 24 hours from now, a week from now, a year from now, ten years from now... In other words, Reasonable Mind helps us consider the future, including consequences and our goals long term. This state of mind helps us be productive and accomplish detail-oriented tasks, organization, and structure. This can also be linked to the left brain, or left hemisphere, given its identification as predominant in logical and analytic thought.

In Reasonable Mind there is no emotion. We thus may be more efficient. However, this can have a cost. Remember, social connection stems from Emotion Mind. Emotion is imperative for intimacy and bonding. Thus, operating purely from Reasonable Mind can keep people out of the tribe, so to speak. Reasonable Mind can be experienced by others as off-putting and cold. For example, have you ever had the most horrible day ever and just wanted someone to listen and commiserate with you and instead they immediately responded with something like "Well, if you just look at it this way, you would see that there is no reason to be upset" or "Well, just do this and you will feel better"? How did this feel? I am imagining it felt unpleasant and unsupportive. And while the person may have been offering these suggestions from a place of caring, their delivery may have left you feeling distanced from the person and not wanting to share more with them. This makes sense because they were not expressing emotion, which is essential for social connection. Research actually shows that people like other people more if they are expressing emotion, whether that emotion is considered positive or negative (Butler et al., 2003; Laurenceau, Barrett, & Pietromonaco, 1998).

Wise Mind

Given that there are pros and cons to both Emotion Mind and Reasonable Mind and that neither provides us the full picture of information, Wise Mind provides a bridge between the two, to guide our actions most effectively. With Emotion Mind we feel a lot of energy or blunting if we are overwhelmed; with Reasonable Mind we feel methodical and focused; with Wise Mind we feel centered, grounded, calm, and at peace, confident in our decisions with assurance that they are "right," meaning that they are consistent with our values and the most effective choice we can make in that moment given the information we have available and what we have learned up to that point in time. If we make a decision in Wise Mind it stands the test of time, unlike Emotion Mind decisions, which can be mired with regret. Wise Mind can be considered our sense of intuition, of knowing. In other words, Emotion Mind says "I feel," Reasonable Mind says "I think," and Wise Mind says "I know."

Of note, sometimes Emotion Mind likes to dress up for Halloween as Wise Mind. Likewise, Emotion Mind can masquerade as Reasonable Mind. So be cautious and challenge your first reactions with radical honesty. For example, Wise Mind is sometimes described as a gut reaction, or intuition. If this is literally experienced in your gut, this may actually reflect Emotion Mind, in particular, anxiety. For example, if you have a gut feeling that you should not take a certain flight, this may be a flying phobia rather than any profound ESP. Likewise, if you are compulsive about your living space being a certain way, and there is an agitated energy to this, you may not be in Reasonable Mind at all, even if you are focused on logical tasks like organization. Rather, your Emotion Mind may be driving you to engage in what could otherwise be considered Reasonable Mind tasks as a way of avoiding or coping. Likewise, one of my mindful eating group members recently joked that it was probably advisable to not refer to Wise Mind as a gut feeling with clients struggling with eating issues, when the gut may be especially vocal and misleading— excellent point! Again, with Wise Mind, you will notice a sense of stillness, a settling, like a pebble resting on the bottom of a river, while the water courses above. Pay attention to this to discern your actual state of mind.

At the same time, as the intersection of Emotion Mind and Reasonable Mind, Wise Mind can straddle both to varying degrees. In the dead center of Wise Mind, the space can feel entirely still and certain, like within the eye of a hurricane or tornado. However, if we are closer to Emotion Mind, we may have more intense energy, but still be in Wise Mind as long as we are incorporating Reasonable Mind. Likewise, the balance may instead be tipped towards the more detached energy of Reasonable Mind if we are leaning more in that direction rather than Emotion Mind, but still be in Wise Mind as long as we are integrating both states of mind. Indeed, sometimes life can demand that we make decisions before we can settle into the core of our Wise Mind. In these cases, we can still do our best to listen to both sides, of Emotion Mind and Reasonable Mind, to inform the most effective, Wise Mind course of action in that moment, given the circumstances.

Also, the goal is not necessarily to always be in Wise Mind. We have each state of mind for a reason and sometimes we need to operate from them independently. For example, again, if you are being attacked by a charging tiger, please be in Emotion Mind so your fight/flight/freeze response can save you! Likewise, if you are my surgeon, please be in Reasonable Mind, following procedure rather than your creative whims in the moment, carving up my organs like an inspired sculptor! Wise Mind can serve as our touchstone to tell us which state of mind will be most effective in any given moment.

Often it is the extremes of Emotion Mind and Reasonable Mind that cause us difficulty, rather than the state of mind itself. For example, again, Emotion Mind gives us love and joy, bonding us to others. This can be wonderful when we are bonding to effective relationships that will nourish and cherish us but can be problematic if they are rushed and towards those who do not have our best interest at heart. Likewise, anger can help protect us from maltreatment, but in its extreme could result in unnecessary aggression, verbal or physical, perhaps cell phones hurtling across the room or even more detrimental injuries. Likewise, anxiety can prompt preparation, such as studying for an exam, but in its extreme can result in shutting down and getting paralyzed in procrastinating and avoiding. Likewise, with Reasonable Mind we can be productive and yet lonely if overly focused on our work, to the exclusion of others in our lives.

It is also a choice. We can choose to disregard what our Wise Mind tells us and regardless of its direction act from Emotion Mind or Reasonable

Mind. There will likely be consequences if this contradicts Wise Mind and yet accepting these consequences with awareness can still align with mindfulness. Over time, however, disregarding our Wise Mind will erode our self-respect, so proceed with caution if you choose to continue acting according to your other states of mind, even if doing so with awareness.

With DBT, in seeking balance, often Reasonable Mind is helpful for getting unstuck from Emotion Mind. As you may have gathered from Chapter 2, many of the core intervention approaches in DBT (such as the diary card, with its detailed ratings and recording of incidents, and behavior chain and solution analysis, with its extreme attention to detail) employ Reasonable Mind. This by nature helps bring in another perspective that can balance out Emotion Mind and, ultimately, foster Wise Mind.

Applying the states of mind to eating-related concerns and body image, what state of mind is most active? Often the answer is Emotion Mind. As we have been discussing, judgments about food as good or bad, forbidden or unforbidden, can drive eating patterns in unhelpful ways, and judgments are a product of Emotion Mind. If we are judging, we are guaranteeing that we will be having emotion. Likewise, a wealth of research now supports the perspective that eating behavior serves as an attempted coping strategy for emotion (Christensen, 1993; Heatherton & Baumeister, 1991; Hohlstein, Smith, & Atlas, 1998; Lynch, Everingham, Dubitzky, Hartman, & Kasser, 2000; Stein et al., 2007; Stickney, Miltenberger, & Wolff, 1999; Wiser & Telch, 1999). Extending this to body image, again, judgments about appearance (e.g., "I'm fat," "I'm ugly") ensure an emotional state that is likely unpleasant and this can further prompt eating behavior to try to cope. Consequently, the Reasonable Mind strategies of DBT and, in general, a dialectical approach are exquisitely positioned to promote effective change with eating-related concerns and body image. Moreover, fostering a Wise Mind stance can soften that harsh emotional voice of criticism. Wise Mind can instead encourage action based on values, which often include living in a kind way—and does it not make sense to include ourselves in a stance of kindness, forgiveness and encouragement?

Values can serve as a compass to guide our action, contrasting with feeling like a ping pong ball responding to Emotion Mind or rigidly focusing on goals in Reasonable Mind. Values are what drive goals. They can be enacted through diverse actions that are possible in any moment rather than ahead of us in the future. Following our values is thus very grounded in the present moment. For example, imagine you have the goal of being a teacher. Achieving this goal may require years and years of tedious education, challenging student teaching, and applying for jobs. Sometimes, especially if this process is difficult (as it inevitably probably will be at times), the goal can feel so distant that it seems unattainable and this can be discouraging. In the extreme, this can lead to not persisting in the process to achieve the goal. In contrast, returning to values is considering what is motivating the goal in the first place. What is it about being a teacher that seems appealing and rewarding, that is inspiring the goal? Perhaps it is helping others learn, reciprocally learning from one's pupils, or empowering others to follow their passions. These are values, or valued directions. To follow these values does not require a degree or credential or position at a school. For example, one could provide a fellow grocery market shopper guidance in how to make soup, passing on helpful tips and encouragement. Or one could provide free workshops or lectures as a volunteer. By focusing on values, we can find joy and fulfillment now, wherever we are. This is living in Wise Mind.

It is also important to note that values are highly personal. They are about what we like and enjoy (e.g., surfing, creating, traveling), not just ideas about esoteric ethics and morality. In fact, focusing on values as a reflection of ethics and morals can actually miss the point, with these ideas often largely stemming from messages we have received from our families or society. We can choose to take on these morals or values as our own. However, we must mindfully, honestly question whether, at our core, these perspectives are in line with our Wise Mind. If the answer that emerges is that they are not, this is an opportunity to go further inward to uncover what our Wise Mind truly believes.

One yardstick that can be helpful for determining whether you are truly connecting to values rather than goals or more externally imposed ethics or morals is whether or not the descriptor is an action verb (e.g., does it end in "ing"?). Values are about the process rather than any endpoint and thus are reflected by action verbs. For example, hiking can symbolize a value; the top of the mountain would be the goal. Likewise, skiing can symbolize a value; the bottom of the mountain would be the goal. There are many ways to reach the top of a mountain or get down a mountain. You could take a helicopter or ski lift, or scale or descend its sheer, rugged face with ropes and gripping cleats. But if you did any of the latter, you would not be hiking or skiing. It is the case, likewise, with values. It is about how you are engaging rather than just getting to the endpoint by any means.

Reflect on this related to unbalanced, disordered eating and body image judgment. Are these patterns consistent with your values? Are they keeping you in the present moment or are they driven by goals, such as achieving a certain number on the scale or a certain clothing size? If you were truly living by your values, what would you be doing? What would your days look like? Would there be any space for unbalanced, disordered eating and body image judgment? Take some time to consider this. Write about what you uncover (see also downloadable Handout 4.1).

Handout 4.1 Values Reflection Worksheet

_____

_____

_____

_____

_____

_____

_____

_____

_____

_____

_____

_____

_____

_____

_____

_____

One last word of validation regarding Wise Mind… When I first heard of it, my thought was "What????" I honestly judged it as hokey and cheesy and could not relate. I was skeptical of it even being possible. And yet, I then continued on my journey in my DBT training and one day, I suddenly felt it—a calm sense of stillness, completely centered, assured, confident in knowing. "Ahhhhhh!!!" I thought. "That is what Wise Mind is." I got it. I share this, in part, to note that Wise Mind needs to be experienced to understand it, and, also, to propose that even if you are not sure what this state might be, you can find it. Everyone has a Wise Mind. We must simply slow down enough to let its voice surface, calming our mind, letting its cognitive webs recede and our emotion dissipate. So I encourage you to stay open to this possibility and be on the lookout. In time, I trust you too will connect to this state of mind.

What Skills

In DBT the What skills are what you do when you are mindful and the How skills are how you do it. In discussing the What skills there is some overlap with the How skills, but for the sake of simplification, they are divided into these two categories. There are three main What skills and three main How skills. For more information, handouts, and homework for the What and How skills, please see Linehan's texts (1993; 2014a; 2014b).

The first What skill is **Observe**. Observing is wordless watching, just noticing, without reaction or labeling or judgment. It is like the stance of a cat, gazing out the window, taking in the world, silently, calmly; only moving out of observation to action if deemed necessary (e.g., a tempting bird prompts a tremoring gurgle in the cat's throat, with the tensing of muscles, preparing to pounce). Again, observation can be of internal or external experience (thoughts, emotions, physical sensations, and urges for the former; environmental stimuli through the five senses for the latter).

Observing is necessary for responding most effectively to reality. Without fully observing we are acting on only limited information, which can often be biased from our own assumptions. For example, I received guest passes to visit a non-profit organization and did not take the time to read on the guest passes that, first of all, the passes were for Wednesdays and Thursdays only, and secondly, that an appointment was necessary. Fortunately, my friend caught the first detail when I shared the cards with him, but then I did not realize the second key detail until we had already driven over an hour to reach the site and we had to reschedule for another day. I clearly did not employ my Observe skill and consequently we expended a substantially greater amount of time and gas money than we would have had I actually read the information clearly written on the guest passes.

When beginning to learn this skill, apply your practice to objects that are unrelated to eating and body image. For example, you can Observe river rocks, seashells, or your breath—anything external or internal. You can listen to music or nature sounds. You can close your eyes and Observe with all your senses but sight and taste objects that a partner or leader provides you.

Over the next week, practice this daily and record what you Observe (see also downloadable Handout 4.2).

Handout 4.2 Observe Practice Worksheet

Monday:_____

_____

_____

_____

Tuesday:_____

_____

_____

_____

Wednesday: _____

_____

_____

_____

Thursday: _____

_____

_____

_____

Friday: _____

_____

_____

_____

Saturday: _____

_____

_____

_____

Sunday: _____

_____

_____

_____

One key application of the Observe skill is **Urge Surfing**. Urge Surfing is applying the Observe skill to urges. With every urge there is a crest and a descent to resolution. There is a peak and a dissipation, as with a wave. What often happens, however, is that we act on the urge before we let it fall because we think we have to act on an urge to get it to go away. Therefore, many of us never learn that urges will naturally go away on their own without action. Now another urge may then arrive, as we would expect if we have ever watched the rise and fall of the ocean or a lake. And yet, that urge will also rise and fall. And although the urges may swell violently and even compose a tsunami, we can ride them out and not get sucked into their riptide. Urge Surfing is watching the rise and fall of the urge, just noticing it, not distracting from it and not getting sucked into it.

To illustrate this skill, I traditionally ask clients to spend about five minutes bringing their attention to any itches they Observe, doing a body scan—and then Observe the urge to scratch the itch—without acting on the urge to scratch, without scratching! Try it now. What do you notice? Record some notes (see also downloadable Handout 4.3).

Handout 4.3 Urge Surfing Practice Worksheet: Itches

_____

_____

_____

_____

Usually what arises in this practice is that itches suddenly spring into awareness and assault the senses... and then dissipate and shift, without any scratching at all. This is a remarkable and powerful demonstration given how automatically we usually scratch an itch without thinking about it. This said, I do not mean to nonchalantly suggest that Urge Surfing is easy. Resisting strong urges, including urges to scratch, can call for a tremendous amount of fortitude.

I experienced this personally after years of teaching this skill when I suddenly developed a diffuse itchiness all over my legs without any clear cause that I could pinpoint. I did my best to surf those urges to scratch—and I succumbed many times! Of course, this only made it worse and in the end, in addition to ample nourishing body wash and lotion, Urge Surfing was essential for the itching to ultimately remit.

So yes, Urge Surfing, whether it is with eating disordered urges or scratching mysteriously itchy legs, can be extremely challenging—and it is possible and imperative for establishing new patterns and not making the situation worse. Applying Observe and Urge Surfing to eating-related concerns and negative body image fosters essential space between urges and actions. In fact, the Observe skill is the bread and butter of mindful eating—bringing awareness to food, truly taking in what it is, in all aspects, based on its substance rather than any cognitive labels imposed upon it, whether self-generated or supplied by a nutrition label, while also noticing thoughts, emotions, bodily sensations, and urges that arise with the experience, just noticing them, and letting them pass without attachment.

Note, for professionals guiding clients through this program, cover any nutrition labels when presenting food. Inevitably clients will immediately turn over food items to check this and ask why it is covered. This points to the critical need to uncouple this knee-jerk reliance on cognitive judgment of food to inform consumption.

Of course, bringing a dialectical perspective to this, nutritional information can reveal what we would otherwise not know and may want to know from a broader health perspective (e.g., if a product contains high fructose corn syrup). And at the same time, turning to nutrition labels in such an automatic way seems to inherently be an evaluative process triggering a cognitive labeling of food that can be so entwined with rules and unhelpful judgments.

Effectively balancing a mindful approach to food with discernment regarding nutritional information is thus an advanced cognitive task. I myself sometimes, when I am emotionally vulnerable, can still get paralyzed in the salad dressing aisle at the grocery store, feeling drawn to certain dressings because of liking their taste and wanting to honor that and yet blocked as if by an invisible force field by all the labels with the dreaded ingredient of high fructose corn syrup. Stepping back from rules about this, psychologically, as we have been discussing, there is still arguably a high value in consuming products that would otherwise be judged based on nutrition labels. Thus, to help wipe the slate clean, I have found it essential to break the immediate turning towards nutrition labels.

With body image concerns in particular, the Observe and Urge Surfing skills can be applied in exposure and response prevention paradigms, which are the most empirically supported treatments for body image (Cash, 2008; Delinsky & Wilson, 2006; 2010; Hilbert, Tuschen-Caffier, & Vogele, 2002; Jansen et al., 2008; Key et al., 2002; Rosen, 1997; Tuschen-Caffier, Pook, & Frank, 2001; Vocks, Wächter, Wucherer, & Kosfelder, 2008), including support for efficacy with eating disorders (Hilbert et al., 2002; Key et al., 2002; Vocks et al., 2008). For example, to disrupt compulsive, critical body checking in the mirror, the Observe and Urge Surfing skills can be applied through the practice of viewing oneself in the mirror, without judgment, observing thoughts, emotions, physical sensations, and urges and letting them go, not attaching to them, and just taking in what is reflected back, without trying to fix or correct or hide, again, and again, and again, until the habituation to the trigger occurs and distress thus abates (Wilson, 1999; 2004).

Another area this can especially help is weighing, to find a middle ground between avoiding the scale entirely and compulsively weighing. From a clinical perspective for working through this, weighing no more or less than once a week is recommended (e.g., Fairburn, 2013). Then, with mindfulness, when the number on the scale is displayed, the task is to Observe it, just notice it, and notice urges that arise with it, letting them rise and fall and pass. This contrasts with the usual pattern that can develop of the scale being the determinant of consumption for the rest of the day or week, to somehow try to compensate for any undesired increases or attempt to maintain and prevent gain. It is also a form of exposure, which can help foster habituation to distress triggered by the scale, with the ultimate possibility of transforming the numbers truly into just lines configured in a particular pattern rather than an arbiter of self-worth and disciplinary action.

In the context of this program, I advise postponing mindful awareness of the scale until after completing the program. This is based on the feedback I received from my treatment trial participants, who found weekly weighing to be, at worst, contraindicated and, at best, not of utility. Understandably, it seemed that focusing on establishing new patterns with eating is challenging enough without extending mindfulness into the arena of body image at this juncture, and while you can apply the skills we are covering to body image, this often requires focusing more in depth with exposure than this program provides related to body image. First focus on really immersing yourself in this process with eating and avoid the scale for now. Put it into storage, out of sight. To continue with weighing if you insist on doing so with the program or to return to it when you complete the program, enlist the support of a professional in applying your mindfulness skills to this process and follow the guideline to weigh no more than once per week.

The next What skill is **Describe**. Describe is nonjudgmentally putting words onto what Observe brings to awareness. Describe is simply stating the facts, as objectively as possible. Again, this can be internal (thoughts, emotions, bodily sensations, urges) or external (environmental stimuli through the five senses).

For example, you can Describe thoughts such as "I am fat" and "I am ugly" using the Describe skill by labeling their designation as thoughts, which is a fact, rather than stating them as if they were fact. In other words, the phrasing would shift to "I am having the thought that I am fat" or "I am having the thought 'I am ugly.'" Similarly, you can Describe thoughts about food (e.g., "I am having the thought 'This food is fattening,' I am having the thought 'If I eat this I will get fat,' I am having the thought, 'If I eat this I will gain 10 pounds'"). This phrasing points out that these are, in the end, just thoughts.

Philosophically, such thoughts—any thoughts—may or may not be true. And they are just thoughts, so we can notice them and let them go or return to evaluate their accuracy through cognitive reframing. This creates space from thoughts, which can be quite powerful, facilitating more opportunity to move away from them, to more effective perspectives. This can help foster different emotions, as outlined in Chapter 3's discussion of CT and CBT, and then alternative behaviors to eating disordered patterns.

Likewise, you can Describe emotions, bodily sensations, and urges to create space and permit more opportunity for effective responding. For example, you may say to yourself "I feel bloated. I feel uncomfortable and anxious with this and have the urge to restrict my intake now to make up for it." In other words, "I am having the bodily sensation of bloating and discomfort, I am having the emotion of anxiety, and I am having the urge to restrict." This has a very different emotional tenor than stating the experience as if it were fact: "I am so bloated. I am so uncomfortable and anxious with this and I should restrict now to make up for it." Can you feel the difference? Again, with this, the action does not necessarily have to be restriction for the urge to go away. Rather, Urge Surfing can ride out the urge, preventing perpetuation of the cycle between unbalanced eating and restricting.

Practice describing your thoughts and judgments as outlined above. Take a few minutes, daily, over the week ahead, to put into words with Describe what you Observe (see also downloadable Handout 4.4).

Handout 4.4 Describe Practice Worksheet

Monday:_____

_____

_____

_____

Tuesday:_____

_____

_____

_____

Wednesday: _____

_____

_____

_____

Thursday:_____

_____

_____

_____

Friday: _____

_____

_____

_____

Saturday: _____

_____

_____

_____

Sunday:_____

_____

_____

_____

The final What skill is **Participate**. To Participate is to enter fully into the present moment, without self-consciousness, noticing any self-consciousness if it arises, or rather perhaps when it arises—since it can be expected to continue visiting us, given learned patterns; likewise, noticing any distractions if, or, again, rather perhaps when, they arise—since our mind, like a golden retriever puppy, inevitably strays—and letting them go, returning to being fully in the moment. This may be likened to being in the zone or flow (Nakamura & Csikszentmihalyi, 2002) or more broadly, a hypo-egoic state (Leary, Adams, & Tate, 2006). Time passes without you realizing it, but not in a zoned out, dissociative way. It feels distinct from the more detached What skills of Observe and Describe.

Participate is perhaps best understood by examples and needs to be experienced to be fully understood. One example that can illustrate this is learning how to swing dance. First you must Observe the steps. Perhaps you watch your teacher demonstrate them. Then you must Describe (e.g., "One two three, rock step, one two three, rock step"). Then after you practice and practice and practice, observing and describing, when you have truly learned a particular variant of swing dance, you need to be fully in the moment, participating, to be most effective. The minute you think about what you are doing, you often mess up (and if you are swing dancing you may end up getting dropped on your head—not effective!). Another example is learning to play a musical instrument or a particular song. First you must Observe the notes or chords in front of you, then you must Describe, labeling them according to their placement within scales and octaves and perhaps finger configurations. Then after you practice these arrangements time after time, imparting them into your muscle memory, to perform you must, again, Participate, being fully in the moment, to be most effective. If instead you think about what you are doing, you will often then botch the notes. I certainly can attest to that from my years of piano playing. My clients who are athletes, musicians, and artists have all related to this as a similar process with their avocation.

How about for you? Do you feel like you have ever been fully present, without self-consciousness, participating? Write down some notes about when you feel this way (see also downloadable Handout 4.5).

Handout 4.5 Participate Reflection Worksheet

_____

_____

_____

Ultimately, the goal is to Participate in your life, no matter what you are doing. If you are fully present, you are innately attuned to the full reality of what is happening, so you can respond most effectively and ultimately experience the most joy. Carried out to the fullest extent, this can create a truly meaningful, valued life that can help counter the distress that may be driving less balanced patterns of eating. Furthermore, by definition, letting go of self-consciousness and judgment can promote a more kind, mindful relationship with food and freedom from harsh self-critical body image.

Be on the lookout for times you Participate over the next week and seek out these opportunities. Take a few minutes, daily, to note what happens (see also downloadable Handout 4.6).

Handout 4.6 Participate Practice Worksheet

Monday:_____

_____

_____

_____

Tuesday:_____

_____

_____

_____

Wednesday: _____

_____

_____

_____

Thursday:_____

_____

_____

_____

Friday: _____

_____

_____

_____

Saturday: _____

_____

_____

_____

Sunday:_____

_____

_____

_____

How Skills

The first How skill—how to do the What skills—is **Nonjudgmental Stance**. First, let us define what a judgment is. A judgment is: a qualitative evaluation; an opinion stated as if it were fact; a subjective shorthand for the more nuanced experience of reality. For example, common judgments include "good/bad," "pretty/beautiful/ugly," "fat," and "stupid"—the list could go on and on: "ridiculous," "horrible"… "Healthy" and "unhealthy," as described earlier in Chapter 1, are also judgments. Everything is relative, and a danger of shorthand is that it loses context and generates rule-governed behavior that can be ineffective (see also Chapter 1 and Chapter 7).

Another danger of judgments is that they can impede true understanding in communication. For example, if you are talking with a friend and they say, "Oh, that restaurant was so good!" you might agree and say, "Yes, totally!" thinking you are sharing a similar perspective, while it is actually entirely unclear why each of you thinks this. One of you could be referring to the food and the other to the ambiance and service. Furthermore, stopping at the judgment, without description of the reasons for it, does not foster very long conversations (e.g., if you ask someone how their day was and they say simply "good" or you ask someone how they are doing and they simply say "fine")! Detail can foster connection through understanding.

With judgment also comes emotion, be it considered positive or negative. For example, the "positive" judgment, "That was so good!" may promote a sense of joy and urges to repeat the associated experience. This may be problematic if the behavior is ultimately not in our best interest or consistent with our values, for example, if we are labeling restriction as good. More "negative" judgments related to a sense of injustice such as "This is so unfair! This shouldn't be happening!" inextricably promulgate anger. With food, judgment such as "This is so unhealthy. I am going to gain so much weight from eating this" can prompt guilt and urges to restrict, which, as we have discussed, is counterproductive (see Chapter 1). Self-judgment in particular, such as "You are so ugly. You are so fat. No one will ever want to be with you," can perpetuate intense emotional reactions such as shame.

Of note, more "positive" self-judgment can still backfire. For example, "positive" self-judgment of appearance reinforces the potentially objectifying process of evaluating appearance to define self-worth. This could then reinforce the belief that being loveable or attractive requires looking a certain way. Thus with mirror exposure, referenced above, the goal is often not to promote body satisfaction or love but rather to remove the judgment from the process of viewing oneself, be it positive or negative in valence—to move away from the subjective to simply the objective, as much as that is possible (given how mirror reflections work, Shafran & Fairburn, 2002, biased by distorting influences, including consumption of a high carbohydrate meal, Crisp & Kalucy, 1974; actual body size, with overestimation increasing the more narrow someone is, Ben-Tovim, Whitehead, & Crisp, 1979; neuroticism, Garner, Garfinkel, Stancer, & Moldofsky, 1976; low perceived self-control and external control orientation, Garner et al., 1976; Pierloot & Houben, 1978; Waller & Hodgson, 1996).

Nonjudgmental Stance, then, is focusing on just the facts. For example, let us take the judgment "I am fat." Clients have asked me, "Well, what if I am? I am obese. That is a fact." To this I respond, "You can say something to the effect that 'According to current medical guidelines, my weight, proportionate to my height, falls into a category that is considered obese. Those are the facts. 'I am fat' is a shorthand, usually with a lot of negative emotional energy attached to it, that is a judgment." Another response to this is to restate the judgment as a thought, with Describe, for example, "I am having the thought that I am fat." If it is true that you are having that thought, then that is a fact.

What about foods? Is it not the case that certain foods are inherently "unhealthy"? Clients will sometimes adamantly argue this point, pointing to research showing connections to dire medical outcomes such as cancer. To this I respond with some variant such as:

> Yes, you can Describe the outcomes of research. And any legitimately trained scientist will very precisely state the outcomes in a manner that is not absolute, to specifically reflect what was found based on the current study design and sample rather than make a sweeping statement that can be assumed to be definitive, to always apply. Research always has limitations and we can state findings as facts but to then make a rule based on the findings is unfounded.

I hope this is beginning to resonate and make sense.

Another judgment to watch out for is "should." There is a joke about this in the therapy field, originating from Albert Ellis, to not "should on yourself!" Think about it. If you say that something should be a certain way that it is not, you are purporting that you know more than the ways of the universe. Rather, the reality is that it is the way it is and in this moment in time, given all the factors that have led up to this very moment in time to make it be that way, it can be no other way. This does not mean that you cannot wish for it to be different or want it to be different or think it is unfair, that you cannot regret it is the way it is or make changes so it can be another way in the future. And yet, right now, in this moment, it is the way it is, so "should" is irrelevant and only perpetuates fighting against reality. The result of "should" is thus remaining mired in suffering, which is defined in DBT as emotional pain and the non-acceptance of that pain. In this human life pain is inevitable, but suffering is optional.

At the same time, you can dislike or even hate something and not be judging it. Likewise, you can like or even love something and not be judging it. Liking and disliking, loving and hating are preferences. Granted, love and hate are strong preferences, but they are still preferences. For example, imagine you say "I love chocolate chip cookie dough ice cream!" Could someone legitimately assert that you do not, if there is no evidence to the contrary? This is different from saying "Chocolate chip cookie dough ice cream is the best ice cream ever!" This is an opinion and a judgment that others may reject, in favor of their preferred ice cream. Again, though, you could restate this as "I have the belief that chocolate chip cookie dough ice cream is the best ice cream ever." This is a belief that you are owning as yours and if it is a belief that you have, this is a fact.

The distinction of judgment from preference is also important when it comes to difficult topics such as trauma. Nonjudgmental Stance towards events that most people would agree are unjust is not approval of the acts. Nor is it indifference to the acts continuing. It is, simply, stating the fact of what has happened. This permits letting go of suffering, while there still may be emotional pain. With Nonjudgmental Stance, facing the pain can be a path to healing and moving forward, including taking steps to prevent the actions from occurring again, if possible. To further practice Nonjudgmental Stance, putting it into words, I encourage you to return to the Describe practice outlined above.

The next How skill is **One-Mindfully**. One-Mindfully is doing just one thing at a time. This again includes internal and external. That is, if you are washing the dishes, just wash the dishes, noticing the sensation of the water and the soap, the washcloth and the dishes, one by one. You may notice the faint iridescent pastels of the bubbles, the smooth surface of the plate in your hand, the warmth of the water, the fabric texture of the washcloth. You may also notice thoughts floating through your head, the bodily sensation of your tense shoulders, the emotion of anxiety, an urge to rush. With One-Mindfully, you would notice these internal sensations and let them go, bringing your attention back to being fully present with simply washing the dishes. Likewise, if you are worrying, just worry. This is actually an essential CBT intervention for generalized anxiety disorder—to set aside time each day (e.g., 30 minutes) to simply worry and nothing else, with research designating CBT as the most empirically supported approach for this disorder and evidence that worry exposure can also stand alone as an efficacious treatment for the disorder (Borkovec, Wilkinson, Folensbee, & Lerman, 1983; Butler, Chapman, Forman, & Beck, 2006; Hoyer et al., 2009). This is a way to counter the White Bear phenomenon (see Chapter 1).

One-Mindfully can be applied to any action. For example, when you are in the shower, just shower, bringing your attention to the sensation and sight and smell of your body wash or soap, your shampoo and conditioner, the water against your skin, rather than going through the motions, meanwhile worrying or daydreaming in your head, so that you then pause and ask yourself if you have washed your hair already (I still do this!). With eating, of course, One-Mindfully is just eating, not getting caught in judgments or other activities, such as watching TV or a movie. That is, when you are eating, just eat.

To begin practicing this, apply this over the week ahead to experiences that do not involve food or body image. Describe what you Observe (see also downloadable Handout 4.7).

Handout 4.7 One-Mindfully Practice Worksheet

Monday:_____

_____

_____

_____

Tuesday:_____

_____

_____

_____

Wednesday: _____

_____

_____

_____

Thursday:_____

_____

Friday: _____

_____

_____

_____

Saturday: _____

_____

_____

_____

Sunday:_____

_____

_____

_____

The final How skill is **Effectiveness**. Effectiveness is doing what works. To do what works you must first define your objective. Then you must ascertain what the rules of the current situation you are trying to navigate to reach your objective are—not what you think the rules should be or what you want them to be, but rather, what they are. To be effective, then you would let go of willfulness and judgment and operate within the rules.

For example, if you are driving and your objective is to get to your destination by a certain time and you are behind a slow-moving car in the fast lane, at a pace that you calculate would reasonably result in being late, and you Observe that there is an opening in the slow lane, you could get willful and assert that the car in front of you "should" get over—that the traffic laws stipulate that that is what the car "should" do, not impeding you from moving forward at a faster speed. However, the "rules" of the situation in front of you are that, to be effective, you could move into the slow lane to move around the car and continue towards your destination at a speed that would permit you to reach your destination as scheduled, barring any further issues. Likewise, we all operate within systems of some sort or other, such as school, work, and the government, and we may disagree with certain requirements, labeling them as senseless "hoops" without any logical bearing. However, if our objective in these arenas is to graduate, maintain employment, and evade wage garnishing or imprisonment, then we need to operate within the rules to achieve our objectives.

Defining our objective is very important because it can alter whether our actions are effective given the same situation. For example, imagine that you are in a job you dislike. You feel you are not being treated fairly or respected or valued and your objective is to have a job that treats you in a manner that you feel is fair and respectful, recognizing your worth. Would walking out of your job be effective? Perhaps. However, at the same time, you likely have the objective of keeping a roof over your head and paying your bills. Given these two objectives, the most effective course of action is thus likely to begin looking for another job, applying and interviewing, making arrangements, until you have another opportunity, then giving your resignation to your current employer.

In contrast, imagine that you are in a job you dislike because you feel it is unethical. Maybe it is engaging in acts that violate standards in your profession and put clients at risk and this is completely against your moral code; by staying you are enabling and even participating in this unethical behavior. Maybe then your objective is to follow your values even if that means struggling to pay your bills for a period of time. Then perhaps walking off the job without first lining up another job is completely effective given your objective.

I think that Effectiveness is one of the most important skills in DBT—and one of the most challenging. It can be extremely difficult to let go of willfulness and a strong drive to change a system, to simply operate within a system. Of course, bringing a dialectical perspective to this, perhaps it is more about knowing how and when to advocate for change within the system and when to sit tight and Observe. It is not always going along with what you disagree with, simply for the sake of getting through the system. And it is not always campaigning to change it or talking out against it. It is tuning into any given moment to determine what is most effective at that moment, with appreciation for the rules you have observed. It is letting go of Emotion Mind urgency to act immediately but also honoring the information being provided by your emotions, to ultimately listen to them and honor the kernel of truth in them.

Effectiveness is also essential when participating in this DBT-based program. DBT is a complex therapy that can be demanding, with expectations for compliance with daily diary card self-monitoring and active engagement in the course material, including homework. It is not uncommon for willfulness to arise in response to the structure. And yet, if your objective is to develop a new relationship with food, and this program has research support to help you do this, how is it helpful to fight against it and not follow the "rules"?

Reflection

With Effectiveness, I invite you to now spend some time reflecting on the material thus far presented in this book, about the evidence for mindful eating and the evidence against restriction. Sit with it. Notice any urges you are feeling to reject these facts and stubbornly persist in the patterns you have established that will keep you stuck. What do you think this is about? Are you in Emotion Mind? What is Emotion Mind saying? Can you access Reasonable Mind to find Wise Mind? Write down your reflections in the space below or by using a supplemental journal or paper (see also downloadable Handout 4.8).

Handout 4.8 Effectiveness Reflection Worksheet

_____

_____

_____

_____

_____

_____

_____

_____

_____

_____

_____

_____

Chapter Summary

In summary, from a DBT perspective, mindfulness involves bringing your attention to your current state of mind, as well as your experience in the environment. We may find ourselves mired in emotion, detached and rational, or centered and grounded. From this framework, when emotion is in control we are in Emotion Mind, when logic is in control we are in Reasonable Mind, and when both emotion and reason are integrated, we are in Wise Mind. With mindfulness we can Observe and Describe these states, as well as the reality around us, to respond with Effectiveness, to Participate fully, One-Mindfully, with Nonjudgmental Stance in life. We can Observe the food in front of us as well as the setting we are in when we are eating, the conversation we are having with our dining companions, and any emotions, judgments, thoughts, physical sensations, and urges that may arise, without acting on urges to escape the experience. Like a symphony blending together yet not erasing the contributions of the separate instruments, we can fully appreciate our relationship with food and life.

5   Expanding the Palate

When I teach mindfulness of urges, my clients, fairly frequently, initially remark that they will go along with the process of monitoring their urges in theory but they are not sure they have any—that they just find themselves acting and do not notice any urges—or they only notice them when it is too late and they have begun binge eating or engaging in other harmful behavior. My response is dialectically validating. Without mindfulness, we often act on autopilot and do not notice what may be driving our behavior—and yet there is always a reason for behavior, an emotion, a thought, an environmental trigger, even if it is elusive. It also makes sense to struggle with identifying the underlying urges, emotions, and thoughts. **Interoceptive awareness**, the degree to which individuals can detect and distinguish internal sensations, such as emotions or physical cues, like anxiety versus hunger and nausea, varies and with disordered eating patterns in particular can be diminished or disrupted (Bizeul, Sadowsky, & Rigaud, 2001; de Zwaan et al., 1994; Pollatos et al., 2008; Sim & Zeman, 2004; van Strien, 2000; van Strien & Ouwens, 2007; Zanetti, Santonastaso, Sgaravatti, Degortes, & Favaro, 2013). Thus, mindfulness is essential for relearning what is going on inside before behavior occurs, to learn how to truly nourish ourselves.

Interoceptive awareness can be disrupted in various ways. With depression, which is often associated with disordered eating, interoceptive awareness can be blunted (Wiebking et al., 2014). Theory and research also points to self-objectification decreasing interoceptive awareness, the latter then mediating self-objectification and disordered eating concerns and depression (Myers & Crowther, 2008; Peat & Muehlenkamp, 2011; Tylka & Hill, 2004). In other words, self-objectification has been shown to decrease interoceptive awareness and decreased interoceptive awareness has then been shown to increase disordered eating concerns and depression. Breaking down these associations further, disordered eating may function as a coping strategy in response to depression. This is supported by research implicating interoceptive awareness as a mediator between negative affect and overeating (van Strien, Engels, van Leeuwe, & Snoek, 2005).

With elevated anxiety, which is also often associated with disordered eating, in particular, restrictive patterns, the role of interoceptive awareness presents as potentially even more complex. That is, anxiety disorders are usually linked to heightened accuracy and intensity of interoceptive awareness, with amplified emotional arousal as a result (Pollatos, Traut-Mattausch, Schroeder, & Schandry, 2007). Interestingly, this could then disrupt processing of emotion in others, related to social anxiety (Pollatos et al., 2011). At the other extreme, low interoceptive awareness has been linked to difficulty interpreting uncertainty (Lamm & Singer, 2010), and depression seems to mute the heightened interoceptive awareness usually associated with anxiety disorders (Dunn et al., 2010). Taken together, when anxiety is involved, disruptions in interoceptive awareness may occur at either extreme, overly sensitive or diminished, ultimately, either way, driving disordered eating again as coping. Indeed, research supports interoceptive awareness as a mediator between anxiety sensitivity and disordered eating (i.e., anxiety sensitivity seems to be linked to decreased interoceptive awareness and then decreased interoceptive awareness is connected to increased disordered eating; Anestis, Holm-Denoma, Gordon, Schmidt, & Joiner, 2008).

These difficulties in interoceptive awareness have been linked to imbalances in activity in specific brain regions, namely, the insula and, in particular, the anterior insula (Critchley, Wiens, Rotshtein, Ohman, & Dolan, 2004; Wiebking et al., 2015), as well as the ACC and ventromedial PFC and lateral PFC (Critchley et al., 2004). Preliminary evidence also exists for a resting functional connectivity disturbance related to the right middle occipital gyrus, which has been implicated in body processing (Lavagnino et al., 2014). Research further suggests that these disruptions in interoceptive awareness may precede disordered eating (e.g., Leon, Fulkerson, Perry, & Early-Zald, 1995), distinguish severity in associated patterns such as set shifting (the ability to move flexibly with change; Abbate-Daga, Buzzichelli, Marzola, Amianto, & Fassino, 2014), and persist after recovery according to other parameters (Klabunde, Acheson, Boutelle, Matthews, & Kaye, 2013), although improvement has also been found with recovery (Matsumoto et al., 2006). Differences in recovery outcomes may be specific to diagnosis, with the latter sample characterized by a history of AN and the former by a history of BN. Further research is needed to elucidate both prospective prediction of interoceptive awareness in disordered eating and the degree of persistence in interoceptive awareness disturbance (Lilenfeld et al., 2006).

Deciphering Hungers

According to Jan Chozen Bays, M.D., author of *Mindful Eating: Rediscovering a Joyful Relationship with Food* (2009), there are seven kinds of hunger. This can be a helpful framework for considering where your urges are coming from and what they may actually be trying to communicate. By looking at the degree to which these hungers apply you can more precisely respond to truly nourish your needs, whether that is by eating food or responding otherwise. You may thus determine that you want to surf the urge to eat a particular food or in a particular way (see Urge Surfing in Chapter 4), but also attend to the underlying need that is not related to food or only tangentially related. The seven hungers (Bays, 2009) are eye, nose, mouth, stomach, cellular, mind, and heart hunger.

Eye Hunger

Imagine walking into a specialty dessert shop. Your eyes fall upon the display case; it is filled with delicacy after delicacy of carefully sculpted creations, swirls and intricate designs. "Everything is almost too pretty to eat!" you think. How will you choose which one you will eat? You carefully ponder the choices and determine which one is the most beautifully appealing to you. With excitement and anticipation you place your order. When it is finally presented in front of you, you hesitate, your spoon or fork hovering above it, still not wanting to desecrate this masterpiece. And then you do. But what if you did not? What is really going on here?

The food industry has evolved to incorporate much emphasis on the element of presentation. Sauces are drizzled in particular patterns. Plating is a major part of food critiquing. I remember being caught off guard by this when I entered a biscuit competition for fun in Mississippi. I was confident that my massive, tender buttermilk biscuits would prevail. However, to my utter dismay, I had not realized that they would be judged, in part, by how I presented them and their simple placement on a metal pan paled in comparison to their competition's elegant wicker baskets with checkered cloths. Needless to say, my biscuits did not win the day, despite their delicate deliciousness! Food staging is even now actually a profession, creating the most visually compelling, eye-catching images of food for consumers. Furthermore, any bustling market provides a feast for the eyes, with vibrant colors and shapes and variety. If you are not hungry before you see such displays, upon encountering them you may suddenly find yourself having an urge to eat. In these cases, the urge may well primarily represent eye hunger. If so, then the question arises, do you need to eat the food to satisfy your hunger? Or could you just soak it all in, observing it with your eyes? After all, the beauty of it has nothing to do with the taste.

Think about what types of eye hunger you experience and how you might respond to this hunger most effectively. Observe this over the week. Take some notes (see also downloadable Handout 5.1).

Handout 5.1 Hungers Worksheet: Eye Hunger

_____

_____

_____

_____

_____

_____

_____

_____

_____

_____

_____

_____

_____

Nose Hunger

Imagine walking into an Indian restaurant. The smell of curry hits you like a wall, enveloping you like a swaddling blanket in its richness. Or walking into a coffee shop. The smell of freshly ground beans and brewed caffeinated nectar fills your nostrils, enlivening your step almost instantly with newfound buoyancy. Or walking into a bakery. The smell of yeasty bread and freshly baked cookies greets you, instantly relaxing you with all its gluten goodness.

If you are not hungry before you encounter such aromas, upon experiencing them you may suddenly find yourself having an urge to eat. In these cases, the urge may likely primarily represent nose hunger. If so, then the question arises, do you need to eat the food to satisfy your hunger? Or could you just soak it all in, observing it with your nose? In this case, the smell may be intimately linked to the taste, given that actually, largely what we call the taste of food is actually its smell—and yet it is a separate entity that could be experienced of its own accord.

Think about what types of nose hunger you experience and how you might respond to this hunger most effectively. Observe this over the week. Take some notes (see also downloadable Handout 5.1).

Handout 5.1 Hungers Worksheet: Nose Hunger

_____

_____

_____

_____

_____

_____

_____

_____

_____

_____

_____

_____

_____

Mouth Hunger

Crunchy. Smooth. The combination of both in a single perfect bite. The symphony of a piece of sushi. These are all ways your mouth can enjoy itself in the mechanics of eating. And your mouth can vary in its craving for these different experiences, based on overall preference as well as associated memories and emotions.

For example, I cannot stand to eat crisp cereal. It feels the same way it may when chalk on a chalkboard screeches. It makes my shoulders tense, the hair on my neck raise, and my spine cringe in its desire for dismissal of the roughness. What makes this so aversive to me? I imagine it stems from my mother's preference for soggy cereal. Perhaps she ate it when I was in the womb so the preference seeped into me from the very beginning, in gestation. Perhaps then she modeled this preference for me and I learned from a young age that that was, quite simply, how cereal was consumed. Likewise, I cannot stand ice cream that is really firm. I like to let it melt a bit, around its edges, and maybe even swirl it around into a type of sweet soup. Can anyone relate?

Other times, I really want a crunchy pretzel or chip. I certainly felt this way after I had my wisdom teeth removed. I had to follow a soft food diet for six weeks. That is a lot of macaroni and cheese and mashed potatoes! Let me tell you, my first potato chip after that was the best potato chip I have ever eaten in my entire life! It was a kettle cooked, waffle weave, so divinely crisp, and also beautiful in its design to satisfy my eye hunger. My mouth was so happy enjoying the resistance of it against my teeth, chomping away.

I also can sometimes see a connection between wanting crunchy foods and feeling frustrated or angry or rebellious. For example, perhaps I feel my voice is not being heard, so chomping away is a form of expressing that angry energy, kind of like yelling without causing any harm in the heat of the moment. Other times it just feels more fun and interesting compared to the less demanding process of barely chewing, then swallowing soft foods, like pudding. Sometimes the less demanding process may be soothing; sometimes it may be boring. Knowing your mouth hunger will help you keep your mouth happy.

Think about what types of mouth hunger you experience and how you might respond to this hunger most effectively. Observe this over the week. Take some notes (see also downloadable Handout 5.1).

Handout 5.1 Hungers Worksheet: Mouth Hunger

_____

_____

_____

_____

_____

_____

_____

_____

_____

_____

_____

_____

Stomach Hunger

Stomach hunger may be what we most commonly refer to as hunger: physical hunger—the grumbling in our belly—the intense demanding, ravenous cavern of constriction that feels like it demands to be fed before life can continue. I can feel overcome by this; when this happens, I need to feed "the monster." Detecting when the stomach is then full is also part of interoceptive awareness.

Deciphering stomach hunger can be confusing. Anxiety can be misinterpreted as stomach hunger. Gastroesophageal reflux, acid causing pain, can also be misinterpreted as stomach hunger. In either case feeding the stomach with food will not address the actual needs (e.g., attending to the anxiety) and can even make it worse. Mindfulness is thus essential for accurately determining whether your hunger is truly stomach hunger or whether, instead, there is an underlying or complicating need—in other words, if you are having a combination of stomach hunger and other experience. For example, when I have been in the emotional turbulence of a new relationship, my body can go rather haywire. It feels overwhelmed by excitement, hormones of connection, hope, elation, and joy—and anxiety! With all this, I am usually a bit off balance, my sleep perhaps decreased from late night conversations or dates, thus running on caffeine and not enough food and maybe a few extra glasses of wine than usual. This can produce the most intense stomach pain, literally like a stabbing in my gut. And navigating this is a nearly impossible undertaking, given that I know I need to eat, and yet the anxiety and excitement and physical vulnerability prevent that pain from dissipating. All that helps this situation is usually time and feeling more comfortable, although, of course, the downside is then that the honeymoon begins to fade! In any case, with mindfulness we can do our best to take care of ourselves and ride out the rest.

Think about what types of stomach hunger you experience and how you might respond to this hunger most effectively. Observe this over the week. Take some notes (see also downloadable Handout 5.1).

Handout 5.1 Hungers Worksheet: Stomach Hunger

_____

_____

_____

_____

_____

_____

_____

_____

_____

_____

_____

_____

Cellular Hunger

Do you ever get into "kicks" with eating a certain type of food? I certainly do sometimes! For example, I may find myself eating seafood tacos and burritos for weeks or alternating between really being into salads, kale and

Brussel sprouts, for weeks, then not really having a taste for salads at all for weeks. I can also go through phases like this with water. Sometimes I get so thirsty and feel like I cannot drink enough water or liquid, like I could drink an entire gallon of lemonade, and other times I am like a camel, feeling like I do not need more than a few cups of water a day. Through my mindfulness practice, I certainly make a committed effort to dialectically still honor what my body needs and nourish and hydrate it adequately despite such extreme variations. For example, even if I am not craving greens, my body probably still needs vegetables. However, it is interesting to contemplate what might be driving such "kicks." It quite possibly could be cellular hunger.

Cellular hunger is your body literally telling you what it needs to be nourished on a nutritional level. For example, I had a stretch of time when I was really into salty sweetness, like salted caramel, and my friend who is a nurse told me it was probably because I was dehydrated and my body was craving salt. This made a lot of sense because I had been cutting back on salt, having recently gone to a farmers' market with a friend and gotten swept up in all the vendors promoting their products to counter the "dangers" of salt, sugar, and gluten. I threw myself into the sampling and had purchased a salt substitute because I really liked the taste and did not think it could hurt— after all, is salt not supposed to be unhealthy? Gosh, even after all of these years of practicing and teaching mindful eating, I got swept into that cognitive mentality, even if subtly, and the result was my not honoring my cellular hunger needing salt. So I continued to listen to my body, fed it sufficient salt and water, and my slight obsession with salty sweetness dissipated.

I also experienced this when I was on my soft foods diet after my wisdom teeth removal. I was eating a lot of carbs because they were soft so I was not getting enough protein. It was really an interesting practice in attending to my needs and figuring out how to adequately nourish them when I was not able to just naturally eat what I usually eat, because of needing to avoid hard foods (even though I generally love my soggy foods!). I learned that to stay balanced with protein I needed to incorporate a range of consistent servings, which included chocolate milk enriched with protein, protein shakes, and mayonnaise-based salads of chicken and seafood.

Think about what types of cellular hunger you experience and how you might respond to this hunger most effectively. Observe this over the week. Take some notes (see also downloadable Handout 5.1).

Handout 5.1 Hungers Worksheet: Cellular Hunger

_____

_____

_____

_____

_____

_____

_____

_____

_____

_____

_____

_____

_____

Mind Hunger

Mind hunger is cognitive hunger—our thoughts influencing our decisions about what we should or should not eat—all the rules and ideas we have about what is healthy and unhealthy, what is "good" and what is "bad." As we have been discussing at length, basing our consumption on this creates a host of issues that backfire. Moreover, operating from our mind detaches us from listening to our senses and all the other hungers we need to be feeding. Mind hunger is thus extremely powerful and dangerous.

At the same time, from a dialectical perspective, I would argue that there is still a place for mind hunger, especially when interoceptive awareness is low. Specifically, mind hunger can help us ensure that we are nourishing our bodies consistently, by making sure, as a rule, to eat at least three meals a day, regardless of how we are feeling emotionally or physically. Even if we are incredibly anxious or ill with the flu, our bodies and minds need to be fed; we need to eat anyway, even if it is just a yogurt for protein or a bowl of soup, clear soda, and crackers to settle our nauseous stomachs and cool our feverish flesh.

Think about what types of mind hunger you experience and how you might respond to this hunger most effectively. With this hunger in particular, remember that acting on mind hunger is not necessarily effective and therefore effectively quenching it may require mindfulness to still the mind and let the thoughts pass without reaction. Observe this over the week. Take some notes (see also downloadable Handout 5.1).

Handout 5.1 Hungers Worksheet: Mind Hunger

_____

_____

_____

_____

_____

_____

_____

_____

_____

_____

_____

_____

_____

Heart Hunger

Perhaps even more than mind hunger, heart hunger may be the most powerful hunger that drives our eating. Heart hunger is all about the emotions that trigger urges to eat, in general and specifically, particular foods and in a particular way. It is about the need to fill the void that can be created by feeling sad, lonely, or rejected. Or other times it can be about wanting to soothe and comfort ourselves in the face of other challenging emotions, such as anxiety, fear, and frustration. This can be because of memories associated with eating particular foods, such as the afterschool snack that would be greeting you when you arrived home from a difficult day among classmates and tests or the foods your mom always brought you in bed when you were sick or the casseroles that arrived from a church family after the death of a loved one, inexplicably instilling such peace with buttered breadcrumbs. Or it can simply be associated with chewing, which stimulates the vagus nerve of the brain and actually triggers the same parasympathetic nervous system that is triggered when we are embraced lovingly by someone (Shiba et al., 2002). Thus it can feel like a way to basically give ourselves a hug when others are not doing that for us.

And yet, of course, no food will nourish that true need for human connection or resolve any emotion. Eating can absolutely be comforting and we may continue to mindfully choose it to, at least partially, address this need. For example, if we are missing a grandparent that has passed away, we may choose to eat their favorite meal as a way of feeling closer to them. However, we can nourish this need in other ways that do not involve food. For example, if we are grieving, we may instead look through old photo albums, watch videos of the person, or visit their grave.

And if we are anxious or frustrated, we may consider what these emotions are trying to tell us and how we can respond to them effectively, if they are justified, taking steps to keep ourselves safe or to reach our objective, respectively; if they are unjustified, like Baby Albert and the white furry objects, approaching the furry objects (whatever they may be for us!) to learn that they are not dangerous (for further discussion of justified versus unjustified emotion and corresponding responses see Chapter 9).

Think about what types of heart hunger you experience and how you might respond to this hunger most effectively. As with mind hunger, in particular, remember that acting on heart hunger by eating is not necessarily effective and may backfire if the eating is followed by judgment and further negative emotions. At the same time, you can choose to eat to nourish this hunger. If you choose to do this, do so mindfully, without judgment, and if this does not fully resolve the heart hunger, consider how you can more completely address your true hunger. Observe this over the week. Take some notes (see also downloadable Handout 5.1).

Handout 5.1 Hungers Worksheet: Heart Hunger

_____

_____

_____

_____

_____

_____

_____

_____

_____

_____

_____

Quieting Emotion Mind

Emotion Mind can demand a lot of attention. Like a toddler it can throw a tantrum if we try to ignore it. Also perhaps like a toddler, if it is hungry or overloaded with foods that are not adequately nourishing; or not well rested; or wants to have more fun; or otherwise is not balanced in its needs being met, it can get cranky, pouting or whining, even whimpering, or, in the other direction, blunted. Likewise, its vocabulary can be diminished when it is struggling, making it hard to know what it needs. Like the volume of a radio, its messages can get distorted, either blaring when cranked as high as it can go or muffled, even inaudible, from being too low. With mindfulness we can increase our ability to sort through this; this can be facilitated by attending to self-care. In DBT, these skills fall under the module of Emotion Regulation and include expanding mindfulness of emotion and attending to factors reducing vulnerability through a set of tools summarized as ABC PLEASE. For more information, handouts, and homework, please see Linehan's texts (1993; 2014a; 2014b). If you are a practitioner, you can use this material to teach and assign homework for practice.

Emotion Model

Have you ever felt a diffuse discontent but been unable to define what it was exactly, simply knowing you were "in a funk," or "in a mood," or "off"? Was this unsettling? It is hard to know what to do with this type of emotional fog because without it being well defined, it is difficult to discern what it is trying to tell us. Increasing our skill in emotional awareness through refined mindfulness can help resolve this.

A basic model of emotions begins with an event that triggers either an automatic emotional reaction or a thought that then produces an emotion (to review theories on the role of thoughts in emotion see Chapter 3). The emotion can then be broken down into multiple components, including physiological activation and bodily sensations, urges, and, ultimately, behavioral action. For example, an event may be an exam. This may trigger the thought "I am going to fail," which then prompts the emotion of anxiety. The anxiety may then consist of a pit in your stomach, a racing heart, increased temperature, and shaking, consistent with the fight or flight response from the sympathetic nervous system. With this, you may have urges to avoid or procrastinate, as attempts at escaping the threat. You can then act on these urges or use Opposite to Emotion Action to approach and take the exam, since it is not a true life-threatening danger and, thus, is actually physically safe to encounter (even if it does not feel that way!; see Chapter 9). Your action is followed by consequences, or aftereffects, such as relief if you approach and take the exam. This would then reinforce the behavior of approaching. Likewise, if you avoid and procrastinate you may experience, at least temporarily, relief, then reinforcing the behavior of avoiding and procrastinating. The choice is yours, even if there is the most infinitesimal space between your urge and action. Whatever you choose, this then will, again, produce consequences, such as thoughts and emotions that can then be similarly deconstructed. For an outline of this basic model see Handout 5.2.

Determining our emotions can be challenging for various reasons. Perhaps you simply are still learning how to do this. Without adequate experience in the skill of mindfulness, you may need more practice. Perhaps you have always struggled with low interoceptive awareness. Perhaps this has been complicated by your unbalanced eating patterns. This also can vary across the components of emotion, for example, perhaps related to culture (e.g., Bernstein, Lee, Park, & Jyoung, 2008; Chentsova-Dutton & Dzokoto, 2014; Dzokoto, 2010; Tsai, Simeonova, & Watanabe, 2004) or overcontrolled family patterns of holding in emotion, focusing on thoughts or physical sensations without realizing how they are related to emotion. For example, sometimes when I ask clients how they feel they respond with thoughts, such as "I feel that it is not fair" or "I feel that I am ugly" and then struggle to identify the associated emotion. Focusing on physical sensations, when we suddenly need to run to the bathroom, feeling sick, we may first wonder if we have food poisoning or are getting sick. Indeed, with panic, clients often initially end up going to the emergency room, thinking they are having a heart attack, not connecting their bodily cues to emotion. In any case, mindfulness within the framework of this Emotion Model can help you improve this.

Another barrier can be overlap in emotional experience. For example, if you have ever been on a first date or had a crush, I imagine you can relate to the confusing rush of emotions that go along with this. You may feel lightheaded, your stomach twisted into knots. Is this anxiety, or fear, or butterflies of excitement and the first blush of love? It may be a combination. Context is thus important for elucidating the specific emotion. For example, if your stomach is upset and you are being chased by an assailant rather than pursued romantically by a flirting suitor, you probably would define this as fear rather than excitement and vice versa (although again there could be a combination in the latter!).

Looking at the context of emotion can also shed light on what it is trying to tell you. For example, if you have experienced a loss, you are likely experiencing sadness; that is what the sadness is trying to tell you. If you have been maltreated or had a goal blocked, you are likely experiencing some variant of anger; that is what the anger is trying to tell you. If you are facing a real or perceived threat, you are likely experiencing fear or anxiety; that is what the fear or anxiety is trying to tell you. If you feel you have acted in a manner that is inconsistent with your values, harming yourself or others, you are likely experiencing guilt; that is what the guilt is trying to tell you. Listen to these messages. Address them to resolve them and they will pass. In doing so consider whether their intensity is being amplified by deficits in the areas of ABC PLEASE (discussed next).

Handout 5.2 Emotion Model

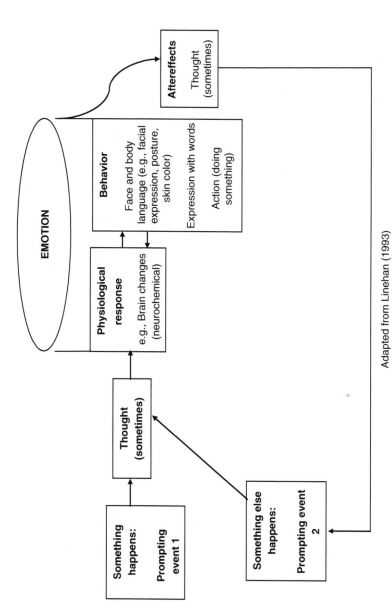

Adapted from Linehan (1993)

Practice deciphering your emotions. Use the following to record your observations over the coming week (see also downloadable Handout 5.3).

Handout 5.3 Deciphering Emotions Worksheet

Monday:

What emotion do I Observe?_____

How do I know?

- What happened (i.e., what event prompted this emotion)? And so what is the emotion trying to tell me?_____

_____

_____

_____

_____

- What thoughts am I having? _____

_____

_____

_____

_____

- How do I feel in my body?_____

_____

_____

_____

- What do I want to do (i.e., what are my urges)?_____

_____

_____

_____

- What do I actually do? _____

_____

_____

_____

• Am I addressing what the emotion is trying to tell me? If not, how can I?

_____

_____

_____

Tuesday:

What emotion do I Observe?_____

How do I know?

• What happened (i.e., what event prompted this emotion)? And so what is the emotion trying to tell me?_____

_____

_____

_____

• What thoughts am I having? _____

_____

_____

_____

• How do I feel in my body? _____

_____

_____

• What do I want to do (i.e., what are my urges)? _____

_____

_____

• What do I actually do? _____

_____

_____

_____

- Am I addressing what the emotion is trying to tell me? If not, how can I?

_____

_____

_____

Wednesday:

What emotion do I Observe?_____

How do I know?

- What happened (i.e., what event prompted this emotion)? And so what is the emotion trying to tell me?_____

_____

_____

_____

_____

- What thoughts am I having? _____

_____

_____

_____

_____

- How do I feel in my body?_____

_____

_____

_____

- What do I want to do (i.e., what are my urges)? _____

_____

_____

_____

- What do I actually do? _____

_____

_____

_____

- Am I addressing what the emotion is trying to tell me? If not, how can I?

_____

_____

_____

Thursday:

What emotion do I Observe?_____

How do I know?

- What happened (i.e., what event prompted this emotion)? And so what is the emotion trying to tell me?_____

_____

_____

_____

- What thoughts am I having? _____

_____

_____

_____

- How do I feel in my body? _____

_____

_____

- What do I want to do (i.e., what are my urges)? _____

_____

_____

_____

- What do I actually do? _____

_____

_____

_____

- Am I addressing what the emotion is trying to tell me? If not, how can I?

_____

_____

_____

Friday:

What emotion do I Observe?_____

How do I know?

- What happened (i.e., what event prompted this emotion)? And so what is the emotion trying to tell me?_____

_____

_____

_____

_____

- What thoughts am I having? _____

_____

_____

_____

- How do I feel in my body? _____

_____

_____

_____

- What do I want to do (i.e., what are my urges)? _____

_____

_____

_____

- What do I actually do? _____

_____

_____

_____

- Am I addressing what the emotion is trying to tell me? If not, how can I?

_____

_____

_____

Saturday:

What emotion do I Observe?_____

How do I know?

- What happened (i.e., what event prompted this emotion)? And so what is the emotion trying to tell me?_____

_____

_____

_____

_____

- What thoughts am I having? _____

_____

_____

_____

_____

- How do I feel in my body? _____

_____

_____

_____

- What do I want to do (i.e., what are my urges)? _____

_____

_____

_____

- What do I actually do? _____

_____

_____

_____

- Am I addressing what the emotion is trying to tell me? If not, how can I?

_____

_____

_____

Sunday:

What emotion do I Observe?_____

How do I know?

- What happened (i.e., what event prompted this emotion)? And so what is the emotion trying to tell me?_____

_____

_____

_____

_____

- What thoughts am I having? _____

_____

_____

_____

_____

- How do I feel in my body? _____

_____

_____

_____

- What do I want to do (i.e., what are my urges)? _____

_____

_____

_____

- What do I actually do? _____

_____

_____

_____

- Am I addressing what the emotion is trying to tell me? If not, how can I?

_____

_____

_____

ABC PLEASE

The skill of **ABC PLEASE** encompasses the following components for reducing vulnerability to Emotion Mind: **A**ccumulating Positive Experiences; **B**uilding Mastery; **C**oping Ahead; Treating **P**hysical Illness; Balanced **E**ating; **A**voiding Drugs and Alcohol; Balanced **S**leep; and Balanced **E**xercise. When these areas are out of balance, Emotion Mind gets stronger, disrupting our ability to adapt to stress. Listen to your experience. If you feel paralyzed and stuck, perhaps getting stuck in details or having trouble shifting, your brain numb and not processing experience, or you grow agitated and restless, or you find yourself suddenly sobbing, this may reflect the influence of inadequate ABC PLEASE. Go through this checklist and assess for deficits in this self-care that could be intensifying your emotions. If you detect imbalance, recognize this and discern the clear piece of the emotions you are experiencing and act only on that. In addition, prioritize getting back into balance with ABC PLEASE. Of course, we may be under many demands or face various barriers to this, and yet, it is imperative to attend to these areas to reduce your suffering. Emotional pain is painful enough. Do not amplify it into unnecessary suffering when you can prevent or adjust this.

- **Accumulating Positive Experiences** reduces vulnerability to difficult emotional experience by promoting more pleasant emotions, such as joy and happiness. This consists of cultivating fun in the short term and also working towards long-term goals to ultimately achieve the life you want. Of course, working towards long-term goals can be arduous and consist of many unpleasant steps that require massive amounts of Opposite to Emotion Action and Effectiveness (see Chapters 9 and 4, respectively). Because of this, it is essential to incorporate short-term positive experiences as you continue towards long-term goals.

For example, I can assure you that the long-term goal of getting a Ph.D. in clinical psychology is not a walk in the park. It is fraught with requirements and politics that can feel insurmountable and imperil nearly all of the ABC PLEASE skills. Indeed, one of the professors in my graduate program was rumored to have said that if you were sleeping you were not working hard enough. Inevitably students succumbed to this pressure and ultimately, when pushed to the limit, ended up dropping out of the program. To not be a similar casualty, in my journey through this, I definitely learned that I needed to prioritize short-term positive experiences to pace myself through the process, to ultimately reach my goal, which was highly important to me. Thus after putting in my first three years of graduate training in a very imbalanced way, I began scheduling time for lunch and coffee breaks around town, movies, and nights off. My strong work ethic did not diminish and I certainly still pulled my share of late nights! However, I was able to do so because I had a reserve of positive experience to buoy me through it. I was driven to keep going because of my passion and vision for becoming a psychologist. I thus was simultaneously Accumulating Positive Experiences in the short term and building my life worth living in the long term.

Likewise, relationships can be long-term positive experiences that come hand in hand with an extensive amount of stress: first developing, then maintaining, resolving conflict and nurturing to grow. Indeed, navigating this arena can toss us asunder at times and attending to intimacy with our loved ones is a daily requirement. The cost of not doing so can be the relationship ending, quietly uncoupling from drifting apart or imploding from unresolved hurt. Given the amount of work that relationships thus require, they do not always feel pleasant in the moment. They may instead be a source of utter frustration and dismay. Yet, as tribal beings, we need connection with other people and a life without others is not usually a life that people want to live. Thus fostering relationships can be part of Accumulating Positive Experiences in the long term, with bolstering needed from short-term positive experiences.

Think about this for you. What brings you joy? What makes you laugh and smile?

When you are struggling with depression, it can feel like nothing will overcome the heaviness, that you will feel hollow whatever you do. This makes sense. One of the main symptoms of depression is loss of interest or pleasure in activities usually enjoyed. At the same time, seeking to cultivate positive experience can signal to our bodies and brains that we are approaching and activating rather than isolating or avoiding. This can thus help at least begin to counter the weight of the depression. Indeed, behavioral activation is one of the most empirically supported interventions in depression treatment (Chartier & Provencher, 2013; Dimidjian et al., 2006; Pagoto, Bodenlos, Schneider, Olendzki, & Spates, 2008; Spates, Pagoto, & Kalata, 2006).

With this also, honor where you are in depression. There are many ways to accumulate positive experiences. They do not have to be highly engaging social interactions, such as parties, which may feel exhausting. Rather, perhaps, consider what might feel less overwhelming, like going to a movie. This can still be accumulating a positive experience and yet require minimal social interaction around your ticket; then you can enjoy the cocoon of the dark theater as you escape into the world on the screen. In taking yourself to the movie you would thus be moving yourself in a positive direction with kindness, in a more feasible manner.

High anxiety can be another barrier to Accumulating Positive Experiences, fueling avoidance, blocking or slowing down even getting to the positive experience, as well as prompting escape from the experience and disrupting participation in the experience. To overcome this, again, Opposite to Emotion Action and Effectiveness, with a graded approach, are essential. For example, perhaps you start with having coffee one on one with someone you feel mostly safe with, then work up to settings with larger groups of people and strangers. You can also accumulate positive experiences independently, for example, curling up with a compelling book, getting lost in its pages; playing music; creating art. Whatever it is, it is most important to be engaging with what you actually enjoy rather than ideas of what you should enjoy.

Guilt can also get in the way, perhaps related to anxiety. For example, if you feel driven to always be productive, perhaps due to external pressure like the professor I mentioned from my graduate training, when you take a break for yourself to have fun, this can produce a sense of guilt. As we will discuss further with Opposite to Emotion Action, this guilt is probably sending you faulty information because everyone deserves to have a little fun. In fact, it is actually essential to our well-being and in any case permits us to experience the full range of the human experience. As long as you are also taking care of your responsibilities and not only having fun, or going too far in that extreme, then please, by all means, have some fun! Again, Opposite to Emotion Action and Effectiveness, with a graded approach, can help you move past this barrier. For example, maybe you start with just a few minutes of fun each day, then work up to an hour, then an evening off, then a full day off, then a full weekend, then a long weekend, until you find yourself on an extended vacation! I assure you, it is worth it and you deserve it.

It is also helpful to have a range of options that will not create financial burden, unless perhaps you have unlimited resources! Think of ways you can have fun that are entirely free or low cost—perhaps going to the beach, walking in the park, exploring a part of town with interesting architecture, window shopping, checking out books at the library, looking through photos to recall fond memories, daydreaming…

Starting with short-term positive experiences, let your mind wander and create a list of inspiration for yourself. This can include experiences that may fall between short-term and long-term, such as taking a vacation. We will then reflect on more distant long-term goals. I challenge you to come up with at least 50 ideas—and feel free to keep going! When you notice or discover a new source of joy, jot it down (see also downloadable Handout 5.4). In the spirit of Accumulating Positive Experiences, have fun with this! Perhaps thinking about having fun and list-making could be your first items!

Handout 5.4   Ideas for Accumulating Short-Term Positive Experiences

1. _____
2. _____
3. _____
4. _____
5. _____
6. _____
7. _____
8. _____
9. _____
10. _____
11. _____
12. _____
13. _____
14. _____
15. _____
16. _____
17. _____
18. _____
19. _____
20. _____

21._____

22._____

23._____

24._____

25._____

26._____

27._____

28._____

29._____

30._____

31._____

32._____

33._____

34._____

35._____

36._____

37._____

38._____

39._____

40._____

41._____

42._____

43._____

44._____

45._____

46._____

47._____

48._____

49._____

50._____

Now further considering long-term goals, think about where you want your life to go. If you went to sleep tonight and woke up tomorrow and everything was how you imagine you want it to be, what would this look like? What would you be doing? Where would you be? How would your day unfold? Your years? Who would be there? Really think about this over the coming week and let it continue to evolve moving forward, adding to it as this unfolds.

With this, remember to be dialectical. Long-term goals can be motivating and crucial to move us towards mindfully creating the life we want. At the same time, rigidly defining long-term goals can be inconsistent with a mindful perspective of openness. It can promulgate comparisons of current experience to future desires according to the definitions we have set. This takes us out of the moment and into a Reasonable Mind stance of thinking (remember that Reasonable Mind is the architect of long-term planning). This may result in premature dismissal of possibilities due to concluding that they do not match the long-term vision. It can also activate Emotion Mind if the future feels too distant, with too many hurdles. Again, this can then result in throwing in the towel, depriving us of the reward of achieving our goals. To retain a dialectical stance in this process, it is thus important to confirm long-term goals with our Wise Mind and remember the values driving our goals, returning to the valued directions we can take this very moment, which, after a series of moments, will lead us to our long-term goals in the end.

Permit yourself space to reflect on this question of what you would like your life to become. Where do you want your life to be moving? What is important to you? What do you want to achieve? This may include professional, personal, and interpersonal goals. While you may want to set health-related goals, I encourage you to move away from goals related to appearance or eating. Focus on the rest of your life here and what you want to be doing with it beyond appearance and eating. Record your thoughts here and return to this as a touchstone as you discern this through your Wise Mind (see also downloadable Handout 5.5).

Handout 5.5 Reflection for Accumulating Long-Term Positive Experiences

_____

_____

_____

_____

_____

_____

_____

_____

_____

_____

_____

_____

_____

_____

_____

_____

_____

_____

_____

_____

_____

_____

_____

_____

_____

- **Building Mastery** reduces vulnerability to difficult emotional experience by promoting a sense of accomplishment and achievement. This can overlap with long-term goal setting as discussed above in Accumulating Positive Experiences. This is especially helpful when your level of authority is pervasively low across your circumstances, such as at school, work, or home. For example, if you are a student, you are under the authority of your teachers, professors, and school administration. Similarly, unless you are the boss, at work you are under the authority of your boss, and, growing up, you are under the authority of your parents. This can feel disempowering, deprived of agency and control. Building Mastery offers a way to counter this, to assert authority in other domains, enabling empowerment and feeling in control.

Building Mastery can vary in scope, contained in playing fields of recreation or chores, or incrementally moving towards expertise. For example, completing a word search, Sudoku, or crossword, or populating an impressive board of Words with Friends can be relatively immediate ways to reign over domains on a smaller scale. Likewise, you can Build Mastery by making your bed and cleaning, in the kitchen rinsing and sterilizing, loading and unloading the dishwasher, accounting for each gadget and utensil; in the bathroom scrubbing each tile and crevice of grout, each spigot, and each rounded curve of sink, toilet, shower, and bathtub until it shines and sparkles. On a larger scale you can learn a new skill, perhaps how to knit or sew or sail or fly a plane or make sushi, perhaps fluency in a foreign language you have not studied before, or perhaps personal growth, such as the very targets of this program, developing a mindful approach to life, emotion regulation, and distress tolerance, letting go of old patterns that do not serve your higher interests. You can also go deeper with a skill you already have, for example, expanding your music or dance repertoire or experimenting with recipes.

For Building Mastery in any of these directions, it is important that the task is challenging but not entirely overwhelming. Approaching this in a graded fashion can, again, help with this. For example, first choose an easier piece of music, then progress gradually to advanced pieces (I can vouch for this practice being much more fruitful than jumping ahead from when I returned to playing piano after falling out of my regular practice over my years in graduate training!). This will help build up a sense of achievement and accomplishment brick by brick, laying the foundation for the next bricks, rather than setting up an expectation of being able to construct a wall overnight. The latter is just not possible. Remember kindness with this. Give yourself time to tend your talents and the garden will bloom.

Research and theory support the need to find a middle ground with self-efficacy and feelings of control to reduce vulnerability to unbalanced eating in Emotion Mind (Cain, Bardone-Cone, Abramson, Vohs, & Joiner, 2008; 2010a; Heatherton & Baumeister, 1991; Rezek & Leary, 1991; Tierney, 2006). For example, low interpersonal self-efficacy has been linked to increased restriction with elevated interpersonal stress and high appearance self-efficacy (i.e., feeling able to alter your weight or shape, e.g., through how you are eating), in particular when interpersonal perfectionism is also high (Cain et al., 2008; 2010a). Finding other sources of self-efficacy by Building Mastery thus seems critical to offset attempts to substitute a sense of control or efficacy in the appearance domain for a lack of control or efficacy in other domains. Furthermore, given the tendency for dieting to backfire into binge eating (see Chapter 1), circumventing dieting by Building Mastery offers a likely diversion for binge eating, as well.

Take a moment here and think about how you use this skill already and how you may build upon this. Jot down some notes (see also downloadable Handout 5.6).

Handout 5.6 Building Mastery Worksheet

_____

_____

_____

_____

_____

_____

_____

_____

_____

_____

_____

_____

- **Coping Ahead** reduces vulnerability to difficult emotional experience by providing a plan of action prior to facing the anticipated stressors, thus enabling more effective responding than might otherwise be possible if caught off guard in Emotion Mind. For example, perhaps you anticipate being alone on a holiday or anniversary date and that this will be difficult for you. Coping Ahead you could research events to attend or think about how you can distract yourself, redirecting your attention, perhaps to a project or movie marathon. With eating-related concerns, you would also want to think about how to approach food that day. For example, will you cook for yourself, perhaps comforting traditional dishes and a favorite dessert to nourish heart hunger, with mindfulness to prevent binge eating, or challenging epicurean recipes to engage your mind with Other Thoughts (see Chapter 6) and Building Mastery? Or will you take yourself out to eat at a fancy restaurant for their special menu? Whatever you choose, what may be issues with the plan? For example, if you decide you want to treat yourself to a fancy restaurant how will you cope when you see couples and families when you are there by yourself? Will you text your friends or family to connect in relationship as much as possible, to reduce your loneliness? Will you distract by reading a magazine? Or will you sit with the emotion as a form of exposure, decatastrophizing that no matter what, you will survive and afterwards feel stronger for it? Perhaps you will do a combination of these options.

Likewise, in general do not leave your calendar blank. Research events related to your interests and make note of them. For example, if you enjoy music, look into upcoming shows or concerts, be they music from live bands or a symphony. If you love art, find openings at local galleries and museums. If you love movies, scout the current releases, keep your eye on upcoming film festivals, and look into independent theaters. Also think about goals or desired positives you would like to accumulate in general, such as learning to surf or sail, creating a piece of art, taking a train trip, shopping for certain items, or getting a massage, and consider when you can add them to your schedule. Then you can look forward to these experiences, to help prevent or decrease depression.

With eating, Coping Ahead for meals can be essential. For example, my colleague used to tease me about being on a sandwich kick when I was traveling between two different offices around dinnertime. Preparing sandwiches to fit into the transition time was my way of Coping Ahead to nourish myself adequately within my time constraints. Similarly, when I had an early morning meeting I would invariably be pushing being on time if I sat at home and ate my usual breakfast, I coped ahead to be on time by having balanced items that I could instead eat in the car or when I got to the meeting. Of course, there were other options to consider in problem solving my tardiness, but cutting out the 15 minutes of my usual breakfast routine was significant and feasible without sacrificing balance, just requiring flexibility and a little creativity. Having food available when it is needed also requires figuring out time to go to the market or store for groceries ahead of time, as well as time to prepare the food. With a busy schedule this can be extremely challenging. Think about how you will do this so you do not default to trying to wing it in the moment, then making ineffective choices or cooking and eating incredibly late at the end of the day.

Think about eating-related stressors that challenge you. Again, these could include how to prepare meals ahead of time and when to get groceries. Consider this in general and for the upcoming week. Note this is not intended to produce a meal plan in the traditional sense, such as may be provided from a dietician, but rather a course of action more focused on timing. Outline your plans here (see also downloadable Handout 5.7).

Handout 5.7 Cope Ahead Worksheet for Meal Preparation and Grocery Shopping

In general, I will take the following steps for meal preparation: _____

_____

_____

_____

_____

In the upcoming week I will take the following steps for meal preparation:

_____

_____

_____

_____

In general, I will take the following steps for grocery shopping (including days and times):_____

_____

_____

_____

_____

In the upcoming week I will take the following steps for grocery shopping (including days and times): _____

_____

_____

_____

_____

Also think about especially triggering situations, such as attending a work party or eating out with friends at a Mexican restaurant or holiday feasting with family. Think about what makes these situations particularly stressful. Is it social anxiety or the endless baskets of tortilla chips and salsa or the dessert table threatening to buckle from the weight of all of the decadence? Then think about all the skills you can use to cope with these situations. Of course, at this point, you are still learning skills, so feel free to read ahead or return to this, in particular after learning the distress tolerance skills. Write out detailed Cope Ahead plans, each with a fresh Cope Ahead Worksheet, for each situation (see Handout 5.8).

Handout 5.8 Cope Ahead Worksheet

Cope Ahead Worksheet

Situation: _____

_____

_____

_____

_____

What makes this particularly stressful? _____

_____

_____

_____

_____

How will I cope with this?_____

_____

_____

_____

_____

_____

_____

After the situation: How well did my Cope Ahead plan work? _____

_____

_____

What was especially helpful (Be sure to do this again next time!)? _____

_____

_____

_____

What was not so helpful; why? _____

_____

_____

_____

What will I plan to do differently next time? _____

_____

_____

_____

_____

- The **PLEASE** skill encompasses self-care in the areas of physical illness, eating, (avoiding) drugs and alcohol, sleep, and exercise.

How do you feel when you are sick or in pain, perhaps suffering from a headache or migraine? Cranky? Numbed out, like you are in a fog? On the verge of tears? Usually you will not be functioning at full capacity, so you respond less effectively to stress. You likely are not able to handle very much stress and it likely affects you more than when you are physically healthy. Treating Physical Illness is thus helpful to reduce your vulnerability to Emotion Mind. This includes taking your medication as prescribed. If you miss a dosage, especially if you are on psychotropic medication, or your medications are being adjusted, this will impact your emotions. Keep this in mind and take extra care of yourself to better cope.

If you struggle with taking care of yourself, remember our friends Opposite to Emotion Action and Effectiveness (see Chapters 9 and 4, respectively). We need to take care of ourselves, so if you are having urges to not do so, go against the urges and take care of yourself! Barriers to this can include the financial cost, such as lost pay or treatment fees. I assure you I can understand this. As a part-time and commissioned employee for several years, I had no sick days or paid vacation time. Any time off was a loss of pay for me or demanded I double up my schedule before or after my absences. Of course, to counter this barrier, consider the potential long-term cost that could result if you put off needed medical care. What may have initially been resolved by a day of rest in bed and chicken noodle soup could develop into a protracted illness that impairs your performance anyway and could then require you to ultimately take multiple days off from work. In other words, in the long run the cost could be higher than if you address the concern more immediately.

It is interesting how we still can have urges to delay taking care of ourselves even when we are rationally aware of the cost benefit analysis. For instance, I used to have severe migraines rather frequently, so now I know when one is coming on and I know full well the suffering that will result if I do not address the situation when it begins by taking medication— and yet, at times I still have a dismissive urge to ignore the pain, the thought that it somehow will be fine. I imagine this comes from my stoic genetic roots and modeling of similar patterns in my family. If you struggle with taking care of yourself, can you relate to this? With mindfulness I then use Opposite to Emotion Action and Effectiveness to address this need before it escalates further; remember this, as well.

Mothers have similarly shared with me that this becomes what they learn from having children, to always put their children first, to the detriment of their own well-being. Challenge this. Consider the metaphor of putting your oxygen mask on first if there is a plane emergency. You cannot help anyone, including the child seated beside you, if you are not taken care of first.

Of course, this entire book is addressing Eating and emotion! This is a reminder to assess how well you are balancing this, not overeating and not undereating. Also, do not eat as a reaction in Emotion Mind. For example, if you are sad or depressed or anxious or otherwise distraught, this does not justify not eating meals. To reduce emotional vulnerability it is essential to consider eating in the same manner as you would medicine. Do not skip doses. Even if you are sick to your stomach with distress, be sure to nourish yourself by eating (see also Mind Hunger above). The metaphor applies to overeating, as well. Follow the prescription as outlined in this program and consider meals and snacks as doses to not be exceeded.

If you have ever had a drink or used drugs or even had a cup of coffee, I am sure you can attest to how these substances can affect your mood. Again, they will either amplify or dull your reactions and interfere with responding as you would if fully balanced in Wise Mind. Thus, Avoiding Drugs and Alcohol can reduce your vulnerability to Emotion Mind, and if you choose to drink or use substances, do so as mindfully as possible and, ideally, in moderation, first solidly Coping Ahead. Think about where you are drinking or using, who you are with, how you will cope with possible stressors that arise, how you will pace your consumption, and how you will keep yourself physically safe otherwise, including how you will get home. Think about drink sizes and consider alternating alcohol with water. Keep in mind guidelines such as having no more than one drink per hour and avoiding binge drinking, if you are a female, keeping your drink total under four drinks for the entire occasion; if you are a male, under five (O'Neill, Parra, & Sher, 2001; Pisetsky, Chao, Dierker, May, & Striegel-Moore, 2008; Stewart, Angelopoulos, Baker, & Boland, 2000; Wechsler, Davenport, Dowdall, Moeykens, & Castillo, 1994; Wechsler & Nelson, 2001). For further guidance and support, especially if you are struggling with alcohol or substance abuse or dependence, seek professional treatment. To complement the dialectical mindful approach you are learning, find a DBT for substance use program if possible and in any case be sure that the therapy is grounded in an evidence-based approach (Courbasson, Nishikawa, & Dixon, 2012; Prendergast, Podus, Finney, Greenwell, & Roll, 2006; Ritschel, Lim, & Stewart, 2015).

Likewise, if you choose to have caffeine, be aware that it will naturally increase your heart rate and increased anxiety can result. Consider if this is going on if you notice you are having increased agitation or anxiety, without a clear cause. It could be that pot of coffee or extra shots of espresso you downed!

On the other hand, if you are a habitual coffee drinker and you do not get your morning fix, this is usually a recipe for emotional imbalance, putting you more on edge or dampening you down in a bit of a fog. Honor where you are with this. Respect your routine of caffeinating in the interest of your emotional balance and recognize how it may be impacting you in unhelpful ways. If the latter ultimately call for reduction or elimination of caffeine, do so with compassion, at a pace that feels effective for you—and brace yourself that the withdrawal will likely be painfully intense. I can empathize! The last time I got myself off of coffee I had the most severe headache I have ever had in my entire life and nothing would touch it—no medication, only time; it lasted for two days. Given the likelihood of withdrawal being painful in this way, time it to minimize disruption, so you can take care of yourself through it. For example, clear a weekend to stay in bed, under the covers, in darkness rather than attempting this in the middle of a demanding work week!

How do you feel when you do not get enough sleep? Or when you get too much? Or when you nap? Disruptions in Sleep can have different effects. For some, getting less sleep is energizing. For others, even slightly less sleep turns them into barely functioning zombies. Personally, I can at least physically run on adrenaline (or so I think!) after a first night with little sleep, but quickly my mind seems to have vacated the premises! I also rapidly become more emotionally vulnerable, numbed out or, in the extreme, susceptible to sudden bursts of crying. Oversleeping can similarly perpetuate emotional imbalance, in particular, depression.

Barriers to sleep likewise include emotion, as well as behavioral patterns and context. For example, rumination from anxiety or depression can keep the mind awake, fending off any hope of falling asleep in the near future. To counter this you can apply many of the skills you are learning in this program, in particular, mindful letting go of thoughts with Observe (see Chapter 4), distracting with Other Thoughts (see Chapter 6), Self-Soothing and Relaxing (e.g., lavender scents; diaphragmatic breathing at six breaths/minute; progressive muscle relaxation; see Chapter 6), and One-Mindfully worrying for a limited time period (see Chapter 4). In extreme crises, non-addictive sleep aids, such as melatonin, may also be worth trying, but generally speaking, avoid sleep medication that can be habit forming and result in a vicious cycle of dependence.

It is also important to consider your emotional patterns to inform the best sleep routines and adjustments for you to reduce vulnerability to Emotion Mind. In particular, if you are experiencing depression, waking up earlier can at least temporarily help brighten your mood (for a review see Giedke & Schwarzler, 2002). Research on sleep deprivation suggests that this can reverse neurobiological underpinnings of depression, including increasing dopamine, normalizing hyperactive metabolism in the orbital medial PFC and in particular the ventral areas of the ACC, and, according to some evidence, increasing activity in the dorsal PFC (Bernier et al., 2009; Gillin, Buchsbaum, Wu, Clark, & Bunney, 2001). This may be enhanced and sustained by, or even attributable to, greater exposure to light, if not from natural sunlight then from bright light therapy (for a further review see Wirz-Justice et al., 2005), with increased light generally linked to improved mood, across time and source (Putilov & Danilenko, 2005). Interestingly, outcomes with bright light therapy have also included decreased binge eating in BN (Braun, Sunday, Fornari, & Halmi, 1999). In contrast, if you are prone to fluctuating moods, from high to low, then it is imperative to, as much as possible, go to bed at the exact same time every night and wake up at the exact same time every day (Frank, 2007; Frank, Swartz, & Kupfer, 2000; Miklowitz, Goodwin, Bauer, & Geddes, 2008; Murray et al., 2011; Swartz, Frank, Frankel, Novick, & Houck, 2009; Swartz, Levenson, & Frank, 2012). This is one of the core components in treatment for bipolar disorder (Frank, 2007; Miklowitz et al., 2008; Murray et al., 2011).

Impediments resulting from behavioral patterns can include stimulation from screens, including electronic devices, such as your phone, tablet, or laptop, and TV; and any associations pairing the bed with activities other than sleep. Think about it. What do you do in bed? Do you eat in bed? Read? Work? Watch TV or movies? The general rule to minimize extraneous associations with the bed besides sleep is to keep the bed only for sleep and sex. By doing this then your brain and body will be triggered to go to sleep more readily than if it is simultaneously triggered to be active, eat, read, work, and watch TV and movies!

Contextual considerations include temperature, sound, and light. Living in Southern California without air conditioning (with the coast nearby, people assert that you do not need it—but, perhaps due to global warming, when it is the height of summer and fall, trust me, you do!), I can certainly vouch for the disruptive influence of heat on sleep. Whew! Sweating when trying to drift off to dream is not pleasant. This is related to heat activating our body's threat system. In other words, when we are hot our bodies think that we are not safe, so they remain vigilant. To counter this, do your best to circulate cool air to decrease the temperature, to then activate your safety system. To do this I succumbed to purchasing a powerful fan.

Unfortunately, I am also especially sensitive to sound and sleep best in dead silence. I thus had to habituate to the whirring noise of the fan. I have, likewise, had to adjust to the muffled roar of the highway when I lived off a major thoroughfare and the sound of the ocean any time I have had the privilege of sleeping beside the Pacific. Returning to temperature, on the other hand, cold extremities can disrupt sleep. In the winter I thus swaddle my feet in cozy slippers or socks to go to bed.

Light can also disrupt sleep. This can be a way to balance your sleep, letting natural light wake you up rather than an artificial blaring alarm. At the same time, if you are not able to get to sleep at night because of light filtering in from outside you may consider investing in more solid window coverings or a sleep mask.

For further guidance in sleep interventions, refer to CBT for insomnia and professionals specializing in this approach, which is the most empirically supported approach for overcoming sleep difficulties (Harvey et al., 2014).

Finally, both too little and too much exercise can cause vulnerability to Emotion Mind. Balanced exercise can reduce depression and anxiety, increase mood stability and feelings of well-being, and even enhance body image (Bowen, Balbuena, Baetz, & Schwartz, 2013; Hausenblas & Fallon, 2006; Strohle, 2009). At the same time, imbalanced exercising or compulsive exercising, driven by the goal of weight loss, can increase our stress and backfire.

To find a middle ground in this, focus on exercise and physical activity that you actually like and want to do. Not everyone needs to run an Ironman or a marathon or half-marathon or even a 10k! Not everyone even needs to run for that matter. Nor do you have to be a member of a gym. There are many ways to move our bodies, so why not choose what you actually might enjoy? This will increase the likelihood that you will follow through with it. For example, perhaps you prefer dance classes or Zumba or yoga. Wonderful! There is even research showing more extensive and sustained benefits of tango on depression, insomnia, stress, anxiety, and mindfulness compared to more traditional aerobic exercise (Pinniger, Thorsteinsson, Brown, & McKinley, 2013). Likewise, yoga has been linked to greater improvement in mood and anxiety, including thalamic GABA levels, than walking (Streeter et al., 2010). Or perhaps you would rather go hiking, surfing or skiing. Whatever it is, honor your true preferences and mindfully let go of judgments about what you "should" be doing.

Likewise, consider the context of your exercise. Do you feel most uplifted working out independently or with others, and if with others, anyone in particular? Do you feel most soothed or energized when taking your exercise outdoors, perhaps to a nature trail or alongside the ocean, compared to the confines of a gym? Relatedly, not all gyms are the same. If you think you would like to join a gym, find one where you feel comfortable and look forward to going. Research suggests that matching exercise context to preferences can account for improved emotional benefit (Plante et al., 2007).

In general, increased physical activity is the goal. In addition to structured exercise, lifestyle choices that promote greater movement count. For example, take the stairs instead of the elevator, or park your car a bit farther away from your destination than the closest parking spot so you walk more, or even walk or bike instead of driving. It all adds up and research supports both as beneficial for physical and emotional health (Strohle, 2009), although exercise, rather than less formal physical activity, does seem to be more advantageous in its impact on mood (Pickett, Yardley, & Kendrick, 2012).

If you struggle with getting started with exercise (perhaps you go through waves, going strong for a while, then stopping, or perhaps you have never really gotten a routine of exercise established), use Opposite to Emotion Action to gradually begin or resume. For example, when I was in graduate school, I literally did not exercise for years (unless you count walking across campus and lifting journal compendiums in the library!), feeling it was too overwhelming with all the other demands and pressure on my time. As I then rehabilitated myself back into life after I graduated, I very mindfully paced my return to exercise. Specifically, I wanted to get back to running, but I knew I was not in any shape to immediately be running for any extended period of time, so I found a graded program that began with increments of alternated walking and running, for just minutes at a time. I listened to my body and when I was ready to progress to the next combination I increased my times. Eventually I was running 5ks.

If you are really struggling with getting moving with exercise, perhaps due to depression, literally start with the first step. If you are in bed, sit up. Put one foot on the ground. Now put the next one on the ground. Now stand up. Now take one step. Now take another. Put on one sock, then another; then one athletic shoe, then another. Put on your athletic shorts and a t-shirt or other athletic top. You are already dressed for working out now, so keep going.

Coping Ahead can also help overcome barriers. For example, when I was a member of a gym, I learned to carry my gym bag in my car. This was after actually going to the gym on multiple occasions forgetting a key item and having to either go home for it and come back or make do with what I had. This included running in a skirt once when I forgot shorts and, another time, in sandals when I forgot my running shoes (until the monitor caught me and informed me that was not allowed!). Likewise, at times, I have toted around my yoga mat in my car. There is a lot to organize. Validate this and have a sense of humor about it if you can. Think of me running in my sandals! You can figure it out, too.

Of note, imbalance in any one aspect of ABC PLEASE can produce a cascade of effects in the other domains. For example, in line with what we can observe anecdotally, research indicates that consumption of alcohol, cigarettes, too much caffeine, and inadequate nourishment can impair sleep, disrupting slow wave and REM cycles (with drinking, in particular, in the second half of the night), delaying sleep onset (with smoking, excessive caffeine intake, and restriction), and cutting short a full night's rest, for example, through early morning wakening, in both clinical and nonclinical populations (with smoking and disordered eating; Bos et al., 2013; Cohrs et al., 2014; Roehrs & Roth, 2001; 2008). Likewise drinking and drug use can disinhibit or impose boundaries on eating, contributing to imbalanced patterns (e.g., Polivy et al., 1984), and caffeine and nicotine can interfere with appetite cues, undermining balanced eating, as well (Anzengruber et al., 2006; Hart, Abraham, Franklin, & Russell, 2011; Jessen, Buemann, Toubro, Skovgaard, & Astrup, 2005). Neglecting aspects of ABC PLEASE can also attenuate the benefit of other self-care. For example, research has found that exercising in the morning before eating (i.e., skipping breakfast, working out first, thus neglecting Balancing Eating although practicing Balancing Exercise) can impair cognitive performance later in the day (Veasey, Gonzalez, Kennedy, Haskell, & Stevenson, 2013). Given interplay across the domains, attending to any one aspect of ABC PLEASE can similarly promote widespread benefit and this will be further amplified as extended across the entire landscape of self-care. For example, research suggests that Building Mastery may be especially critical in producing the emotional benefits of exercise and physical activity through its bolstering of self-efficacy (Bodin & Martinsen, 2004).

Reflect on your PLEASE skills in general and over the coming week. Think about how you can move to greater balance in general and Observe how practicing or neglecting the PLEASE skills impacts your vulnerability to Emotion Mind this week. Record some notes (see also downloadable Handout 5.9).

Handout 5.9 Emotion Regulation PLEASE Worksheet

In general, I see the following opportunities for growth with my PLEASE skills:

Physical Illness: _____

_____

_____

_____

_____

Eating: _____

_____

_____

_____

Avoiding Drugs and Alcohol: _____

_____

_____

_____

Sleep:_____

_____

_____

_____

_____

Exercise: _____

_____

_____

_____

_____

PLEASE monitoring this week:

Physical Illness

Monday:_____

_____

Tuesday: _____

_____

Wednesday: _____

_____

Thursday:_____

_____

Friday: _____

_____

Saturday: _____

_____

Sunday:_____

_____

Eating

Monday:_____

_____

Tuesday: _____

_____

Wednesday: _____

_____

Thursday: _____

_____

Friday: _____

_____

Saturday: _____

_____

Sunday: _____

_____

Avoiding Drugs and Alcohol

Monday: _____

_____

Tuesday: _____

_____

Wednesday: _____

_____

Thursday: _____

_____

Friday: _____

_____

Saturday: _____

_____

Sunday: _____

_____

Sleep

Monday: _____

_____

Tuesday: _____

_____

Wednesday: _____

_____

Thursday: _____

_____

Friday: _____

_____

Saturday: _____

_____

Sunday: _____

_____

Exercise

Monday: _____

_____

Tuesday: _____

_____

Wednesday: _____

_____

Thursday: _____

_____

Friday: _____

_____

Saturday: _____

_____

Sunday: _____

_____

Chapter Summary

In summary, hunger is complex. When we feel hungry it can be for many different reasons. With mindfulness we can better discern what these reasons are in any particular moment and then more effectively decide whether we want to eat, at all, or in a particular way, or a particular food. Mindfulness is especially critical to counter low interoceptive awareness, which can regularly accompany disordered eating, clouding detection and distinction of internal cues—emotion or physical sensations such as hunger. The Emotion Model outlined in this chapter can provide a guide to help sharpen this awareness.

Emotion Mind can also be clouded by imbalanced self-care. With the skill of ABC PLEASE we can reduce our vulnerability to this, Accumulating Positive Experiences, Building Mastery, Coping Ahead, Treating Physical Illness, Balancing Eating, Avoiding Drugs and Alcohol, Balancing Sleep, and Balancing Exercise. With daily attention to these areas we can cultivate both greater resilience in the moment and, ultimately, the life we want to be living.

So, before you eat, pause. Think about what you are responding to, what your true hungers may be. Are you drawn to a particularly beautiful presentation? Did a particular smell captivate you? Are you angry and want to chomp away at a mouthful of crunchiness? Are you trying to quench your aching stomach? Do you need to nourish a particular nutritional deficit, such as protein, carbohydrates, or dairy? Is it simply time to eat, according to the clock? Or do you think you need to eat certain foods each day because of research you have read? Or is your heart aching from despair, broken by love lost?

In any of these cases, if you choose to eat, simply do so mindfully, providing yourself what can best quench your hunger in that moment. It is a choice and you need not feel shame about it. At the same time, remember that, depending on the hunger, needs may remain for you to meet otherwise. When you truly feed your needs fully, then your hunger will be satisfied and pass, until the next hunger arises. Each hunger is a new opportunity to nourish what you need. Be kind to yourself and honor this.

6   A Balanced Meal

As introduced in Chapter 1, Dialectics refers to the acknowledgment and balancing of polarities, fostering a middle ground. For example, we can completely accept ourselves in this moment as we are and we can work on moving forward in valued directions. Indeed, acceptance is the first step to change, and only with acceptance can we change. Similarly, dialectics lets go of rules to permit behavior that is adaptive in the current situation rather than based on an imposed structure that may or may not apply. Mindfulness from a dialectical perspective balances internal and external observation to permit Effectiveness in the current situation. Thus we can be alternately mindful of our internal thoughts, emotions, urges, and physical sensations and of our external surroundings. At any given moment in time, Effectiveness may call for more or less of either focus. Mindful eating from the dialectical perspective moves beyond the plate in front of us to see the entire space around us, as well as our internal urges, motivations, emotions, and thoughts, to help us most effectively nourish ourselves. It calls upon distress tolerance for Effectiveness depending on the situation.

Distress tolerance skills provide strategies for tolerating high emotion, urges, and crises. These skills do not directly resolve the source of the emotion, urges, or crises. Rather, they take the edge off the situation enough to permit riding it out until the intensity lowers or circumstances shift to permit more directly addressing the situation. For example, if you experience a stressor right before going to work or school, perhaps right before a major meeting or exam, and you need to focus on the meeting or exam, you may not have the space to first fully sit with the stressor and resolve it. Rather, you may need to set the situation aside for the length of time it takes to complete the meeting or exam, then return to the situation afterwards. Under these circumstances, you would want to employ distress tolerance skills to effectively complete the meeting or exam.

Likewise, some stressors can be completely overwhelming, triggering high urges, and cognitively, accessing Reasonable Mind and Wise Mind is just too daunting in that moment. This, in essence, can define a crisis. When this occurs distress tolerance skills can help you move from the state of feeling overwhelmed, shutting down, or vulnerable to urges (for disordered eating or other destructive actions) to a less intense state, with greater accessibility to Reasonable Mind and Wise Mind. Basically, distress tolerance skills buy you time to make a more effective choice than you may make in the height of Emotion Mind.

Moreover, distress tolerance skills help you get through a situation without making it worse. That is, given that disordered eating or other destructive behavior does not resolve what is driving the crisis but rather only serves a temporary function of emotional coping, still leaving the situation to address, if you are in a crisis and you act on urges for disordered eating or other destructive behavior, you are left with not only the situation but also the aftermath of having engaged in the disordered eating or other destructive behavior. As explored in Chapter 2, the cons of this can be extensive. Distress tolerance helps you not have to then deal with those consequences on top of the initial crisis.

Importantly, distress tolerance skills, by definition, also incorporate acceptance and willingness to return to the source of the emotion, urges, or crisis. Radical Acceptance not only stands alone as a specific distress tolerance skill but also can be considered a part of the very practice of distress tolerance. That is, distress tolerance involves momentarily stepping away from emotion, to then return to the emotion and address the source. In contrast, if you simply turn away from emotion, with no intention of returning to the emotion, you are engaging in avoidance. Avoidance is not distress tolerance. As we have been discussing, avoidance will inevitably backfire, strengthening the intensity and persistence of emotion.

To help increase accessibility in the height of intense emotion, urges, and crisis, most distress tolerance skills in DBT are defined by acronyms (Linehan, 1993; 2014a; 2014b). These acronyms are like handles to tools, helping you more quickly pull them out of your toolbox when you need them. I highly encourage you to memorize these acronyms to help with their accessibility when you need them the most—when your Reasonable Mind and Wise Mind are more remote.

To further increase accessibility, I also recommend practicing these skills when you are not in a crisis. When done mindfully, this can fall under the category of Emotion Regulation. For example, when practiced outside of a crisis situation, Activities can include Accumulating Positive Experiences and Building Mastery (see Chapter 5). Opposite to Emotion Action similarly can be considered either Emotion Regulation or Distress Tolerance (see the "E" of ACCEPTS), depending on the context in which it is applied. In general, the more you practice, the more you will increase your chances of connecting to these alternatives with Reasonable and Wise Mind when your Emotion Mind is in control. When professionally guided, coaching calls can then provide a further bridge to Reasonable Mind and Wise Mind in the face of a crisis, when Emotion Mind interferes with remembering alternatives.

Also, after reading and writing about these skills, gather together items you might use for the skills (e.g., puzzles, yarn, knitting needles, books) so they are ready when you need them! This can be a way of Coping Ahead. It is definitely not nearly as effective to be searching for items to use when in the midst of emotional intensity and high urges, so Cope Ahead by preparing these items, having them accessible and ready to go when you need them, including placing them in key locations. For example, you may transport a distress tolerance toolbox around in your car or perhaps store one in your kitchen, by the refrigerator. Wherever they are going to be most helpful, be sure to have options available.

For further description and guidance in teaching these skills in general, as developed and further revised by Linehan, please see Linehan's standard DBT manuals (1993; 2014a; 2014b). The following will highlight the distress tolerance skills that have been researched within DBT adapted for mindful eating. If you are a practitioner, you can use this material to teach and assign homework for practice.

Distraction

ACCEPTS

The skill of ACCEPTS consists of Activities, Contributing, Comparisons, Opposite Emotion, Pushing Away, Other Thoughts, and Strong Sensations.

- With **Activities**, mindfulness is being redirected from distressing emotion, urges, or crisis to engagement in other pursuits. This can be helpful as long as the alternative focus is not harmful and not approaching the emotion, urges, or crisis—and it can be especially helpful if the activities are pleasant events, promoting more positive emotions, Building Mastery, or furthering valued directions. With this it is also important to think about activities that are inconsistent with the behavior you are trying to block. For example, watching TV can be an activity. However, this may not be entirely helpful if you are trying to not binge eat because it leaves your hands free to plow through bags of chips and shovel spoonful after spoonful of ice cream. In contrast, perhaps knitting or lathering up lotion may be a more effective choice with this urge. Take a moment here and think about how you use this skill already and how you may build upon this. Jot down some notes (see also downloadable Handout 6.1).

Handout 6.1 Distress Tolerance ACCEPTS Worksheet: Activities

_____

_____

_____

_____

_____

_____

_____

- With **Contributing**, mindfulness is being redirected from distressing emotion, urges, or crisis to engagement in acts of kindness towards others. This can range from formal volunteering to less structured interactions, such as asking your grocery store clerk how they are doing, or smiling at a stranger you pass on the street. Let go of any attachment to elaborate ideas of volunteering if this is not possible, in general or in the moment, and move instead towards flexibility, with varied options to permit feasibility. Take a moment here and think about how you use this skill already and how you may build upon this. Jot down some notes (see also downloadable Handout 6.1).

Handout 6.1 Distress Tolerance ACCEPTS Worksheet: Contributing

_____

_____

_____

_____

_____

_____

_____

- With **Comparisons**, mindfulness is being redirected from distressing emotion, urges, or crisis to observation of others. This can bring perspective and inspiration. This can also foster a more easy manner regarding your own situation. Thinking about this skill may call to mind the classic comment from parents to think of the starving children in Africa, intended to prompt gratitude. Unfortunately, when Comparisons is suggested in a manner like this, it can be invalidating, for example, by implying that you should not feel the way you feel because others have it much worse. This is not the spirit of Comparisons. With Comparisons, we are bringing our awareness to the spectrum of human suffering and experience while not diminishing the validity of our own experience. Some more helpful ways to practice this can be reading about others who have overcome adversity, perhaps similar to your own, to seek connection to their story and inspiration that you, too, can move past your current trials. Another more helpful way to practice this can be enjoying entertainment with a comedic tone. For example, if you watch a movie or some reality TV with really outrageous characters you can take solace in knowing that at least you are not them! Take a moment here and think about how you use this skill already and how you may build upon this. Jot down some notes (see also downloadable Handout 6.1).

Handout 6.1 Distress Tolerance ACCEPTS Worksheet: Comparisons

_____

_____

_____

_____

_____

_____

_____

- With **Opposite Emotion**, mindfulness is being redirected from distressing emotion, urges, or crisis to activities that promote contrasting emotions. For example, to use Opposite Emotion when you are sad, instead of listening to sad music and watching sad movies with your box of tissues, perhaps watch a movie that always gets you laughing or listen and sing along to empowering, inspiring, upbeat music. Likewise, if you are angry, instead of engaging in attacking behavior, such as yelling or throwing things, perhaps practice kindness or relaxation (see also Self-Soothing for this, below); if you are nervous, instead of ruminating and catastrophizing, perhaps create a safe emotional space and cheerlead yourself (see also Self-Soothing for this, below). Take a moment here and think about how you use this skill already and how you may build upon this. Jot down some notes (see also downloadable Handout 6.1).

Handout 6.1 Distress Tolerance ACCEPTS Worksheet: Opposite Emotion

For Sadness:_____

_____

_____

_____

_____

For Anger: _____

_____

_____

_____

_____

For Anxiety/Fear: _____

_____

_____

_____

_____

For Guilt/Shame: _____

_____

_____

_____

_____

- With **Pushing Away**, you are mindfully setting aside distressing emotion, urges, and thoughts, describing them and perhaps transforming them using Imagery. For example, try literally writing down the emotions, urges, and thoughts that you are having and then put the piece of paper somewhere for safekeeping to return to later; or use Imagery, perhaps making your emotions, urges, and thoughts into clouds, blown away, or tennis balls volleyed over the net (see also Imagery, below). Take a moment here and think about how you use this skill already and how you may build upon this. Jot down some notes (see also downloadable Handout 6.1).

Handout 6.1 Distress Tolerance ACCEPTS Worksheet: Pushing Away

_____

_____

_____

_____

_____

_____

_____

- With **Other Thoughts,** mindfulness is being redirected from distressing emotion, urges, or crisis to alternative cognitions and images. This can be anything that fills your mind with other thoughts. You could count internally (e.g., in intervals of 7; if you lose track or make a mistake, starting over again) or externally, objects in the environment. For example, when I once was subject to a particularly painful washing of my hair at a salon (it seemed like it would never end, my poor neck starkly propped upon the cold porcelain of the sink, with no comfort from any cushioning!), I counted the lamps overhead and the tiles in the ceiling. Whew, that was rough—and a perfect opportunity for this skill! I have also used this when I have been experiencing escalating anxiety on a plane, redirecting my attention to the colors, shapes, and textures of the fabric of the seat in front of me. This can be especially helpful in such situations, when you may not have access to other more concrete tools for distress tolerance and you essentially have to rely on your mind. Take a moment here and think about how you use this skill already and how you may build upon this. Jot down some notes (see also downloadable Handout 6.1).

Handout 6.1 Distress Tolerance ACCEPTS Worksheet: Other Thoughts

_____

_____

_____

_____

_____

_____

_____

- With **Strong Sensations,** mindfulness is being redirected from distressing emotion, urges, or crisis to sensations that are particularly intense but not harmful. Physiologically, this skill can shock you into a different state. This skill can be extremely helpful in dire situations when less extreme skills are not helping, in the face of highly intense emotion, urges, and crisis.

A classic way of practicing this skill is to hold an ice cube until it melts. Hold one or more than one. Squeeze them in your palms or position them over thinner skin, such as the skin of your neck, below your ears. I personally find bare ice cubes most helpful, but others prefer to soften the intensity by using ice covered with a cloth or other barrier, such as the plastic of a frozen water bottle, or various ice packs. Pay attention to what works for you. If you feel pain, this is not necessarily unhelpful. In fact, again, this skill is meant to help in dire situations and if all you can think about is the pain of the ice, then it is arguably doing its job. Variants of this include sucking on ice, taking an ice-cold shower, jumping into an ice-cold pool, and walking barefoot on the beach in the cold water along the sand. Spa products can also be helpful to generate intense contrasts, such as mud masks that tighten up your face and grainy facial and foot scrubs.

With taste, try mindfully eating spicy or sour foods, such as Thai food that is so spicy it has you in tears or Sour Patch kids that make you pucker. With smell, perhaps jolt yourself with the classic reviver of smelling salts or other strong scents through oils. With sound, see what happens when you turn up the volume on your music, just momentarily, as loud as possible, to create a sense of numbness in your head. With movement, release energy in sudden bursts, such as a spurt of sprinting (but not in a punishing way to compensate for eating).

Take a moment here and think about how you use this skill already and how you may build upon this. Jot down some notes (see also downloadable Handout 6.1).

Handout 6.1 Distress Tolerance ACCEPTS Worksheet: Strong Sensations

Touch: _____

_____

_____

_____

Taste: _____

_____

_____

_____

Smell: _____

_____

_____

_____

Sound:_____

_____

_____

_____

Sight:_____

_____

_____

_____

Movement:_____

_____

_____

_____

Self-Soothing

Self-Soothing consists of soothing ourselves through the five senses, promoting a state of enhanced relaxation. For example, perhaps you look at the ocean, waves rolling in (sight), hearing their rhythm of cresting and folding back into themselves (sound), feeling the softness of the sand sinking below your feet, embracing them (touch). Perhaps you appreciate the smell of curry permeating the air from a kitchen that has created an Indian delight (smell) and mindfully savor the coconut milk of that curry (taste).

Of course, if you are working on mindful eating, honor where you are in the process of learning this. If you do not feel ready to mindfully self-soothe with food at home, seek out contexts that provide a structured containment, such as sampling at the grocery store or farmers' markets (I am imagining that the promoters and vendors will deter you from unlimited sampling!), cheese tasting classes, or gelato sampling with those tiny spoons.

With time, as you bring your awareness to your experience of eating, it can be interesting to discover what you truly find soothing. Many clients have shared that they have learned that they actually are not soothed at all by foods they thought were soothing, such as stereotypical binge or comfort foods (e.g., chips, ice cream, cake) and may even find the foods unenjoyable when eaten mindfully; instead they may actually find a fresh salad or cup of tea soothing. Discovering then what is truly soothing can help actually nourish those needs.

Take a moment here and think about how you use this skill already and how you may build upon this. Jot down some notes (see also downloadable Handout 6.2). Again, then gather together items you might use for this skill (e.g., pictures, lotion, candles) so they are ready when you need them!

Handout 6.2 Self-Soothing Worksheet

Sight:_____

_____

_____

_____

_____

Sound:_____

_____

_____

_____

Touch: _____

_____

_____

_____

_____

Smell: _____

_____

_____

_____

Taste: _____

_____

_____

_____

IMPROVE

The skill of IMPROVE consists of Imagery, Meaning, Prayer, Relaxation, One Thing in the Moment, Vacation, and Encouragement. Like Other Thoughts, this skill (specifically, Imagery, Meaning, Prayer, and Encouragement) can be especially helpful when more concrete tools are unavailable.

- **Imagery**. Like Other Thoughts, this skill is substituting images for the difficult thoughts connected to high emotion, urges, and crisis. It is painting a scene of another place, ideally one that is more compelling or soothing. For example, if you cannot go to the beach, imagine you are there. Soak it in. Or if you do not have access to ice to practice Strong Sensations, imagine yourself plunging into an ice-cold pool. For this skill, it can be especially helpful to imagine places you have been, so you can bring them more fully to life with vivid memories. Take a moment here and think about how you use this skill already and how you may build upon this. Jot down some notes (see also downloadable Handout 6.3).

Handout 6.3 Distress Tolerance IMPROVE Worksheet: Imagery

_____

_____

_____

_____

_____

_____

_____

- **Meaning** involves finding wisdom in pain. This can involve connecting to a lesson for growth or understanding of how the current situation came to be. This can be especially challenging in the face of intensely painful situations that feel like they are not understandable. And yet, everything happens for a reason in the sense that everything preceding that moment led up to that moment in that precise way such that it could be no other way. This skill can call upon spirituality and philosophy about the universe. And full meaning may not be realized until the crisis has fully passed.

Whatever the situation, I encourage remembering that emotions, however painful, are there for a reason, to provide important information. Sadness tells us we have had a loss, whether it is an actual loss of a loved one passing away, a loss of a dream or expectations, or the loss of a favorite item of clothing. Listening to this emotion we can grieve the loss and honor what we have had and then ultimately seek further connection to address our needs as tribal human beings. Anger tells us that we are not being treated how we feel we deserve to be treated, perhaps that we are being judged, or we are judging a situation, or that a goal we have is being blocked. For example, if we are driving and our goal is to reach a certain destination by a certain time and there is construction or a traffic jam that slows us down, we can expect to get frustrated. Listening to this message can help us advocate for ourselves, to be treated in a manner consistent with our values, or help us learn, to perhaps prevent a recurrence of the situation (e.g., prompting leaving earlier to allow for possible unexpected delays). Fear and anxiety tell us that we are in danger or may be in danger in the upcoming future (respectively); listening to this message can keep us safe. Guilt tells us that we feel we acted in a manner that was inconsistent with our values and can motivate repair and, again, steps to prevent a recurrence in the future. With such important messages, our emotions are there to protect us, not hurt us, even when they are excruciatingly painful. It is fighting against them and judging them that creates suffering.

Quotes or songs can serve as perhaps more tangible reminders to foster connection with Meaning in the midst of crisis. For example, to Cope Ahead in advance of a crisis, to serve as cues for this skill, my clients have written meaningful quotes on their mirrors and created playlists. Returning to spirituality, if this resonates with you, can also provide a pathway to Meaning. Perhaps go to a service or meditation for insights that may be helpful in this area. Another idea is to seek out mentors who have walked before you, gleaning their wisdom.

Take a moment here and think about how you use this skill already and how you may build upon this. Jot down some notes (see also downloadable Handout 6.3).

Handout 6.3 Distress Tolerance IMPROVE Worksheet: Meaning

- **Prayer** can be interpreted in different ways. It can mean prayer in the traditional sense of a reaching out to a higher power. It can also mean finding stillness within. In either sense, the stance is of openness rather than pleading. Perhaps a classic representation of this is the Serenity Prayer: "Grant me the serenity to accept the things I cannot change; courage to change the things I can; and wisdom to know the difference." To foster an open stance through your body, turn your palms upward, extending your fingers and resting your hands on your thighs, slightly raising the corners of your mouth into a **Half-Smile** (for inspiration, reference the Mona Lisa!), breathing in and out deeply (see Relaxation below for further guidance in pacing your breath and diaphragmatic breathing). You can also embody this through open forms in yoga, your toes spread apart.

Again, perhaps attend a service or meditation, without being overly attached to this structure, with less formal, more direct forms of Prayer also helpful and perhaps more feasible, depending on the circumstances. One variant of meditation I have especially enjoyed discovering is kirtan, a musical meditation of chanting, as well as singing, ringing bells, and clapping, extending across the major world religions. If you have access to this in your community, I highly recommend trying it, as well as ultimately developing it into a regular forum for participation. If you are new to this, I especially encourage you to enter the process mindfully. Notice any judgments or anxiety that may arise through the experience, from the perhaps unfamiliar, repetitive sounds to the pauses of silence as you engage with those around you in the call and response. In my experience any initial judgment or anxiety has shifted to a deep appreciation for the collaborative resonating of tones and stillness.

Yoga can also open your heart consistent with this skill. Try restorative yoga, Iyengar yoga, or yoga facilitated by live music. I remember the first time I tried restorative yoga. At first I was disappointed by the pace of the class, having thought I wanted an aerobic workout. I was not even breaking a sweat! And yet, I was nonetheless having envious judgments towards the woman on the mat beside me, seemingly effortlessly stretching her leg above her head and otherwise contorting her form into positions that would qualify her for the Cirque de Soleil! And then something mysteriously beautiful happened. The instructor had us hug our bolsters and be still in a particular pose, designed, she said to open us. She let us know that this could cause emotion to arise and to let this happen if it did. I was then overtaken with a welling of emotion, deep sadness releasing, and tears began to silently fall on that bolster, as I clung to it like a life raft. I was able to access that emotion cleverly stored deep within me. I have been similarly moved by Iyengar yoga, which I have found to be more solidly grounded in cultivating meditation through the body, with patient guidance from the instructor, rather than often faster paced mainstream yoga offerings. Likewise, I have found that combining yoga with music can tap into emotions that seem to be otherwise blocked. I encourage you to bring mindfulness to your own journey in these areas and to how they can serve you spiritually. Kirtan is traditionally donation-based and free yoga classes are available, so finances need not be a barrier.

Take a moment here and think about how you use this skill already and how you may build upon this. Jot down some notes (see also downloadable Handout 6.3).

Handout 6.3 Distress Tolerance IMPROVE Worksheet: Prayer

_____

_____

_____

_____

_____

_____

_____

- **Relaxation** encompasses practices that foster a greater sense of calm and centeredness, involving the pathway of your parasympathetic nervous system to counter stress and anxiety. For example, diaphragmatic breathing (one form of Relaxation) contrasts with shallowly breathing from the chest, which can result in an elevated state of anxiety and even chronic hyperventilation. Relaxation can also include Self-Soothing (see above), yoga, and progressive muscle relaxation (tightening and then relaxing, sequentially, muscles, from head to toe or toe to head; for scripts, an Internet search will quickly provide ample examples; for an excellent review on its background and research support see McCallie, Blum, & Hood, 2006). By first increasing tension, then relaxing, progressive muscle relaxation can be a more accessible strategy than simply trying to just relax your body.

One helpful strategy for determining if you are breathing from your chest or diaphragm is to place one hand on your chest and one on your belly and then breathe in and out. Diaphragmatic breathing is sometimes referred to as "belly breathing." If you are breathing from your diaphragm, when you breathe in the hand on your belly will go out and when you breathe out it will go in; meanwhile, if you are breathing entirely from your diaphragm, the hand on your chest will not go up and down. If the hand on your chest does not remain still, but rather moves with your breath, then you are still breathing, at least partially, from your chest. Breathing in this way when lying down can let gravity help you move to more completely breathing from your diaphragm, enabling your chest to better rest—and it is an excellent opportunity to shift how you are feeling as you are trying to go to sleep or trying to wake up, when perhaps your mind decides to ruminate or be filled with unwanted thoughts of the past, or perhaps difficult emotion creeps in, prompting urges to stay in bed in an ineffective way.

More specifically with breathing, increasing attention is being directed to resonant frequency breathing for biofeedback. This corresponds to a particular characteristic of cardiac functioning known as heart rate variability, with greater variability associated with more effective functioning between sympathetic and parasympathetic states. To determine your precise resonant frequency, seek out a biofeedback practitioner who can determine this for you with the appropriate equipment. Generally speaking, otherwise, an average recommended pace is six breaths per minute, with some support for the specific ratio of five seconds for your inhalation and five seconds for your exhalation in a 10-second cycle per breath (e.g., Lin, Tai, & Fan, 2014; Prakash, Ravindra, Madanmohan, Anilkumar, & Balachander, 2006).

Take a moment here and think about how you use this skill already and how you may build upon this. Jot down some notes (see also downloadable Handout 6.3).

Handout 6.3 Distress Tolerance IMPROVE Worksheet: Relaxation

_____

_____

_____

_____

_____

_____

_____

- **One Thing in the Moment.** This skill echoes the Mindfulness How skill of One-Mindfully—doing one thing fully in the moment, whether that is internally or externally focused—so when you are showering, shower; when you are worrying, worry. When using this for distress tolerance, you would want to focus on thoughts or external experiences that are not related to the distress you are trying to tolerate. For example, in other words, if you are worried about a relationship situation, you would not ruminate on those thoughts. Rather, you might One-Mindfully read a book or the news. Likewise, if you are distressed about a relationship situation, you would not focus on pictures and memorabilia of that person. Rather, you would redirect to other environmental stimuli, like washing the dishes, one dish, one stroke at a time. Take a moment here and think about how you use this skill already and how you may build upon this. Jot down some notes (see also downloadable Handout 6.3).

Handout 6.3 Distress Tolerance IMPROVE Worksheet: One Thing in the Moment

_____

_____

_____

_____

_____

_____

_____

- **Vacation.** This skill is a way of participating that provides a break from the current crisis, a break from the responsibilities and demands of maturity. This can literally mean taking a vacation, whether a weekend trip or a longer trip further afield, or can be more brief escapes through various Activities or Imagery. For example, you cannot always get on a plane to France on the spur of the moment when you are having a stressful day, but you could probably daydream at least for a few minutes about the Eiffel Tower and Café Les Deux Magots; you could look at travel books or search online for hotels; you could look at pictures and videos from your past travels.

Another fun way to practice this skill is to connect with favorite childhood hobbies or passions. For example, I loved Mark Twain growing up, so to practice this skill I could literally visit his hometown of Hannibal, Missouri (which I have!) or read one of his books. Another example of this could be to watch your favorite movie from childhood or stay in your pajamas all day and maybe watch some cartoons Saturday morning with sugary cereal.

Take a moment here and think about how you use this skill already and how you may build upon this. Jot down some notes (see also downloadable Handout 6.3).

Handout 6.3 Distress Tolerance IMPROVE Worksheet: Vacation

_____

_____

_____

_____

_____

_____

_____

- **Encouragement.** This skill consists of cheerleading yourself that you can get through the difficult situation, that this too shall pass, that you can overcome. You can practice this skill with positive affirmations or even play music that pumps you up, like the infallible classic theme from *Rocky*, as he trains in the streets of Philly, culminating in his climbing the stairs of the Museum of Art. I highly recommend having a playlist of personal favorites for inspiration and empowerment (e.g., "I Will Survive," "Eye of the Tiger," "We Will Rock You," "Get Ready for This"). Take a moment here and think about how you use this skill already and how you may build upon this. Jot down some notes (see also downloadable Handout 6.3). And put together a playlist so it is ready to go when you need it!

Handout 6.3 Distress Tolerance IMPROVE Worksheet: Encouragement

_____

_____

_____

_____

_____

_____

_____

Alternate Rebellion

Alternate Rebellion can be considered a form of Opposite to Emotion Action for the feeling of rebellion. Rebellion is a normal human feeling that can especially arise if we feel a constricted sense of control, at the mercy of external constraints. Unfortunately, acting on this sense of rebellion can often have harmful consequences. For example, engaging in binge eating may feel like a way of rebelling against judgment from others or societal expectations and yet simply generates temporary relief from uncomfortable emotions, then producing a host of further difficult emotions, such as shame and guilt. With Alternate Rebellion you can feel that sense of rebellion with no negative consequences.

For individuals with high perfectionism, there can be a multitude of truly harmless ways to practice this. For example, perhaps you feel like you always have to wear earrings or a belt—so you do not as a way of practicing Alternate Rebellion. Or perhaps you feel like you always have to have your nails perfectly filed or done, that the instant the polish starts chipping or looking somehow otherwise less than immaculate, you need to do them over—so you let them go without filing or purposely do not re-do them immediately. Or perhaps you feel like your bra and underwear need to match—so you purposely combine different colors and patterns. Another fun example is to wear shirts with messages that may be considered provocative in the setting you are entering—wearing the shirt under a prim and proper suit jacket or cardigan, buttoned up, so only you, with your slight smile, know what you are wearing under that polished, conservative surface. Perhaps with eating you actually nourish yourself and eat a well-balanced meal, with gluten and dairy, amidst a culture obsessed with "clean eating."

Over the years I have collected ideas for Alternate Rebellion from clients. See the included list (Handout 6.4) for this inspirational archive. When reviewing it keep in mind that Alternate Rebellion is a very individual practice. What feels rebellious to one person may not feel rebellious at all to another person. Also, the idea is to feel rebellious, not guilty or anxious. Of course, if you are not used to going against the rules, whether they are self-imposed or imposed by others, doing so can generate some anxiety or guilt. However, to effectively practice Alternate Rebellion this anxiety or guilt needs to be minimal and superseded by a sense of rebellion. If you try an idea and feel intensely anxious or guilty, try another idea that may be less challenging. Also, the list is certainly not exhaustive. Rather, it is a sample to serve as a springboard for your own unique Alternate Rebellion.

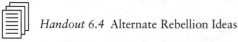

ALTERNATE REBELLION

Ideas

1. Throw ice cubes into the bathtub
2. Drive just to drive
3. Shop just to shop
4. Just sit
5. Listen to loud music
6. Stay in your pajamas all day
7. Wear jeans
8. Leave your cell phone at home
9. Say no to someone at work
10. Turn off the TV
11. Wear scrubs
12. Don't shower
13. Don't go to a meeting
14. Don't always agree to volunteer
15. Buy something to wear that you really like that is a bit frivolous
16. Get your hair cut before it's long enough to give to Locks of Love
17. Ask for what you want
18. Share your true feelings
19. Throw out files of materials without looking
20. Don't apologize for taking time for a walk
21. Buy and read a gossip magazine, e.g., *People*
22. Write a letter or email to a restaurant when food or service is not satisfactory
23. Read a book instead of watching a major event on TV with everyone else (e.g., the Oscars, the Superbowl)
24. Read banned books
25. Order non-alcoholic when everyone else orders beer
26. Wear the same clothes more than one day in the same week
27. Watch *Pretty Woman*
28. Wear white before Memorial Day, after Labor Day
29. Wear built-in bra tanks and camisoles
30. Go barefoot
31. Take your shoes off in the office
32. Wear a t-shirt that makes a statement/supports a cause
33. Don't blow dry your hair
34. Don't wear make-up
35. Get rid of old plastic containers
36. Get rid of old make-up
37. Flush expired pills
38. Wear a spoon ring
39. Sing loudly along to the radio or music: Alanis Morissette, "Bitch" by Meredith Brooks, or "I Will Survive" by Gloria Gaynor...
40. Wear pajamas throughout the day Saturday—then change into different pajamas for the evening
41. Wear your favorite, ratty jeans
42. Don't wear a belt
43. Wear a t-shirt or tank under a coat or sweater for work
44. Wear dress pants to church
45. Get a henna tattoo
46. Wear a hippy skirt
47. Watch your favorite sitcoms in the morning on a weekday
48. Don't immediately clean up, do the dishes, or take the trash out

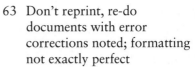

49 Don't walk on the sidewalk
50 Walk on the grass
51 Walk in the rain without an umbrella
52 Don't immediately open emails
53 Don't immediately respond to emails
54 Get rid of old receipts and bill statements
55 Don't balance your checkbook daily
56 Don't get the mail daily
57 Don't check personal emails daily
58 Don't shave your legs daily
59 Don't paint your nails
60 Paint your nails different colors
61 Don't wear earrings
62 Wear expressive earrings
63 Don't reprint, re-do documents with error corrections noted; formatting not exactly perfect
64 Take care of yourself
65 Don't wear underwear
66 Buy and wear sexy/frivolous underwear
67 Internet shop
68 Waste time
69 Ebay
70 Window shop
71 Throw laundry; other safe items
72 Show up late to meetings without consequences for being late
73 Surf the Internet
74 Sleep in
75 Wear sunglasses you like that are not the current trend

Take a moment here and, reviewing the list of ideas and brainstorming beyond the list, think about how you use this skill already and how you may build upon this. Jot down some notes (see also downloadable Handout 6.5).

Handout 6.5 Alternate Rebellion Worksheet

_____

_____

_____

_____

_____

_____

_____

_____

_____

_____

Radical Acceptance

Radical Acceptance is complete, full openness to what is—letting go of fighting against reality, instead embracing it from deep within. Imagine a tree stretching up from your being, the branches reaching out through your arms and the crown of your head, the roots extending through your stomach, to the soles of your feet. This is Radical Acceptance—a grounded, full stance to what is, be it rain or snow falling on your leaves, the wind pushing against you, making your limbs sway, or the brilliant sun warming your bark. This is reflected in the Latin origin of the term "radical," which literally means "root."

Radical Acceptance can also be considered radical because it calls upon us to accept everything, even what we do not like or even hate. We can dislike or even hate something and still radically accept it. For example, my cat once got an ear infection. To treat this I had to give her ear drops; she hated them and fought against them nearly every time. The process was trying. I would hold her in my arms and as I would try to squeeze the drop into her ears she would writhe and squirm, shaking her head so severely that the drops would often fly out of her ears into her eyes; one time she got the drops into my eyes and whew, they stung! Of course getting ear drops is not necessarily a fun time and may well be uncomfortable. However, fighting against this made it so much worse. And then one day, seemingly miraculously, my cat was so still as I held her, slightly trembling, and, with apparently timid trust, she let me smoothly squeeze those drops into her ears and the whole process was over in seconds, unlike the minutes of usual protracted agony. I am quite certain she still did not like those ear drops and maybe even hated them—and yet in that interaction she radically accepted the drops and did not make the situation worse.

An important point to emphasize here is that pain—be it from eye drops or situations with difficult emotions like sadness, anger, guilt, and fear—is inevitable, but suffering—the non-acceptance of pain—is optional. We will all have loss in this life—relationships end, dreams are not always realized or maintained, loved ones die, and material objects tatter and break—so we will inevitably feel the pain of sadness. For many reasons we will not always get what we want (as lamented by Robert Burns and Steinbeck: "The best laid plans of mice and men..."), and we will all inevitably experience conflict as we interact with others who are unlike ourselves and so will not necessarily agree with us; and there will be miscommunication based on our perceptions of the world and our unique learning history—so we will inevitably feel the pain of anger; and when we harm others we will probably feel guilt. And in this world there are many dangers, real or imagined, so we will not always be safe or feel safe—so we will inevitably feel the pain of fear or anxiety, anticipating danger. These pains are painful enough. We do not need to make them worse by refusing to accept them, fighting against them, making them linger and amplifying them, miring ourselves in suffering.

Also, importantly, acceptance and Radical Acceptance are not resignation—not giving up or giving in, but rather choosing to let go of the fight against what is; this can be an extremely courageous act, especially when we do not like or even hate something. Moreover, acceptance is the first step to change. First, we must radically accept the entirety of what is happening, to know how to effectively move forward with change. For example, if we have a swarm of flies in our kitchen but refuse to acknowledge this and instead try to just ignore it, the swarm of flies will keep swarming and even multiply. Instead, if we radically accept the swarm of flies we can then take measures to eliminate the swarm of flies if we decide we no longer want the flies. This is likewise with any difficult situation. First, we must radically accept it. Perhaps this applies to your relationship with food. Contemplating letting go of old patterns can feel daunting so we may try to just continue as if they are not happening, as if somehow ignoring them will magically solve them. Or we may be willful about not wanting to do what is effective to actually change (as the reflection at the end of Chapter 4 encouraged you to consider). If we get stuck in this, we will never change. So first we must radically accept and then move with willingness into effective responding.

In addition, consistent with the wisdom of the Serenity Prayer (see Prayer above), sometimes we truly cannot change a situation. Perhaps it has already irrevocably happened or others are not willing to change despite our skillful requests and they are just too powerful against our influence. In such cases, Radical Acceptance perhaps becomes even more critical for our own well-being, to move forward because, again, reality is what it is and fighting against it only keeps us stuck in suffering and makes the situation worse.

So, with Radical Acceptance we find ourselves at a crossroads. It is a choice. You can choose to continue to suffer. Or you can choose to move through the pain, listen to it and address what it is telling you. You can choose to do nothing with stubborn pouting or attempted ignoring. Or you can choose to humbly embrace the steps you need to move on with whatever life has handed you. In DBT the skill of turning towards the path of acceptance is called **Turning the Mind**. Then walking down the path, taking the necessary steps in Effectiveness, is known as **Willingness**. Not taking the steps is the opposite, i.e., **Willfulness**, or fighting against reality with resistant energy.

At the same time, it can be incredibly helpful to remember Meaning (see above). From a behavioral perspective, everything really does happen for a reason and it can be no other way than it is in this exact moment in time. And we can only learn if we fully open ourselves up to this experience, to learn from it and move on.

Take a moment and think about what you are fighting against accepting. How is this serving you? Is it time to let go and accept? What would it mean if you were to radically accept what you are fighting against? How do these concepts apply to your relationship with your body and food? (See also downloadable Handout 6.6.)

Handout 6.6 Radical Acceptance Reflection Worksheet

_____

_____

_____

_____

_____

_____

_____

_____

_____

_____

_____

_____

_____

_____

_____

_____

_____

_____

_____

_____

_____

Chapter Summary

In summary, mindful eating from the dialectical perspective includes not only attention to the food in front of you but also a balance of attention to any distress with redirection of attention to promote Effectiveness; this is not avoidance because there is still the Willingness and intention to return to the emotion, to listen to it and address the information being provided by it. Moreover (with the potential exception of Strong Sensations), unlike avoidant coping such as binge eating, distress tolerance will often not entirely stop an emotion, short term or long term. Rather, you are making space for both the emotion and other experience, taking the emotion along for the ride so to speak, but in the backseat rather than the driver's seat, perhaps blaring your music, the windows rolled down, driving along the ocean, in your mind or reality, to give yourself a break from that rowdy passenger and get them to be a little quieter so you can then attend to them more effectively. You are driving the car and can turn down the path of distress tolerance and ultimately acceptance with any distressing passenger, any judgmental voice or upsetting feeling about food or how you look. Check your windows periodically, fasten your seatbelt, and keep driving. The road ahead is yours.

7 Setting the Table

So pull up a chair. In your actual life, what does that chair look like? Is it an elegant seat at a table set with fine china and an exquisite white linen cloth? Or the driver's seat of your car as you navigate traffic? Are you surrounded by others or alone? Is the TV droning on in front of you or are you listening to the waves lapping against the shore from your picnic blanket at the beach? Or are you even sitting? Are you standing over the sink or in front of the fridge?

Context matters. Creating a kind environment can relax you to more mindfully enjoy your food. The very same food consumed in different settings can be experienced in vastly different ways. Indeed, there is a whole art behind restaurant décor and ambiance, as well as the plating of food. Think about it. How do you feel when you are eating in the different ways outlined above? Do you feel more anxious or zoned out in some than others? What contexts foster a more soothing atmosphere? Write some notes (see also downloadable Handout 7.1).

Handout 7.1 Context Reflection Worksheet

_____

_____

_____

_____

_____

_____

_____

_____

_____

Think about this over the next week. Use your mindfulness skills to Observe and Describe what you notice and seek out environments that you think will be soothing. Record your observations here (see also downloadable Handout 7.2).

Handout 7.2 Context Monitoring Worksheet

Monday:_____

_____

_____

_____

_____

Tuesday:_____

_____

_____

_____

_____

Wednesday: _____

_____

_____

_____

_____

Thursday:_____

_____

_____

_____

_____

Friday: _____

_____

_____

_____

_____

Saturday: _____

_____

_____

_____

_____

Sunday:_____

_____

_____

_____

_____

Context can also include your emotion and a variety of factors at any given moment that would determine what would be most effective to eat. Sometimes your body needs comfort. Sometimes your body needs salt. Sometimes your body needs protein. Sometimes your body needs a hearty meal. Sometimes light is best. Through mindfulness you can hear cues for this and respond flexibly and adaptively. In contrast, basing what you eat on cognitive guidelines and rules can leave you hungry for what you really need.

Rule-Governed Behavior

As discussed in Chapter 1, judgments about food can serve as rules. Rules provide a shorthand strategy for making decisions across situations more efficiently. For example, if one has a rule that gluten is forbidden, this quickly eliminates a number of items on most menus, narrowing down the choices to what is gluten-free. Similarly, if one has a rule that dairy is forbidden, this quite rapidly diminishes the options at any standard ice cream parlor. Basing decisions on such rules speeds up cognitive processing. This serves a purpose, since we usually have many other demands on our time beyond food and eating. However, when we use rules to make decisions, this takes us out of the present moment and the specific, unique context of that moment, and especially when it comes to eating, it can backfire. Although it may make sense, rule-governed behavior is usually not effective.

Rules can take many forms. Take a few moments and think about what your rules are around food. Examples could include not eating after a certain time of day, not eating unless hungry, or not eating certain types of food, such as food with particular content. List them here (see also downloadable Handout 7.3).

Handout 7.3 Rules Reflection Worksheet

_____

_____

_____

_____

_____

_____

_____

_____

_____

_____

_____

_____

_____

_____

_____

Now, over the course of this week, use your mindfulness skills to bring your attention to these rules and practice labeling them as thoughts, then return to the present moment you are in, to base what you eat on the actual context, rather than any of the rules in your head. Write some notes here about this experience (see also downloadable Handout 7.4).

Handout 7.4 Rules Monitoring Worksheet

Monday:_____

_____

_____

_____

Tuesday:_____

_____

_____

_____

_____

Wednesday: _____

_____

_____

_____

_____

Thursday:_____

_____

_____

_____

_____

Friday: _____

_____

_____

_____

_____

Saturday: _____

_____

_____

_____

_____

Sunday:_____

_____

_____

_____

_____

Constructing a Forbidden Foods Hierarchy

As referenced above, your rules may include not eating certain foods and, as we have been elaborating, challenging this to create a new relationship with food is essential. Basically, if your urges are to avoid certain foods and, as theory and research would predict, that avoidance is ineffective, then you need to approach the foods to establish a new pattern. In other words, you need to create a new learning association to counter your existing conditioning. In DBT language, this can be an example of Opposite to Emotion Action. The alternative attempts at avoidance ultimately only perpetuate harmful consequences, such as backfiring in your intake or experiencing painful emotions, such as guilt or shame, that you would otherwise not need to experience from your behavior.

Remember Baby Albert and his conditioning that taught him that soft, white, furry objects were harmful? To break free from this he needed to approach the actually harmless furry objects. Your forbidden foods are the same. Your forbidden foods are Albert's harmless, soft, white, furry objects—even if they are not cotton candy and as long as they are not spoiled, moldy food!

So where do we start with approaching all of these foods that we have learned to fear and try to avoid? Let us start with a list. First, really think about all the foods you think or feel you should not eat. You may have generated overarching rules about this above, in the rules practice, like "I should not eat sugar or sweets" or "I should not eat gluten or carbs." Now get more specific. Literally break down the foods into specific variants. For example, sweets could include cookies, cakes, ice cream, pie, donuts, and candy. Then cookies could include a multitude of various delicacies, such as brownies, chocolate chip cookies, and store-bought pre-packaged cookies, and then the latter could include a range of options, such as Oreos, Nestle Tollhouse, Nilla Wafers, and on, and on. Write them all down. Being so specific is important because you may need to challenge various components of one broad category.

Use the space provided in Handout 7.5 to engage with this process and see Handout 7.6 for an example (see also downloadable Handouts 7.5 and 7.6). For this first step of generating your list, do not get stuck in organizing. Just record what you identify, letting it flow. Perhaps even start with just a blank paper, then organize and transfer your list to Handout 7.5. Take your time to really scour your experience to create as complete a list as possible. Perhaps carry this list with you over the next week and jot down more notes as you think of or notice a new food to add to the list.

When you do put your list into the format demonstrated by Handout 7.6, initially focus on the first four columns. Then, once you have what seems to be a complete list of foods to work on challenging, consider to what degree you feel they are forbidden, 0 to 100, with 100 being the most forbidden and 0 being not forbidden at all. At first, just rate them as best you can. In this process you may have foods that tie (e.g., multiple 100s). That is O.K. Just start linking the foods to a general rating.

Once you have completed your initial ratings, go through your list again and get more specific. Refine the list, really adding in gradation. For foods that you have rated as the same, think of what would happen if you were confronted with those foods at the same time and you had to eat one of them. Which would be easier, if only slightly? If you need a more hands on strategy for organizing, perhaps create small sheets of paper or note cards with all of the foods and then organize them in front of you, forming a line from least forbidden to most forbidden, shuffling them around as needed.

Again, take your time working through this process. At the same time, do your best to not get stuck in trying to get the ratings perfect. The goal here is to create a general graded list that can inform your practice of mindful eating, so that you are gradually increasing the degree to which you are challenging yourself.

Once you have your list organized and fully ranked, you have your roadmap for the mindful eating practice ahead of you. Simply start at the bottom of your list, with the food you ranked least forbidden, and prepare to get reacquainted with this food. This food is no longer your enemy. This food is also no longer a conspirator. This food is an opportunity to pause and Observe and be present with what is, whatever that is, to nourish yourself truly, emotionally and physically, based on what you are needing in that moment. If that emotion is anxiety or fear, remember to breathe and come back to the food. The morsel of food in front of you is not in and of itself a threat. It is a gift. Unwrap it and welcome it in with nonjudgment.

If you are a professional guiding clients through this process in therapy, it is essential to bring the foods to life as much as possible, simulating what clients would encounter in the real world and perhaps even going into the real world. For example, if mindfully eating popcorn, present it right in its microwavable bags, as a client would likely encounter it and struggle to not eat the entire bag. In this way they will be able to interact with the packaging, hearing it rustle, feeling its greasy insides against their fingers, and reaching into its ragged edges for the kernels. It can also be helpful to accompany clients to eat out in restaurants and bring in take-out and fast food. Basically, the exposure will be most helpful if it reproduces as many triggers as possible.

Handout 7.5 Forbidden Foods List: Worksheet

General category	Subcategories	Further specifics	Further specifics, if needed	Forbiddenness (0–100)

Handout 7.6 Forbidden Foods List: Example

General category	Subcategories	Further specifics	Further specifics, if needed	Forbiddenness (0–100)
Sweets	Cookies	Brownies	Baked from box	90
			Massive brownie at a café	72
			Brownie a la mode	80
		Iced, cut-out cookies	Bakery section plastic container, holiday decorated	70
			At Christmas cookie party	89
		Pre-packaged	Oreos	65
			Nestle Tollhouse Soft-bake chocolate chip	48
	Cake	Bakery section slices		47
		Decorated layer cake		54
	Ice Cream	Ben & Jerry's		79
		Half gallons	Chocolate chip cookie dough	87
	Pie	Mom's butterscotch pie		74
		Mom's apple pie		75
	Donuts	Cream-filled		77
		Donut holes		52
		Chocolate-glazed		82
	Candy	Holiday candy	e.g., Halloween, Easter, Valentine's, Christmas	92
		Candy bars	Nutty	98
			Caramel	69
Crunchy snacks	Potato chips	Store-bought bag	Reduced-Fat	15
			Regular, kettle cooked	94
	Popcorn	Movie theater, butter		56
		Microwave popcorn		35
	Crackers	Ritz		37

Category	Item	Detail	Value
	Tortilla chips	At Mexican restaurant	38
		Store-bought bag	28
		Nachos at game	64
Carbs	Pasta	Pasta with red sauce	25
		Pasta with alfredo	49
		Pasta with pesto	55
	Potatoes	French fries; fast food	60
		Baked potato — With butter	58
		With cheese sauce	78
Pizza	Homemade	Cheese	53
		Pepperoni	85
		Sausage	93
	Pizza Hut	Cheese	86
		Pepperoni	88
		Sausage	99
	Specialty	Cheese	76
		Pepperoni	91
		Sausage	95
Cheese	Hard cheese	Sliced	68
	Soft cheese	Goat cheese	45
		Brie	66
		Cheese spreads	62
Eggs			100
Pork	Bacon		50
	Ham		32
	Barbeque		63
	Bratwurst		97

It is also helpful to have a variety of foods within any particular category to choose from, to compare and contrast. For example, if you are practicing mindfully eating potato chips, try several kinds, perhaps kettle cooked, ridged, and baked. Notice which you truly prefer. I was quite surprised the first time I did this practice and discovered that those baked chips I had been so attached to eating over regular chips all those years, because of my cognitive rules about what was acceptable, were really quite manufactured and lackluster beside the crisp sweetness of kettle cooked. I also learned that my favorite flavor is barbeque rather than cheddar and that I also enjoy salt and vinegar. All of these nuances I had missed because of my thoughts and judgments about branding and packaging. See what you find. You may also be surprised!

So what exactly do you do once you have your food to mindfully eat in front of you? Quite simply, use your mindfulness What skills of Observe and Describe to first bring your full attention to the food, what it looks like (e.g., its colors, gradations, and patterns), smells like, feels like (texture and temperature), and sounds like (e.g., break it apart and see if it makes a noise!). As you do this, notice any urges, emotions, thoughts, and physical sensations that arise—notice them and bring your attention back to your food. Once you have fully observed the food with all of your senses except taste, go ahead and taste the food. Again, as you do, notice any urges, emotions, thoughts, and physical sensations that arise—notice them and bring your attention back to your food.

If you are choosing from multiple food items, Observe what led you to select the specific food items you did and what led you to eat them in the order you did. This can reveal interesting patterns. For example, perhaps you notice that you tend to go for the largest piece or the piece that looks the most perfect. Perhaps you start with the item you think you will like the most or you save that one until the end so it can be your last bites. When reflecting on the practice, think about where these patterns may have developed.

Also Observe the process of eating. For example, do you pick up the next bite or forkful after you have just put the previous bite into your mouth or while you are still chewing? If you notice this and Observe the urge rather than acting on it, does an emotion of anxiety arise? What might this be about?

Notice your preferences. Remember preferences are not judgments. You can like or dislike, or love or hate and not be judging. Notice if you truly like what you thought you did or if you actually like something you thought you did not. For example, I have many thoughts about fruit, what I do and do not like. For instance, I am convinced that berries have fur. Truly. And yet recently I was presented with very large beautiful blackberries. So I gave them a chance and tried them. Wow—they tasted like heaven in my mouth! I am now sold and seek them out in local farmers' market, savoring them with deep joy and appreciation. Likewise, for years I have judged pears as mealy and avoided them unless they were canned in that sweet syrup; then I tried a perfectly fresh one and "wow." I was converted. In the same way, I opened myself up to mango after deciding they tasted like soap and had the most divinely delicious experience, the fruit melting in my mouth. And I found further joy in an heirloom tomato that made me wonder what I have been thinking was a tomato all these years. Food can truly be incredible. Do not let your thoughts deprive you of this gift.

Bringing mindfulness to eating with others is also important, given that eating in community is so intimately woven into our cultures. Also, I would argue, we would not want to refuse ourselves the connection that can occur when we are with others, perhaps over spoonfuls of sinfully delicious shared chocolate mousse or an outrageously satisfying entrée. Eating together can be an event—a celebration—a solace. And we will only enjoy it more if we bring mindfulness to this process, taking it all in, from the conversation to the plate in front of us. Therefore, be sure to include practices with others. Notice how your practice changes compared to when you are mindfully eating alone. Notice what prompts urges to talk and what prompts actual talking. Do you feel uncomfortable and anxious if you are simply eating in silence? What might this be about? Does this change with more practice? Do your discomfort and anxiety decrease over time? Does your experience differ depending on who you are eating with? How so?

Practicing in a group, after mindfully eating the foods, group members and leaders Describe their experience to each other. It is invaluable for facilitators to model openness to this process and support clients by engaging in the eating and sharing with them. If you are practicing independently, perhaps keep a mindful eating journal, describing your observations in writing.

Also, I highly recommend that you be as inclusive as possible in your exposure to forbidden foods, letting go of any ideas about certain nutritional composition, such as gluten, dairy, and processed foods. As we have extensively discussed, psychologically, avoiding any food can backfire. Therefore, it is imperative to actually be open to all foods, to ultimately eat in a balanced way that may include at least minimal gluten, dairy, and processed foods. Furthermore, it is an interesting question to ponder what the source of any physical discomfort from eating certain foods may be. I would argue it may not necessarily be a physical intolerance but rather the product of judgment, generating a distressing emotional response manifesting in physical symptoms. The main point here is to be open. By being open you can truly set yourself free.

This process can take many weeks or months or even years, depending on the individual. Typically the progression of foods for a group (and this can, likewise, mirror individual hierarchies) begins with more discrete food items, like fruit or popcorn, then moves into meals, like pizza or pasta, then finishes with desserts. The standard length for a group hierarchy is approximately 12 weeks. However, clients can continue after this, since, clearly, all forbidden foods cannot be covered in 12 weeks.

As you proceed, honor your process. You do not need to pressure yourself to try more challenging foods until you feel ready, as long as you are not medically compromised or continuing to engage in frequent or severe bingeing and purging behavior, as long as you are adequately nourished. And eventually, you can truly overcome every food on your list. I assure you. And when you do, you will feel unbelievably empowered.

Chapter Summary

With mindfulness, we can elevate and transform our experiences with food. Instead of being mired in judgment, guilt, and shame, or eating as a chore, in haste, wherever we happen to be, we can create and seek out environments for eating that soothe our senses and establish more enriching associations to eating, to more fully appreciate the gift of nourishing ourselves through food. Then working through your individualized forbidden foods hierarchy will challenge and unravel your beliefs and judgment about food, freeing you to choose the more balanced path of mindful eating, letting go of feeling controlled by food to instead being empowered to embrace whatever it is that you need in a particular moment. Take your time. Be, always, patient and kind with yourself. Realize this may take years. And keep going. I assure you that you can truly master any food that is on your list. And when you do, embrace that most amazing feeling for you will have truly earned it, with courage that many others will never know.

8 Bon Appétit!

As you embark on mindful eating, there is much to notice. It can be a fun adventure and practiced in many nuances. As I like to joke with my sister, when you discover a symphony of exquisitely complementary flavors and perhaps contrasting textures combined into one glorious mouthful, it can be a "taste sensation." Deconstructing this can also expand your practice, to heighten your attention to specific aspects. The following practices offer inspiration for your continued exploration. For each of them, remember to use your Mindfulness What and How skills and seek a stance of Wise Mind.

Mindfulness of Liquids

Tangelo Juice

When I begin a mindfulness hierarchy with a group, it is a tradition to start with mindful drinking of tangelo juice. First, at the beginning of the group session, group members and I use all of our senses except taste to fully experience the tangelo—its fragrance, the dimples in its peel, the contrast of the softness of the inner fruit, its varied shades and hues of orange, the sound of puncturing the peel with your thumb and fingers and it slowly unraveling from its fruit. Then during the group break, I juice the tangelos, pouring the juice into Dixie cups. Then at the end of the group session we toast the beginning of our mindful eating hierarchy and mindfully drink the juice.

Unless they are impossible to find due to being out of season, I like to use tangelos because their peel is so fun to Observe, often staying in one whole spiraling piece, prompting urges to maintain this unbroken ribbon, culminating in the finale of popping off at the top, like a cap! Tangelos are also especially juicy, making them particularly well-suited for juicing. The juiciness is also interesting to Observe. Clients have said they have felt badly giving up the fruit to juice later because it looked so delicate, as if it were crying. The white substance so commonly adhering to oranges and their peel is also missing, reducing common disgust, frustration, or urges to obsessively free the fruit from this casing.

Taken together, this mindfulness of tangelos and their juice can thus be a rewarding introduction to developing a new relationship with food. Indeed, I have been astounded over the years when group members share that they have never eaten a tangelo before, instead just going through the motions of buying and eating "regular" oranges, which are such a different experience. In these cases the mindfulness with the tangelo truly expands their awareness of the possibility of food being a frontier anew to explore.

Try this practice. Notice what you Observe. Record any reflections here (see also downloadable Handout 8.1).

Handout 8.1 Eating Mindfulness Practice Record: Tangelo Juice

_____

_____

_____

_____

_____

_____

_____

_____

_____

_____

_____

Water Taste Test

I remember watching an episode of late night TV when the guest was a water tasting expert. The expert lined up a tasting menu of varieties, as if it were a wine tasting. Like the host, I found myself laughing at the idea that there could be such subtle nuances in taste among waters. The whole idea seemed like a highly pretentious exercise for the affluent.

Yet, when I was growing up, I lived in the country and my family had a spring for water. I did not think twice about how the water tasted... until I went to college and was subjected to city water on campus. Wow. I found the taste so appalling I would actually bring large bottles of my parents' spring water to college. Then I moved away from the state I grew up in, to go to graduate school, and carting large bottles of water across several state lines or through airports became an impracticality, so I started drinking city water regularly. Over six years of graduate school, guess what happened. I began to strongly dislike the taste of my parents' spring water. This has persisted to this day, since I have remained away from my childhood home. I can tell there is a strong, distinct difference.

Think about all the bottled water available. There are so many different brands, and people tend to have their favorites and brands they avoid. With packaging of mountain vistas and inviting waterfalls, it is interesting to consider what we are really responding to when we assert our likes and dislikes in water.

To bring new awareness to water, conduct your own water tasting. Select three different brands or varieties of water, consistently either sparkling or still; pour them into Dixie cups labeled on the bottom with the identity of the water. If you are a facilitator, you can then present them to clients without them knowing the true identities. If you are doing your own tasting, do your best to shuffle the cups so that you cannot link the cups to their identities. Then sip away! Notice any subtle nuances in the waters—brightness, smoothness, minerals. Determine which you like the best and why you think this is. Determine what makes you not like the water you do not like. When you have fully sampled the waters, peek at the bottom of the cups to unveil their identities. Are you surprised by what you find? Think about what this teaches you about our assumptions concerning what we think we like and do not like. Record any reflections here (see also downloadable Handout 8.1).

Handout 8.1 Eating Mindfulness Practice Record: Water Taste Test

_____

_____

_____

_____

_____

_____

_____

_____

_____

_____

_____

Soda Taste Test

The basic structure of the water taste test can be applied to a variety of other liquids. In particular, soda (or pop, depending on what part of the U.S.A. you may be from!) can be a fun practice. This can be useful for challenging rules about drinking this beverage. For example, I was really quite struck by how adamantly opposed to soda my clients were when I first presented this practice in Southern California. Having previously lived and practiced in the Midwest primarily, soda was basically a normal beverage to consume. I remember holidays at my one grandparents' house. To this day, it is a tradition in the afternoon for my one uncle to take orders for the soda that each family member would like, from the basement refrigerator, where my grandma keeps the treasures perfectly chilled. The main question was not whether you drank soda but rather if it was Pepsi or Coke, then diet or regular. There are definitely major divisions on this topic. I am still used to diet being the preferred choice due to it having no calories, but that tide has now received a backlash of proponents for regular because of the natural sugar. Then, of course, there is the stevia camp within the diet contingent, or the absolute rejection by many now with the current food movement.

When I was teaching Nonjudgmental Stance once to a multifamily DBT skills training course, I had quite a response from a mom who insisted the research proved that soda was entirely unhealthy, without any redeeming qualities of worth. Yet, I would still argue that any food product needs to be approached from a nonjudgmental position with openness to the possibility of consumption due to the wealth of research that I have been outlining in this book. Moreover, I can personally attest that soda can feed heart hunger in many ways.

For example, when I am sick or need Self-Soothing, clear soda, like Sierra Mist, can perfectly pair with a warm bowl of chicken noodle soup or even standing alone conjure up a similar sentiment. It instantly transports me back to childhood and being taken care of by my mom when I was little. I also have a great fondness for orange Fanta from Europe. I am a firm believer that it tastes utterly different from the abnormally orange, artificial variants that are sold here in the U.S.A. or Mexico. It instead has a soft, more natural orange hue, suspending the most delicate subtle bubbles of carbonation. Every time I return to Europe I am so excited to order that Fanta.

Mindfully drinking soda can also be a form of Alternate Rebellion against cultural condemnations of these liquids, despite their continued persistence lining entire grocery store aisles. I definitely felt a sense of rebellion when I bought three glowing orange two-liter bottles of soda for that first soda taste test I presented in Southern California. I imagined raised eyebrows of judgment from the clerk and the customers behind me, much more than any time I have bought alcohol! This seems silly and yet I can definitely attest to the reality of the feeling.

For all of these reasons, I recommend practicing a soda taste test. Select three varieties of a similar soda, for example, three clear sodas or three orange sodas; pour them into Dixie cups labeled as outlined for the water taste test and then compare and contrast, noticing the different colors, degrees of carbonation, smoothness; seeing what you are really drawn to among the choices. You may be surprised. You can, of course, do the classic Coke versus Pepsi test. I also encourage you to be creative. Try different international varieties or brands you have not tried before and may even judge. Bring an open mind. Record any reflections here (see also downloadable Handout 8.1).

Handout 8.1 Eating Mindfulness Practice Record: Soda Taste Test

_____

_____

_____

_____

_____

_____

_____

_____

_____

_____

_____

_____

Other Beverage Taste Tests

Of course, you can expand the water and soda taste tests to any beverage. The key is to match on overall similarity and then focus on subtle distinctions. For example, you could do a coffee tasting or a tea tasting of three different brands of the same type of tea.

You may also challenge ideas about juices or smoothies. For example, when I went to a local farmers' market for the first time, I had been strictly opposed to drinking anything green or composed of vegetables simply because of my cognitive judgments of what it would taste like and a mental block on drinking vegetables. My rule was that fruit is to be juiced for drinking, not salad! Imagine my surprise when a vendor convinced me to try his green concoction, blended with grapefruit juice. It was lovely! It tasted like apple juice, almost! I similarly discovered that I love carrot juice and am enjoying finding specific versions that I prefer. I have also learned that I do not like beet juice, but I feel much better having given it a chance than simply continuing to dismiss it based on preconceptions.

Another variant is to do a milkshake taste test. For this you can compare various flavors from the same source, e.g., the same fast food restaurant, or the same flavor from different sources, e.g., vanilla milkshakes from different fast food restaurants. Again, compare them to each other. With this, you can also mix flavors to see how this affects your experience and create a whole new taste sensation.

Record any reflections here (see also downloadable Handout 8.1).

Handout 8.1 Eating Mindfulness Practice Record: Other Beverage Taste Tests

_____

_____

_____

_____

_____

_____

_____

_____

_____

_____

_____

_____

_____

_____

_____

_____

_____

_____

_____

_____

_____

_____

Mindfulness of Smells

Edible Versus Inedible

I discovered this practice in Pavel Somov's lovely book of inspiration *Eating the Moment* (2008). In fact, I encourage you to turn to Dr. Somov's book for further detail to draw on for the practices in this chapter, as well as other creative ideas. The practice of edible versus inedible focuses on our sense of smell. For this, you will need a variety of inedible objects and corresponding edible counterparts and at least one partner. For example, candles can smell strikingly real, so perhaps you get a red velvet cake candle and pair it with a slice of red velvet cake or a red velvet cupcake. Likewise, you could pair a coffee candle with real coffee, a lemon candle with a real lemon. You can also find deceptively real smells with lotions and body washes. Once you have assembled your items, instruct your partner or group members to close their eyes. Then bring the items under their nose to smell and guess edible or inedible. Let everyone smell before taking the vote so it will not be influenced by others' responses. To be really pure on this you can have everyone write down their votes, waiting until all have committed to a guess before sharing. This is a fun practice for early in the process of embarking on the mindful eating hierarchy, to help foster a stance of curiosity rather than anxiety, to begin building a new, more relaxed yet enlivened relationship with food. As a partner, group member, or leader of the practice, record any reflections here (see also downloadable Handout 8.1).

Handout 8.1 Eating Mindfulness Practice Record: Edible Versus Inedible

_____

_____

_____

_____

_____

_____

_____

_____

_____

_____

_____

Mindfulness of Eating Mechanics

Sitting Versus Standing

One of my clients teases me about being a professional sitter and expresses amazement at how I can sit in my therapy chair all day. Likewise, someone recently told me that sitting is the new smoking. Health fanatics have yet again found a target for attack, and standing desks are being heralded as the new wave in office furniture for those who are aware of the dangers. Of course, there is probably value in considering the warnings. And yet, like anything, I would argue it must be taken with a grain of salt.

I mention this related to mindfulness of eating mechanics because, like working in a sitting position compared to a standing position, there can be different cognitive rules about this. Indeed, interestingly, it is almost universally considered unhealthy to eat while standing. And yet, how does the experience actually differ? If you are enjoying morsels of fruit or ingredients with your partner as you prepare breakfast or cook a meal, is this really an act to avoid or is it more about the *way* you are eating, for example, shoveling in food in front of the glaring refrigerator light in the middle of the night? Similarly, what happens when you are trying to balance a cocktail plate and drink, mingling at a party, compared to sitting down at a table or sofa to eat and drink?

For this practice, compare your experience eating the same foods sitting, then standing, then perhaps sitting again. Usually this works best with a meal so you have more to eat, to permit ample time in each position. You can also create a party scene with finger foods and really bring your attention to what happens when you are sitting compared to standing. What do you notice? I have noticed that I instantly feel more anxious when I am standing. It is interesting to contemplate what this might be about, perhaps an association with social anxiety at parties, or simply the discomfort of having to balance everything? Record any reflections here (see also downloadable Handout 8.1).

Handout 8.1 Eating Mindfulness Practice Record: Sitting Versus Standing

_____

_____

_____

_____

_____

_____

_____

_____

_____

_____

_____

_____

Eating at the Table Versus on the Floor

Like comparing eating while sitting to eating while standing, it can be interesting to compare eating at the table and eating while sitting on the floor. Again, usually this works best with a meal so you have more to eat, to permit ample time in each position. Perhaps start by eating at the table, then move to the floor. Notice what changes. How do you feel in the different locations?

I have discovered that I almost instantly feel lighter and more relaxed on the floor. It feels more fun. I have used this as inspiration to throw myself a picnic on the floor of my place on a three-day weekend holiday, laying out a picnic blanket and spreading out my festive personal potluck. Likewise, if I am feeling like I need a bit of rejuvenation during a day at the therapy office, I will sit on the carpet of my office to eat my lunch, then maybe carry on there, typing up paperwork, until my next session.

Variants of this can include observing eating while sitting at different types of tables, for example, formal dining room tables, high tops, tiny wrought iron café tables, picnic tables, or low Japanese tables, sitting on pillows. You can also experiment with sitting on different floors or grounds, such as grass, sand, tiles, or carpet. What do you notice?

Record any reflections here (see also downloadable Handout 8.1).

Handout 8.1 Eating Mindfulness Practice Record: Eating at the Table Versus on the Floor

_____

_____

_____

_____

_____

_____

_____

_____

_____

_____

_____

Use of the Non-Dominant Hand

Another aspect of the mechanics of eating that can be automatic and instinctive is the hand we use. To bring greater awareness to this process, try eating with your non-dominant hand (i.e., if you are right-handed, use your left hand and vice versa). Notice what arises. Do you feel awkward, frustrated, or more present? How does it feel using the muscles in your non-dominant hand? Record any reflections here (see also downloadable Handout 8.1).

Handout 8.1 Eating Mindfulness Practice Record: Use of the Non-Dominant Hand

_____

_____

_____

_____

_____

_____

_____

_____

_____

_____

_____

_____

Likewise, if you are American and right-handed, you likely cut meat or other food with your right hand, your fork in your left, then switch the utensils to eat the bite with your right hand. As a parallel practice, try eating in the European style, with your fork remaining in your left hand and the knife in your right as you cut *and* eat the food (if you are right-handed). Again, notice what arises. Do you feel awkward, frustrated, or more present? Record any reflections here (see also downloadable Handout 8.1).

Handout 8.1 Eating Mindfulness Practice Record: American Versus European Style

_____

_____

_____

_____

_____

_____

_____

_____

_____

_____

_____

Not Using Utensils

Moving even further past awareness with utensils, what happens when you abandon utensils altogether? To really practice this I encourage not just bringing awareness to foods you typically would eat without utensils (e.g., sandwiches, fries, popcorn) but interacting with food that you would traditionally eat with utensils. I like to assign this as homework to my groups: to go to an Ethiopian restaurant, to eat meat, potatoes, and vegetables with nothing more than spongy injera. Have fun with it. Notice what arises. Record any reflections here (see also downloadable Handout 8.1).

Handout 8.1 Eating Mindfulness Practice Record: Not Using Utensils

_____

_____

_____

_____

_____

_____

_____

_____

_____

_____

_____

_____

You can also bring awareness to how it feels to use utensils with items typically eaten without utensils. The classic *Seinfeld* association here, of course, is when George eats a candy bar with a fork and knife. Give it a try and see what happens! You may just discover another form of Alternate Rebellion. Record any reflections here (see also downloadable Handout 8.1).

Handout 8.1 Eating Mindfulness Practice Record: Unusual Use of Utensils

_____

_____

_____

_____

_____

_____

_____

_____

_____

_____

_____

_____

Chapter Summary

There are so many ways to heighten your awareness with food in a mindful, creative way. I hope this chapter serves as inspiration for further practices. Eating can be such an adventure. It is a path to both self-exploration and connection to other traditions. By expanding your openness to all its nuances and possibilities, you can take a trip into and beyond your current circumstances without ever stepping foot in an airport or stamping your passport (although of course, travel can be a wonderful forum for further exploration!). Embrace it all, and have fun!

9 Moving Past Barriers

Given the complexity of contributing factors to eating patterns, change can be extremely difficult. As we have discussed, behavior serves a function and eating in particular ways can serve many important functions, in particular, related to emotion regulation. Therefore letting it go and establishing new patterns can be extremely difficult.

It can be incredibly discouraging to continue to repeat patterns of mindless eating despite your best efforts. If you find yourself struggling with this, you are certainly not alone. Be patient with yourself. Change can take years—and perhaps the most important ingredient for change is to continue—to take that next step, then the next, to crawl if you need to, to rest if you need to, but to ultimately keep going. Do not give up on yourself. I have worked with women who have struggled with eating disordered patterns their entire life, for decades and decades, including those aged in their 70s—and even then, this program has helped them leave their disordered patterns behind. I trust it can for you, as well.

Perhaps the main barrier that can impede moving forward is emotion. It can be paralyzing. It can also be associated with powerful, self-defeating thoughts, such as "I can't do this." To overcome this barrier, the DBT skill of Opposite to Emotion Action can be imperative.

Other barriers include environmental triggers, cuing patterns that have become automatic, as well as external demands, creating practical issues, and interpersonal difficulties. In addition, if you are a professional leading this as a group-based program, group heterogeneity in diagnosis can create issues. The closed nature of the group can also be a barrier to starting the program.

Emotion

As human beings we are hardwired to avoid pain—and emotions are painful. Indeed, they have been literally found to trigger the same pain pathways as physical pain (Papini, Fuchs, & Torres, 2015). If you have suffered extreme heartbreak, you know this. Your heart can literally feel like it is broken or shattered. Hence, behaviors that help us escape or avoid pain are strongly reinforced. We, therefore, are extremely prone to persist in those behaviors. This includes eating patterns.

To overcome this barrier, we thus need to bring our Reasonable Mind to bear, to check the facts of the situation, and to evaluate what we are really trying to feed. Remember, if we are experiencing heart hunger, we may choose to feed it with food—and yet, we may need to feed it in other ways to truly, fully nourish it.

First, use your mindfulness skills to identify the emotion you are feeling, then reflect on where this may be coming from and what it might be trying to tell you. Are you afraid of changing? Are you afraid of letting go of the familiarity and comfort of your eating patterns? Are you afraid you will fail and then it will feel even worse or just be the same anyway?

Are you angry that you have to deal with this? Are you feeling willful? Does it not seem fair?

Are you feeling sad for all the time you feel you have lost from your eating patterns, what they have taken from you?

Write about what is coming up for you here (see also downloadable Handout 9.1).

Handout 9.1 Barriers to Mindful Eating: Problem Solving Worksheet: Emotion

_____

_____

_____

_____

_____

_____

_____

_____

_____

_____

_____

_____

Whatever you are feeling, it is valid. That means it makes sense. It is understandable. At the same time, this does not mean that you need to then continue with your eating patterns. To move past the emotions you are feeling, if they are keeping you stuck, you need to employ the DBT skill of Opposite to Emotion Action.

Opposite to Emotion Action is the skill of moving opposite to the urge associated with an emotion. This is indicated when an emotion is unjustified or ineffective. Deeming an emotion unjustified does not mean it is not valid. All emotions are valid. They make sense. They are there for a reason. However, they may not entirely fit the actual facts of the situation and may therefore be unjustified. Justified emotion fits the facts of the situation, while unjustified emotion does not fit the facts.

For example, returning to Baby Albert, it makes complete sense that he was afraid of white furry objects. His fear was 100 percent valid. And yet, his fear was unjustified. That is, white furry objects are not inherently life-threatening or dangerous and fear communicates that there is a true threat. Therefore, his fear does not match the reality of the situation about the threat. He is experiencing fear about objects that are actually not threatening. Therefore, recall from Chapter 3, he needs to take the opposite action to the urges caused by the fear: to approach the object to habituate and learn that it is not threatening. In contrast, if Albert were afraid of tigers and he suddenly encountered one charging at him on safari, then his emotion would be entirely justified and he would want to act on his emotion to keep himself safe, to run away from that tiger or otherwise escape it, to keep himself alive and safe!

With Opposite to Emotion Action it is also important to ask whether acting on the urge associated with the emotion is effective or ineffective. For example, if Albert is afraid of tigers (which is justified, given their ability to devour us!), but he has chosen the profession of zoologist, specializing in tigers, then it would probably not be effective for him professionally to be panicking and running away from every tiger he encounters on the job. Thus sometimes our emotions are entirely justified, but acting on the urges we have with them is not effective, at least in the moment.

Opposite to Emotion Action can be applied to any emotion, not just fear, and often the key question with other emotions is not whether the emotion is justified or unjustified but whether acting on the urge associated with the emotion is effective or ineffective. For example, if we feel sadness because we have experienced the loss of a loved one's death; romantic breakup or disillusionment, in dating, separation, or divorce; the end of a friendship; a previously enjoyed state; hopes or dreams; or a favorite item, our emotion is justified. However, with sadness and grief can come strong urges to isolate, withdraw, and immobilize. If we need to continue to pay our bills, acting on these urges all the time would lead us to not show up to work and this would not be effective. It would also perpetuate our sadness, not allowing us to Accumulate Positive Experiences and ultimately develop new connections to fill our relationship needs. Therefore, it is essential to balance mindfulness and acceptance of the emotion with Opposite to Emotion Action to keep us moving forward.

Likewise, if we are in a toxic environment or relationship and feel we are not being treated fairly, our anger may be entirely justified. However, given that leaving an abusive relationship can place us in one of the most risky positions we may ever encounter, it is essential to prepare to leave in a planned way, to keep ourselves safe. We therefore would want to use Opposite to Emotion Action to be effective in the current circumstances, to develop a safety plan, before then enacting our departure from the situation.

Applying this to difficulty engaging in this mindful eating program, if your emotions feel overwhelming and strong, you will be vulnerable to continuing to act on your urges for eating patterns that are ultimately ineffective. Likewise, if your urges feel just too strong to resist, this could feel like too much and you may capitulate. To get past these barriers, it is thus critical that you use Opposite to Emotion Action, Urge Surfing, and Willingness. This is extremely challenging. And you can do it. Remember the skill of Encouragement (from IMPROVE, see Chapter 6) and cheerlead yourself.

Take some time and reflect on what emotions might be coming up for you, interfering with moving forward, past your patterns, instead repeating your ultimately ineffective patterns. Look at your diary card emotion ratings and how these connect to what you have been doing with eating on the corresponding days. Write some notes here, including how you will then apply Opposite to Emotion Action to move past these barriers (see also downloadable Handout 9.1).

Handout 9.1 Barriers to Mindful Eating: Problem Solving Worksheet: Emotion (Continued)

_____

_____

_____

_____

_____

_____

_____

_____

_____

_____

_____

If you discover that part of your emotional barrier involves feeling a desire to still maintain a connection to your eating pattern—that losing it will be anxiety-provoking, perhaps pushing you from what feels like a safety net—validate yourself. Again, behavior serves important functions. If it did not meet important needs, we would not continue doing it.

At the same time, review your pros and cons from Chapter 2. Ultimately, in your Wise Mind, do you really want to continue this pattern? Can you move forward even with your fear and anxiety, into the unknown? This takes courage. And I believe in your strength in being able to do this. To maintain eating patterns usually actually requires perseverance, commitment, and energy. Imagine what you could do if you applied that to moving past the patterns. You would likely be limitless. To remind yourself of the cons of mindless eating and pros of mindful eating, to counter the powerful pull of those short-term pros of mindless eating, post your pros and cons where you can see them when you need to, to block urges for mindless eating. For example, perhaps post them on your refrigerator, in your bathroom, as the wallpaper on your phone, laptop, or tablet, or as highlights with Post-It notes on the steering wheel of your car or your debit card, to block trips to the store to purchase binge foods. If you live with others and do not feel comfortable posting the details in this way, create a symbol that will represent the reasons you want to not act on urges for mindless eating. For example, if a major reason is the impact it has on your loved ones, post a picture of your family; you know what this means and yet anyone else would just think it was a picture of your family.

Sometimes to help truly let go of your attachment to a pattern, it can also be helpful to write it a letter, to thank it for all it has done for you, then wish it well, letting it know the reasons it cannot continue to be a part of your life. When a relationship ends, this can help recognize and honor both the helpful and unhelpful roles the companion has served and foster a better sense of closure. Take some time and use the space here to write this out in depth, reflecting on all the memories you have, painful and enjoyable. There are both and that is O.K.—and you can move on, no matter how difficult that feels. (See also downloadable Handout 9.2.)

Handout 9.2 Letter for Closure to Mindless Eating Patterns

_____

_____

_____

_____

_____

_____

_____

_____

_____

_____

_____

_____

_____

_____

_____

_____

_____

At the same time, consider the possibility that you are pushing yourself too hard. Change takes time and if you are trying to tackle foods that are higher in your hierarchy before you are ready, you will likely be struggling with intense emotion and this can overwhelm and paralyze you. Take a step back and allow yourself to continue practicing at lower levels of the hierarchy.

Also remember mindfulness with the difficult thoughts that can accompany intense emotion, such as despair. Remember thoughts are just thoughts. They may or may not be true. And in either case we can detach from them and let them go, so they do not stand in our way. Or we can put them in our pocket and take them with us. Use your Mindfulness Describe skill to step back from them (e.g., say "I am having the thought 'I can't do this.' I am having the thought 'This will never change.'"). To review this, return to Chapter 4.

Environment

Another powerful barrier to change is the environment. Any time that you engage in a behavior, that behavior is paired with the environment around you. If you engage in this behavior repeatedly, it strengthens the association. This association can then be generalized. For example, if you overeat at home, at night, on the couch, in front of the TV, when certain programs are on, this can trigger urges when you are at home in general, when it is nighttime in general, when you are on couches in general, when you are in front of a TV in general, with similar programs in general.

Times of day can be especially triggering, perhaps related to emotional underpinnings. For example, a common cycle that can develop is being "good" during the day, distracting by focusing on work, not feeling difficult emotions, and eating in a balanced or even restrictive way, then with dusk the distractions fall away, opening the door for emotions to surface and, perhaps, confused hunger cues to emerge. This can then prompt overeating to cope.

These cycles can be difficult to circumvent and may require at least temporary changes to your routine and living space. For example, if you find melancholy creeping in predictably when your work day is done, think about what that emotion is trying to tell you. If it reflects your life outside of work not being what you want it to be, then seriously consider what you need to do to fill that need, as best you can.

This may require short-term and long-term strategies. For example, in my process of recovering from a difficult divorce, I would inevitably experience the cycle of melancholy at the end of the day. I made space for it, but after some time, I knew it had to be about more than grieving and moving on from the one particular lost relationship, to a new partnership, and in any case it would take time to establish a healthy, lasting new connection. I then more effectively responded to this emotion by increasing ABC PLEASE as a priority; mindfully reaching out to friends during the evening; expressing my emotion and creating joy in returning to piano playing, which I had put aside in my focus on my training, early career, and former marriage; and reading books of interest to my passions, especially travel, and self-help to further my healing. I then began looking forward to the quiet of going home and having time to get back in touch with what I value and love. I also found myself again more motivated to mindfully cook and enjoy the food I prepared to nourish my many hungers.

Another consideration is your physical environment. If you are extremely triggered in particular contexts, such as your home, think about when you are most vulnerable and Cope Ahead by planning to not be at home at those times. This is a short-term solution, given that ultimately you will need to habituate to the environment to develop a new association. However, bringing a dialectical perspective to this, when you are first trying to establish new patterns you may need to minimize time in the triggering environment. In such cases, perhaps you delay going home after work, for example, until your roommate is home, since you know that having another person there keeps you accountable and reduces your likelihood of engaging in unbalanced eating. If you are delaying, think about what would be the most helpful alternative. For example, perhaps staying late at work is helpful, so that the worst that happens is that you are more productive, or perhaps you schedule self-care, such as a massage or walk on the beach.

To counter triggering cues in the physical environment you can also recreate your space. For example, when I was still struggling with separation I was surrounded by so many reminders of my previous relationship, every piece of home furnishing seemingly seared with painful nostalgia, but still present because of not being in a financial position to replace everything and not wanting to simply exist as a minimalist, with no belongings! My friend came over and in less than an hour, moving around some pieces, she created a new energy and I instantly felt such a sense of rejuvenation. I then realized anew how essential it was to create fresh associations with my living space and began acquiring, as I was able, new pieces. With each new lamp and item of furniture, I felt so much more empowered and at peace. With peace comes greater Wise Mind and a greater capacity to not engage in patterns of eating in unbalanced ways or otherwise being self-destructive or stuck.

For my clients, I often work specifically on recreating their bathrooms, due to the rooms' association with purging. This can be as simple as getting a new shower curtain or bringing in soothing or inspiring new touches, such as creating a beach theme instead of a previous floral theme. The kitchen, office space, and car are also common areas that benefit from a makeover.

You do not need to spend a lot of money on this. Do not let money be a barrier, if that is a concern. Check out consignment stores or garage sales or see if any of your friends have pieces they would be willing to contribute. You can also simply post encouraging messages to yourself, in signs or with mirror markers. Whatever it is, the point is to create a new environment to be associated with new patterns of behavior. Of course, Opposite to Emotion Action for unjustified guilt can also help overcome any cognitive or emotional barriers here. If you are a therapist, assign this as homework to your clients and ask them to send you pictures of it to promote accountability and encouragement.

Think about this for yourself. What are your patterns? Where do you tend to have urges or engage in unbalanced eating patterns? What might this be about? What hungers might you really be having? How can you feed those hungers? How can you give your environment a facelift? Record your thoughts here (see also downloadable Handout 9.1).

Handout 9.1 Barriers to Mindful Eating: Problem Solving Worksheet: Environment

_____

_____

‒‒‒‒‒‒‒‒‒‒‒‒‒‒‒‒‒‒‒‒‒‒‒‒‒‒‒‒‒‒‒‒‒‒‒‒‒

‒‒‒‒‒‒‒‒‒‒‒‒‒‒‒‒‒‒‒‒‒‒‒‒‒‒‒‒‒‒‒‒‒‒‒‒‒

‒‒‒‒‒‒‒‒‒‒‒‒‒‒‒‒‒‒‒‒‒‒‒‒‒‒‒‒‒‒‒‒‒‒‒‒‒

‒‒‒‒‒‒‒‒‒‒‒‒‒‒‒‒‒‒‒‒‒‒‒‒‒‒‒‒‒‒‒‒‒‒‒‒‒

‒‒‒‒‒‒‒‒‒‒‒‒‒‒‒‒‒‒‒‒‒‒‒‒‒‒‒‒‒‒‒‒‒‒‒‒‒

‒‒‒‒‒‒‒‒‒‒‒‒‒‒‒‒‒‒‒‒‒‒‒‒‒‒‒‒‒‒‒‒‒‒‒‒‒

‒‒‒‒‒‒‒‒‒‒‒‒‒‒‒‒‒‒‒‒‒‒‒‒‒‒‒‒‒‒‒‒‒‒‒‒‒

‒‒‒‒‒‒‒‒‒‒‒‒‒‒‒‒‒‒‒‒‒‒‒‒‒‒‒‒‒‒‒‒‒‒‒‒‒

‒‒‒‒‒‒‒‒‒‒‒‒‒‒‒‒‒‒‒‒‒‒‒‒‒‒‒‒‒‒‒‒‒‒‒‒‒

‒‒‒‒‒‒‒‒‒‒‒‒‒‒‒‒‒‒‒‒‒‒‒‒‒‒‒‒‒‒‒‒‒‒‒‒‒

External Demands

Another area that clients have commonly identified as a major barrier to their progress in mindful eating is external demands, in particular, at work and school. For example, one of my clients repeatedly talked about struggling with her work schedule and the limited breaks she got. She described always feeling under pressure to eat while she kept working or even skip lunch. Of course, I encouraged her to consider her perspective on this as apparently irrelevant behavior—and at the same time, of course, our work environments can be demanding and can at the very least make it challenging, if not impossible, to practice mindful eating as fully as we would like.

I can definitely relate. I remember distinctly a boss who thought it was completely acceptable to demand that I work through my lunch break and expected this. I had to really consider how to be effective under that pressure, how to prioritize my well-being while also keeping my paycheck. My solutions included portable meals, like sandwiches, chips or crackers, and pieces of fruit that I could eat as mindfully as possible when driving between worksites.

Relatedly, in my therapy with college students over the years, a major issue for problem solving has been navigating course schedules and university meal environments consisting of food courts, markets, and cafeterias. With teens and families, as well, the demands of an extremely packed schedule, with school and activities, can compromise the dinner hour, resulting in fast food shoved down mindlessly. Countering these barriers often requires quite a concerted, committed effort to plan ahead, to have food prepared and accessible, balancing meeting demands with still prioritizing mindful eating as much as possible, even if the meal being eaten is a burrito on the run.

Think about your patterns with this. What pressures do you feel from demands and time? How is this interfering with eating in a more mindful way? How can you further plan ahead to navigate this more effectively? Record your thoughts here (see also downloadable Handout 9.1).

Handout 9.1 Barriers to Mindful Eating: Problem Solving Worksheet: External Demands

_____

_____

_____

_____

_____

_____

_____

_____

_____

_____

_____

Other People

The patterns of others can also impede progress in mindful eating. Clients report this time after time. For example, clients talk about struggling with eating out with others who engage in mindless eating or restriction, or living with someone who eats in an unbalanced way. This can be especially difficult if the people engaging in unbalanced eating are your parents, both if you are still living at home and if you are just returning for holidays. After all, as children we turn to our parents for how to behave, looking to their behavior as a model. Thus when they do not teach us balanced ways and we have to establish them ourselves, we can be going up against years of behavioral conditioning—and it often does not matter how many years go by, or how old we get, when we go back to our childhood home or spend time with our parents, we can feel just as we did when we were living there as a child or adolescent. It is also not uncommon for disordered eating to run in families (e.g., Marcos, Sebastian, Aubalat, Ausina, & Treasure, 2013; MacBrayer, Smith, McCarthy, Demos, & Simmons, 2002).

Taken together, it is thus essential to consider how the people in your life may be supporting or impeding your progress in mindful eating. Have you shared your history and current process with those with whom you have close, intimate relationships, whether they are friends, family, or romantic partners? How did they react? If you have talked to them, so they can understand that you are working on eating in a mindful way and why this is important to you, and their behavior is still not supportive, consider whether it may be best for you to avoid eating with them, at least when you are just beginning your journey in mindful eating. Perhaps also consider whether their lack of support reflects a broader issue that may suggest the relationship needs further repair or may even need to be given up. These are difficult questions. Take some time to reflect on them and record your thoughts here (see also downloadable Handout 9.1).

Handout 9.1 Barriers to Mindful Eating: Problem Solving Worksheet: Other People

_____

_____

_____

_____

_____

_____

_____

_____

_____

_____

_____

_____

Group Heterogeneity

For therapists conducting this group-based program, I would strongly advise against placing a client with AN who is newly weight-restored into a group of clients primarily struggling with binge eating, especially when the other clients are overweight or obese. Anecdotally, this has been the one major barrier I have found to clinical effectiveness related to group dynamics in my experience developing this approach. I hesitated to try this combination but in the geographic region where I was conducting my randomized research trial, other resources were limited and a mother begged me to let her daughter participate. So I tried it. And the daughter did not even last through the first group session, not even to the break of the first group session! She left the room sobbing, terrified to be surrounded by so many embodiments of her worst nightmare of being fat. There was no overcoming this barrier at that point. She did not continue in the group.

This said, I have had clients successfully participate in such heterogeneous groups when they have had a history of AN, reflected in their weight being on the low side of normal, but weight-restored, and further along in their journey, perhaps years into it, shifted more to binge eating and, at times, also purging. Thus it is important to consider clinical fit for each client individually. In the orientation and commitment process be sure to raise any possible concerns to promote open discussion ahead of time, including a plan for how the client will handle any feelings of being triggered that do arise.

Group Recruitment

Finally, in the private practice realm, in my experience, another major barrier can be the closed nature of the group. This means that after a group starts it is closed to new group members. This is because of the graded mindful eating hierarchy, which requires sequencing. Starting the group is thus contingent on a cohort being ready to start at the same time. To form a cohort in a timely manner, with group recruitment, can be a challenge. This can thus leave clients waiting, then when enough clients have been screened and committed, clients who had been waiting may find their circumstances or motivation have changed, so they retract their commitment and decline participating after the time has passed, causing the group to still remain on hold. This is very frustrating and is best addressed clinically by working with clients individually while they are waiting for the group to start. When barriers to providing the bridge of individual sessions, such as financial constraints, exist, continuing to remain in communication with clients on the group waitlist can, at times, help reduce attrition through maintained connection.

For professionals going through this process, I recommend practicing your own distress tolerance, Radical Acceptance, and Opposite to Emotion Action to persist! Cheerlead yourself. This is an important and needed intervention and by not letting the barriers derail you, you can truly help change lives with this treatment.

I have tried to adapt and implement this program instead as an open group within higher levels of care, in the setting of intensive outpatient treatment and partial hospitalization, and its success still appeared mostly dependent on the extent to which clients were able to progress through the process together, in a graded fashion. One exception to this that I have found to work well in my private practice has been permitting new group members to join the group after it has started if they already have had an extensive background in DBT (e.g., having graduated from other DBT groups) and are far enough along in their recovery or mindful eating experience otherwise to be able to join the group at the point reached in the mindful eating hierarchy. Even then, in my experience, it was still important that the group was relatively near the beginning of their hierarchy, no more than a few weeks into it.

Chapter Summary

In summary, some of the main barriers to mindful eating include emotion, the environment, external demands, and interpersonal difficulties; professionals leading the group-based program will want to consider implementation barriers from the closed group structure and diagnostic heterogeneity, in particular related to time from weight stabilization in AN. However, do not be discouraged. Or if you are, notice the emotion, validate it, and let it pass, then redirect to moving past these barriers. None of these barriers are walls that cannot be dismantled or overcome. Changing these patterns may be one of the most challenging undertakings you ever face. And you can overcome it. I assure you. Just keep going. Know that, although your path is unique in its own way, just as you are a unique being that will never be entirely exactly replicated, many have walked before you and achieved freedom from these patterns. You can, too.

10 Taking Inventory and Moving Forward

Congratulations! You have reached the final chapter in this program. If you have been applying yourself to the process, taking your time with the practices, and working your way through your mindful eating hierarchy, I trust that you are now well on your way down the path of mindful eating. And yet the path still lies ahead of you. Mindful eating requires continued application, returning your awareness with each meal, each bite. As you prepare to continue on this path after you close the pages of this book, take this opportunity to pause and review the material we have covered. In reflecting on your journey, for each area, consider what you have learned and the next steps for continued growth (see also downloadable Handout 10.1). We will then discuss final closing reflections.

I   Returning to the beginning of our discussion, there is now ample theory and evidence supporting the paradoxical impact of thinking on eating. That is, in particular, the more we create rules about food to guide our eating, the less likely we are to succeed in eating in a certain way. Instead, to effectively nourish ourselves according to certain guidelines, we actually must be nonjudgmentally open to all foods.

Furthermore, mindfulness from a dialectical perspective integrates a critical role for distress tolerance and refocusing from each morsel of food in front of us to the context surrounding us. We can choose to mindfully Observe the waves crashing in front of us as we sit at a table overlooking the ocean, or notice the décor of the restaurant where we are dining, or listen to our dining partner. This requires the most advanced attunement to both our internal and external experience to inform what is most effective for us in any given moment. To achieve this awareness we must move out of our heads and how we think about food to foster the ability to listen to our bodies and our hearts, to nourish what we actually need.

Handout 10.1 Reflections and Next Steps Worksheet (I)

What I have learned:_____

_____

_____

_____

_____

_____

_____

_____

Next steps for continued growth: _____

_____

_____

_____

_____

_____

_____

_____

II   As with any behavior, eating in an unbalanced, disordered way serves a function. As human beings, we do not engage in behavior for no reason, and with unbalanced eating, the attempted function is often coping in response to difficult, painful emotions. However, this behavior provides only short-term relief that often backfires, since it is not fully addressing underlying emotions but rather simply providing a temporary break from them.

To move past these patterns, the research-based approach for mindful eating from the dialectical perspective includes consistent, full engagement with self-monitoring and skills practice. To facilitate this, tools include daily diary cards turned in weekly, Binge Record Sheets, skills assignments, behavior chain and solution analysis, and, for participants working with professionals, coaching calls. Not completing these components is considered therapy-interfering behavior and targeted for resolution through problem solving. Therapy-interfering behavior is the second target in the DBT treatment hierarchy, after life-threatening behavior (which includes self-harm, suicidality, and medically compromising eating-related behavior) and before quality-of-life-interfering behavior (in this case, namely, other eating-related behavior). To adhere to the program requires commitment before moving forward. This commitment is mirrored by facilitators and this author.

Handout 10.1 Reflections and Next Steps Worksheet (II)

What I have learned:_____

_____

_____

_____

_____

_____

_____

_____

_____

Next steps for continued growth: _____

_____

_____

_____

_____

_____

_____

_____

_____

_____

III   Retracing the development of mindful eating from the dialectical perspective, this approach is grounded in the heritage of behaviorism, cognitive theory and research, and Eastern philosophies of acceptance and detachment. As a Third Wave treatment, it rests upon a foundation of research and wisdom that now includes empirical accounts of neurobiological underpinnings and diverse treatment trials. Current understandings of temperament suggest that disordered eating patterns that are primarily restrictive, such as restricting AN, may slow the pace of progress in mindful eating— and yet from the dialectical perspective, mindful eating remains a powerful pathway for change across the spectrum of eating.

Handout 10.1 Reflections and Next Steps Worksheet (III)

What I have learned:_____

_____

_____

_____

_____

_____

_____

_____

_____

Next steps for continued growth: _____

_____

_____

_____

_____

_____

_____

_____

_____

IV   Core mindfulness skills include the states of mind of Emotion Mind ("I feel"), Reasonable Mind ("I think"), and Wise Mind ("I know"), as well as the What and How skills. The What skills consist of Observe (just noticing), Describe (putting words on what is observed), and Participate (being fully present in the moment, responding intuitively from Wise Mind). Urge Surfing is an important variant of Observe to create space between urges and action. The How skills consist of Nonjudgmental Stance (without evaluation, just the facts), One-Mindfully (being one with your experience, internal or external), and Effectiveness (doing what works).

Handout 10.1 Reflections and Next Steps Worksheet (IV)

What I have learned:_____

_____

_____

_____

_____

_____

_____

_____

_____

Next steps for continued growth: _____

_____

_____

_____

_____

_____

_____

_____

_____

V   With mindfulness we can more clearly discern the driving forces and motivations prompting our hunger and then more effectively nourish our needs. This can be complicated by deficits in interoceptive awareness, the ability to detect and distinguish between internal sensations, such as anxiety versus hunger. Disordered eating and related difficulties with emotion, such as depression and anxiety, promulgate disruptions in this capacity. These can be overcome through mindfulness, with the aid of the Emotion Model as discussed. It is also critical to decrease vulnerability to Emotion Mind through self-care in the areas of ABC PLEASE: Accumulating Positive Experiences, Building Mastery, Coping Ahead, Treating Physical Illness, Balancing Eating, Avoiding Drugs and Alcohol, Balancing Sleep, and Balancing Exercise.

As outlined by Jan Chozen Bays, M.D. (2009), seven main hungers to consider are eye, nose, mouth, stomach, cellular, mind, and heart hunger: What pleases or enlivens your sight? What appeals to your smell? What does your mouth want to experience: crunchy or soft? Is your stomach empty? What nutrients do you need? What are your thoughts telling you about it being time to eat or needing to eat certain foods? And, perhaps the greatest question of all, what does your heart want and need? In answering these questions you may choose to eat or you may find that you ultimately can or need to quench these hungers in ways that have nothing to do with food.

Handout 10.1 Reflections and Next Steps Worksheet (V)

What I have learned:_____

_____

_____

_____

_____

_____

_____

_____

_____

Next steps for continued growth: _____

_____

_____

_____

_____

_____

_____

_____

_____

_____

VI From a dialectical perspective, mindfulness moves beyond the plate in front of us to consider how to most effectively focus our attention to manage our emotions, thoughts, and urges. At times this means that we will direct our attention to other objects in our environment or internal experience. With distress tolerance, we are giving ourselves temporary relief from overwhelming crisis, with the Willingness to return to that emotion when we are more centered. Distress tolerance tools include redirecting through Activities, Contributing, Comparisons, Opposite Emotion (e.g., watching a funny movie when we are sad), Other Thoughts, Strong Sensations, Self-Soothing, Imagery, Meaning, Prayer, Relaxation (including diaphragmatic breathing paced at six breaths/minute and Half-Smiling), One Thing in the Moment, Vacation, and Encouragement.

Radical Acceptance is also critical. That is, we must embrace reality to be able to move through it and not be paralyzed by fighting against it. Quite simply, as harsh as this may sound, it is what it is. Saying it should be another way and trying to protest or deny it only keeps us stuck in suffering. And of course, reality can be incredibly painful. And yet, we must have the courage to take off any blinders or armor and open ourselves to it, to let it in and let it be so we can let it go.

This process of Radical Acceptance is continuous. Once we radically accept, we quite often will drift back to non-acceptance. We must then turn the mind back to the path of acceptance and willingly move into action with Effectiveness. This can feel insurmountable. And yet, when you reach a true place of Radical Acceptance, it can be unbelievably freeing.

Handout 10.1 Reflections and Next Steps Worksheet (VI)

What I have learned:_____

_____

_____

_____

_____

_____

_____

_____

_____

_____

Next steps for continued growth: _____

_____

_____

_____

_____

_____

_____

_____

_____

VII   Bringing awareness to the context of our eating can further enhance the process of creating a new relationship to food. Then, perhaps the most critical vehicle for overcoming rule-governed behavior around foods judged as unhealthy or forbidden is to work through approaching those very foods through your individualized forbidden foods hierarchy. In this process it is imperative to pace yourself and honor where you are. Likewise, professionals working with clients on this process need to recognize that it is essential to balance encouragement to move forward with respect for where clients are in their readiness for the next steps. Make sure you or your clients are first and foremost engaging with this task from a stance of kindness and patience. And keep going. I assure you that you can eventually check off every single item on your list. And for you or your clients it will be more empowering than you can imagine.

Handout 10.1 Reflections and Next Steps Worksheet (VII)

What I have learned:_____

_____

_____

_____

_____

_____

_____

_____

Next steps for continued growth: _____

_____

_____

_____

_____

_____

_____

_____

VIII Deconstructing mindful eating offers a multitude of options for practice. In my mindful eating groups, a tradition is to embark on the forbidden foods hierarchy with first mindfully observing, then juicing and drinking, tangelos. Other possibilities for mindfulness of liquids include water, soda, and milkshakes. Isolating mindfulness to smell can also be a fun option with a partner or group, and exploring mechanics can be interesting, including sitting versus standing and experimenting with the use of your hands and utensils.

Handout 10.1 Reflections and Next Steps Worksheet (VIII)

What I have learned:_____

_____

_____

_____

_____

_____

_____

_____

Next steps for continued growth: _____

_____

_____

_____

_____

_____

_____

_____

_____

_____

IX   Roadblocks to mindful eating can include emotion, the environment, external demands, and interpersonal difficulties; professionals can encounter issues from the closed group structure and diagnostic heterogeneity, in particular when clients with AN are early in weight stabilization. This process may thus feel fraught with difficulty. Yet, these barriers are not insurmountable and with Opposite to Emotion Action, in particular, can be problem solved and overcome. The reward of mindful eating—and, ultimately, mindful living—is well worth it.

Handout 10.1 Reflections and Next Steps Worksheet (IX)

What I have learned:_____

_____

_____

_____

_____

_____

_____

_____

_____

Next steps for continued growth: _____

_____

_____

_____

_____

_____

_____

_____

_____

Future Directions

As detailed across the preceding chapters, as individuals and professionals moving on in the path of mindful eating from the dialectical perspective, we are preceded by many researchers, theorists, and traditions extending back decades and even centuries, providing us a firm foundation and compass for where to go from here. The opportunity for further research, to improve our understanding of this process and how to best extend it across the spectrum of eating even more, is exciting. For example, as the field continues to move more into neurobiological investigation, greater attention to locating associated brain functioning and regions of specificity in BED and grazing would be beneficial, with most studies in this arena to date focused on AN and BN. In general, research on grazing is lacking, despite the common reporting of this pattern of eating.

Further clinical trials are also needed. In particular, samples of restrictive eating disorders and of adolescents are currently underpowered or unavailable, with most studies of mindful eating to date instead focused on patterns involving binge eating and adults. This calls for investigations to elucidate the efficacy and effectiveness for mindful eating extended to these presentations. With this, active comparisons to other more established treatments, such as family-based treatment for AN and adolescents (Lock & Le Grange, 2012; Loeb & Le Grange, 2009), as well as consideration of how mindful eating may be incorporated into these existing protocols, will be critical. Investigating the integration of mindful eating from the dialectical perspective and RO DBT in particular would be invaluable for potentially expanding the efficacy of these two approaches for overcontrolled, restrictive presentations. In general, support for mindful eating across the spectrum of eating would be strengthened by active comparisons to more established treatments. Likewise, dismantling designs remain limited and are indicated to understand incremental efficacy and mechanisms of change, and extending follow-up would inform the extent to which change is maintained.

It would also be interesting to compare DBT-based mindful eating to interpersonal psychotherapy (IPT), in particular, for BN and BED, given the status of IPT as one of the other main treatments for BN and BED (Arcelus et al., 2009; Fairburn, Jones, Peveler, Hope, & O'Connor, 1993; Hilbert et al., 2012; Murphy, Straebler, Basden, Cooper, & Fairburn, 2012; Wilfley et al., 2002). Indeed, the Interpersonal Effectiveness module of skills typically taught in DBT was originally omitted from the adaptation for BED and BN not because the researchers considered it unindicated for the population, but rather because of an intention to eventually permit comparison in a randomized trial to IPT. This remains to be conducted. Relatedly, it could be informative to investigate any incremental efficacy from including the Interpersonal Effectiveness module in DBT-based mindful eating.

Burning Bridges

The act of burning can powerfully symbolize letting go. I have experienced this as part of a meditation circle. The leader asked us to reflect and write down that which no longer serves us and, when we were ready, present it to a candle flame, to be released. It was incredibly moving, committing certain struggles to that humble sheet of paper, then watching them disintegrate into wisps of black and gray, tinged with glowingly bright orange sparks. As I then tossed the scrap, billowing smoke, into a receiving bowl, I felt a burst of glee, as if so much heavy weight was lifted and gone. Forever. To no longer torment me. I was free.

The act of burning bridges can be similarly profound. The phrase may have a negative connotation, with warnings against burning bridges personally and professionally. However, when you are leaving behind toxicity, this can be empowering and even essential. The origin of the skill is rooted in the historical practice of armies burning bridges after crossing bodies of water to block retreat. Basically, the idea was that after burning the bridges the soldiers had to press on into battle, to fight for victory. A similar concept is the point of no return, which stems from a flight reference to the point when a plane does not have enough fuel to return to where it departed. Again, the spirit of the phrase is that there is no turning back.

In a group setting I walk clients through this imagery at the end of our last session together, before we celebrate the completion of the course and process closure. I will ask you to do the same. The practice is a form of Imagery, so get into a comfortable position, feet flat on the floor, eyes closed if you are being guided or gently focused on the page in front of you, to read through it on your own.

Now take a few moments to reflect on the behaviors, thoughts, and patterns you have been working on over the course of this program. They may be many. Recall when you began this journey how you committed to building a new relationship to eating and food, moving towards mindfulness. As best you can, consider which specific aspect of your former relationship with eating and food you are now ready to completely release and let go, to leave in the past. This may be an entire behavior, such as binge eating, overeating, or restricting, or it may be a specific rule, such as rigid attachment to judgments about forbidden foods. Look inward and see what arises. Listen to what your Wise Mind suggests.

When you have selected your specific behavior, thought, or pattern, imagine that you are on an island with it. Look around. Notice what the island looks like. Perhaps there are towering palm trees or perhaps the island is barren, with dead trees fallen and jagged boulders lining the shore, angry waves crashing against them. Whatever your mind creates, really place yourself there.

Once you have fully examined your island, turn around and look towards the mainland in the distance. Ahead of you there is a bridge connecting the island to the mainland. The bridge may be rickety, a suspension bridge, twisting in the wind. Or it may be a more solid structure. But in any case it is made of a combustible material, wood or rope. Really take in what it looks like.

Once you have fully examined the bridge ahead of you, turn your attention to the behavior, thought, or pattern you are ready to leave behind. Perhaps you have made it into a symbolic object. Or perhaps it is just words. Or perhaps it is memories, a recollection of both regrets and benefits. It has served a function for you and been part of your journey. Do not judge it. Thank it for any ways it has served you. And then set it down.

Choose where you will place it. Perhaps you will rest it upon the rocks. Or perhaps you will bury it in the sand. Wherever you choose to place it, Observe this as long as you feel is sufficient. For you are saying goodbye. You are about to walk across that bridge and not look back, leaving this friend yet foe behind.

Once you have fully given space to the behavior, thought, or pattern, perhaps giving it one last kiss or caress, get up. Turn around. And start walking.

Do not look back. Raise your head up. Take one step forward. Then another. If you need to pause or kneel, perhaps to let emotion swell, do so. Honor what you need. And then keep walking. Walk across the bridge until you reach the solid embrace of the mainland.

On the mainland, feel the firmness of the ground, holding you up, spreading before you, welcoming you to its new life. Breathe in the air, its freshness. Observe what surrounds you. Perhaps a bustling harbor. Perhaps a sweeping landscape. Whatever it is, take it all in.

Then, once you have fully examined the mainland ahead of you, notice that by the foot of the bridge there is a torch ablaze, resting in its sconce, waiting for you. Pick it up. Feel its heft. Notice how the flame glows, its faceted pigments dancing in front of you. Feel its warmth and even heat, breathing in its depth.

And when you are ready, bring the torch down upon that wooden bridge, setting it on fire. Then step back safely to the mainland and watch it burn. It may burn quickly. It may burn slowly. Whatever you imagine is fine. Just notice what you imagine and let the fire continue, plank by plank, or fiber by fiber, crackling, folding into the water below it, until it reaches the island, where your behavior, thought, or pattern waits.

Notice whatever emotion arises. Make space for it. Feel it fully. It makes sense. And you are safe. Likewise the behavior, thought, and pattern is safe. You have simply set it free.

When the bridge has fully collapsed, its smoldering embers submerged into the water, and when you have fully felt the emotions that have arisen, turn around, returning your gaze to the mainland ahead of you. And start walking again, anew and free.

References

Abbate-Daga, G., Buzzichelli, S., Marzola, E., Amianto, F., & Fassino, S. (2014). Clinical investigation of set-shifting subtypes in anorexia nervosa. *Psychiatry Research, 219(3)*, 592–597. doi: 10.1016/j.psychres.2014.06.024

Abramowitz, J.S., Tolin, D.F., & Street, G.P. (2001). Paradoxical effects of thought suppression: A meta-analysis of controlled studies. *Clinical Psychology Review, 21(5)*, 683–703. doi: 10.1016/S0272-7358(00)00057-X

Aittasalo, M., Miilunpalo, S., Kukkonen-Harjula, K., & Pasanen, M. (2006). A randomized intervention of physical activity promotion and patient self-monitoring in primary health care. *Preventive Medicine, 42(1)*, 40–46. doi: 10.1016/j.ypmed.2005.10.003

Albers, S.A. (2010). Using mindful eating to treat food restriction: A case study. *Eating Disorders: The Journal of Treatment and Prevention, 19(1)*, 97–107. doi: 10.1080/10640266.2011.533609

American Psychiatric Association. (2013). *Diagnostic and statistical manual of disorders* (5th edition) Washington D.C.: Author.

Andersen, A.E., Bowers, W.A., & Watson, T. (2001). A slimming program for eating disorders not otherwise specified. Reconceptualizing a confusing, residual diagnostic category. *Psychiatric Clinics of North America, 24(2)*, 271–280. doi: 10.1016/S0193-953X(05)70223-9

Anderson, D.A., Williamson, D.A., Duchmann, E.G., Gleaves, D.G., & Barbin, J.M. (1999). Development and validation of a multifactorial treatment outcome measure for eating disorders. *Assessment, 6(1)*, 7–20. doi: 10.1177/107319119900600102

Anestis, M.D., Holm-Denoma, J.M., Gordon, K.H., Schmidt, N.B., & Joiner, T.E. (2008). The role of anxiety sensitivity in eating pathology. *Cognitive Therapy & Research, 32(3)*, 370–385. doi: 10.1007/s10608-006-9085-y

Anzengruber, D., Klump, K.L., Thornton, L., Brandt, H., Crawford, S., Fichter, M.M., Halmi, K.A., Johnson, C., Kaplan, A.S., LaVia, M., Mitchell, J., Strober, M., Woodside, D.B., Rotondo, A., Berrettini, W.H., Kaye, W.H., & Bulik, C.M. (2006). Smoking in eating disorders. *Eating Behaviors, 7(4)*, 291–299. doi: 10.1016/j.eatbeh.2006.06.005

Arcelus, J., Whight, D., Langham, C., Baggott, J., McGrain, L., Meadows, L., & Meyer, C. (2009). A case series evaluation of the modified version of interpersonal psychotherapy (IPT) for the treatment of bulimic eating disorders: A pilot study. *European Eating Disorders Review, 17(4)*, 260–268. doi: 10.1002/(ISSN)1099-096810.1002/erv.v17:410.1002/erv.932

Arndt, J., Greenberg, J., Solomon, S., Pyszczynski, T., & Simon, L. (1997). Suppression, accessibility of death-related thoughts, and cultural worldview defense: Exploring the psychodynamics of terror management. *Journal of Personality and Social Psychology, 73(1),* 5–18. doi: 10.1037/0022-3514.73.1.5

Avena, N.M., Rada, P., Moise, N., & Hoebel, B.G. (2006). Sucrose sham feeding on a binge schedule releases accumbens dopamine repeatedly and eliminates the acetylcholine satiety response. *Neuroscience, 139(3),* 813–820. doi: 10.1016/j.neuroscience.2005.12.037

Avena, N.M., Rada, P., & Hoebel, B.G. (2007). Evidence for sugar addiction: Behavioral and neurochemical effects of intermittent, excessive sugar intake. *Neuroscience and Biobehavioral Review, 32(1),* 20–39. doi: 10.1016/j.neubiorev.2007.04.019

Baiano, M., Salvo, P., Righetti, P., Cereser, L., Baldissera, E., Camponogara, I., & Balestrieri, M. (2014). Exploring health-related quality of life in eating disorders by a cross-sectional study and a comprehensive review. *BMC Psychiatry, 15,* 165. doi: 10.1186/1471-244X-14-165

Baker, R.C., & Kirschenbaum, D.S. (1993). Self-monitoring may be necessary for successful weight control. *Behavior Therapy, 24(3),* 377–394. doi: 10.1016/S0005-7894(05)80212-6

Bays, J.C. (2009). *Mindful eating: A guide to rediscovering a healthy and joyful relationship with food.* Boston, MA, US: Shambhala Publications, Inc.

Beck, A. (1963). Thinking and depression: I. Idiosyncratic content and cognitive distortions. *Archives of General Psychiatry, 9(4),* 324–333. doi: 10.1001/archpsyc.1963.01720160014002

Beck, A. (1964). Thinking and depression: II. Theory and therapy. *Archives of General Psychiatry, 10(6),* 561–571. doi: 10.1001/archpsyc.1964.01720240015003

Beck, A. (1970). Cognitive therapy: Nature and relation to behavior therapy. *Behavior Therapy, 1(2),* 184–200. doi: 10.1016/S0005-7894(70)80030-2

Beck, A. (1993). Cognitive therapy: Past, present, and future. *Journal of Consulting and Clinical Psychology, 61(2),* 194–198. doi: 10.1037/0022-006X.61.2.194

Beck, A.T., Steer, R.A., & Brown, G.K. (1996). *Manual for Beck Depression Inventory—II.* San Antonio, TX, US: Psychological Corporation.

Beevers, C.G., Wenzlaff, R.M., Hayes, A.M., & Scott, W.D. (1999). Depression and the ironic effects of thought suppression: Therapeutic strategies for improving mental control. *Clinical Psychology: Science and Practice, 6(2),* 133–148. doi: 10.1093/clipsy.6.2.133

Ben-Tovim, D.I., & Walker, M.K. (1991). The development of the Ben-Tovim Walker Body Attitudes Questionnaire (BAQ), a new measure of women's attitudes towards their own bodies. *Psychological Medicine, 21(3),* 775–784. doi: 10.1017/S0033291700022406

Ben-Tovim, D.I., Whitehead, J., & Crisp, A.J. (1979). A controlled study of the perception of body width in anorexia nervosa. *Journal of Psychosomatic Research, 23(4),* 267–272. doi: 10.1016/0022-3999(79)90029-1

Bernier, D., Bartha, R., Devarajan, S., MacMaster, F.P., Schmidt, M.H., & Rusak, B. (2009). Effects of overnight sleep restriction on brain chemistry and mood in women with unipolar depression and healthy controls. *Journal of Psychiatry and Neuroscience, 34(5),* 352–360.

Bernstein, K.S., Lee, J., Park, S., & Jyoung, J. (2008). Symptom manifestations and expressions among Korean immigrant women suffering with depression. *Journal of Advanced Nursing, 61(4),* 393–402. doi: 10.1111/j.1365-2648.2007.04533.x

Birgegard, A., Clinton, D., & Norring, C. (2013). Diagnostic issues of binge eating in eating disorders. *European Eating Disorders Review, 21(3),* 175–183. doi: 10.1002/erv.2227

Bizeul, C., Sadowsky, N., & Rigaud, D. (2001). The prognostic value of initial EDI scores in anorexia nervosa patients: A prospective follow-up study of 5-10 years. *European Psychiatry, 16(4),* 232–238. doi: 10.1016/S0924-9338(01)00570-3

Bodin, T., & Martinsen, E.W. (2004). Mood and self-efficacy during acute exercise in clinical depression. A randomized, controlled study. *Journal of Sport and Exercise Psychology, 26(4),* 623–633.

Bonifazi, D.Z., & Crowther, J.H. (1996). In vivo cognitive assessment in bulimia nervosa and restrained eating. *Behavior Therapy, 27(2),* 139–158. doi: 10.1016/S0005-7894(96)80011-6

Borkovec, T.D., Wilkinson, L., Folensbee, R., & Lerman, C. (1983). Stimulus control applications to the treatment of worry. *Behaviour Research and Therapy, 21(3),* 247–251. doi: 10.1016/0005-7967(83)90206-1

Bos, S.C., Soares, M.J., Marques, M., Maia, B., Pereira, A.T., Noguiera, V., Valente, J., & Macedo, A. (2013). Disordered eating behaviors and sleep disturbances. *Eating Behaviors, 14(2),* 192–198. doi: 10.1016/j.eatbeh.2013.01.012

Boutelle, K.N., Kirschenbaum, D.S., Baker, R.C., & Mitchell, M.E. (1999). How can obese weight controllers minimize weight gain during the high risk holiday season? By self-monitoring very consistently. *Health Psychology, 18(4),* 364–368. doi: 10.1037//0278-6133.18.4.364

Bowen, R., Balbuena, L., Baetz, M., & Schwartz, L. (2013). Maintaining sleep and physical activity alleviate mood instability. *Preventive Medicine, 57(5),* 461–465. doi: 10.1016/j.ypmed.2013.06.025

Braun, D.L., Sunday, S.R., Fornari, V.M., & Halmi, K.A. (1999). Bright light therapy decreases winter binge frequency in women with bulimia nervosa: A double-blind, placebo-controlled study. *Comprehensive Psychiatry, 40(6),* 442–448. doi: 10.1016/S0010-440X(99)90088-3

Brownstone, L.M., Bardone-Cone, A.M., Fitzsimmons-Craft, E.E., Printz, K.S., Le Grange, D., Mitchell, J.E., Crow, S.J., Peterson, C.B., Crosby, R.D., Klein, M.H., Wonderlich, S.A., & Joiner, T.E. (2012). Subjective and objective binge eating in relation to eating disorder symptomatology, negative affect, and personality dimensions. *International Journal of Eating Disorders, 46(1),* 66–76. doi: 10.1002/eat.22066

Brunstrom, J.M., Yates, H.M., & Witcomb, G.L. (2004). Dietary restraint and heightened reactivity to food. *Physiology and Behavior, 81(1),* 85–90. doi: 10.1016/S0195-6663(88)80018-7

Bulik, C., & Reichborn-Kjennerud, T. (2003). Medical morbidity in binge eating disorder. *International Journal of Eating Disorders, 34,* S39–S46. doi: 10.1002/eat.10204

Bulik, C., Sullivan, P.F., & Kendler, K.S. (2002). Medical and psychiatric morbidity in obese women with and without binge eating. *International Journal of Eating Disorders, 32(1),* 72–78. doi: 10.1002/eat.10072

Burke, L.E., & Dunbar-Jacob, J. (1995). Adherence to medication, diet, and activity recommendations: From assessment to maintenance. *Journal of Cardiovascular Nursing, 9(2)*, 62–79. doi: 10.1097/00005082-199501000-00007

Butler, A.C., Chapman, J.E., Forman, E.M., & Beck, A.T. (2006). The empirical status of cognitive-behavioral therapy: A review of meta-analyses. *Clinical Psychology Review, 26(1)*, 17–31. doi: 10.1016/j.cpr.2005.07.003

Butler, E.A., Egloff, B., Wilhelm, F.H., Smith, N.C., Erickson, E.A., & Gross, J.J. (2003). The social consequences of expressive suppression. *Emotion, 3(1)*, 48–67. doi: 10.1037/1528-3542.3.1.48

Butow, P., Beumont, P., & Touyz, S. (1993). An experimental study of the relationship between thoughts and eating behavior in bulimia nervosa. *Behaviour Research and Therapy, 31(8)*, 749–757. doi: 10.1016/0005-7967(93)90005-F

Cain, A.S., Bardone-Cone, A.M., Abramson, L.Y., Vohs, K.D., & Joiner, T.E. (2008). Refining the relationships of perfectionism, self-efficacy, and stress to dieting and binge eating: Examining the appearance, interpersonal, and academic domains. *International Journal of Eating Disorders, 41(8)*, 713–721. doi: 10.1002/eat.20563

Cain, A.S., Bardone-Cone, A.M., Abramson, L.Y., Vohs, K.D., & Joiner, T.E. (2010a). Prospectively predicting dietary restraint: The role of interpersonal self-efficacy, weight/shape self-efficacy, and interpersonal stress. *International Journal of Eating Disorders, 43(6)*, 505–512. doi: 10.1002/eat.20740

Cain, A.S., Epler, A.J., Steinley, D., & Sher, K. (2010b). Stability and change in patterns of concerns related to eating, weight, and shape in young adult women: A latent transition analysis. *Journal of Abnormal Psychology, 119(2)*, 255–267. doi: 10.1037/a0018117

Cain, A.S., Epler, A.J., Steinley, D., & Sher, K. J. (2012). Concerns related to eating, weight, and shape in young adult men: A latent transition analysis. *International Journal of Eating Disorders, 45(6)*, 768–775. doi: 10.1002/eat.20945

Carter, F.A., & Jansen, A. (2012). Improving psychological treatment for obesity. Which eating behaviours should we target? *Appetite, 58(3)*, 1063–1069. doi: 10.1016/j.appet.2012.01.016

Cash, T. (2008). *The body image workbook: An eight-step program for learning to like your looks, 2nd edition*. Oakland, CA, US: New Harbinger Publications.

Chartier, I.S., & Provencher, M.D. (2013). Behavioral activation for depression: Efficacy, effectiveness, and dissemination. *Journal of Affective Disorders, 145(3)*, 292–299. doi: 10.1016/j.jad.2012.07.023

Chentsova-Dutton, Y., & Dzokoto, V. (2014). Listen to your heart: The cultural shaping of interoceptive awareness and accuracy. *Emotion, 14(4)*, 666–678. doi: 10.1037/a0036193

Christensen, L. (1993). Effects of eating behavior on mood: A review of the literature. *International Journal of Eating Disorders, 14(2)*, 171–183. doi: 10.1002/1098-108X(199309)14:2<171::AID-EAT2260140207>3.0.CO;2-U

Clark, D.A., & Beck, A.T. (2010). Cognitive theory and therapy of anxiety and depression: Convergence with neurobiological findings. *Trends in Cognitive Sciences, 14(9)*, 418–424. doi: /10.1016/j.tics.2010.06.007

Cohrs, S., Rodenbeck, A., Riemann, D., Szagun, B., Jaehne, A., Brinkmeyer, J., Gründer, G., Wienker, T., Diaz-Lacava, A., Mobascher, A., Dahmen, N., Thuerauf, N., Kornhuber, J., Kiefer, F., Gallinat, J., Wagner, M., Kunz, D., Grittner, U., & Winterer, G. (2014). Impaired sleep quality and sleep duration in smokers—Results from the German Multicenter Study on Nicotine Dependence. *Addiction Biology, 19(3)*, 486–496. doi: 10.1111/j.1369-1600.2012.00487.x

Conn, V.S., Valentine, J.C., & Cooper, H.M. (2002). Interventions to increase physical activity among aging adults: A meta-analysis. *Annals of Behavioral Medicine, 24(3)*, 190–200. doi: 10.1093/geront/gnu090

Cooley, E., & Toray, T. (1996). Body image and personality predictors of eating disorder symptoms during the college years. *International Journal of Eating Disorders, 30(1)*, 28–36. doi: 10.1002/eat.1051

Cooley, E., & Toray, T. (2001). Disordered eating in college freshmen women: A prospective study. *Journal of American College Health, 49(5)*, 229–235. doi: 10.1080/07448480109596308

Cooper, J., Kapur, N., Webb, R., Lawlor, M., Guthrie, E., Mackway-Jones, K., & Appleby, L. (2005). Suicide after deliberate self-harm: A 4-year cohort study. *American Journal of Psychiatry, 162(2)*, 297–303. doi: 10.1176/appi.ajp.162.2.297

Courbasson, C., Nishikawa, Y., & Dixon, L. (2012). Outcome of dialectical behavior therapy for concurrent eating and substance use disorders. *Clinical Psychology and Psychotherapy, 19(5)*, 434–449. doi: 10.1002/cpp.748

Crisp, A.H., & Kalucy, S. (1974). Aspects of the perceptual disorder in anorexia nervosa. *Psychology and Psychotherapy: Theory, Research, and Practice, 47(4)*, 349–361. doi: 10.1111/j.2044-8341.1974.tb02300.x

Critchley, H.D., Wiens, S., Rotshtein, P., Ohman, A., & Dolan, R.J. (2004). Neural systems supporting interoceptive awareness. *Nature Neuroscience, 7(2)*, 189–195. doi: 10.1038/nn1176

Crow, S.J., Agras, W.S., Halmi, K., Mitchell, J.E., & Kraemer, H.C. (2002). Full syndromal versus subthreshold anorexia nervosa, bulimia nervosa, and binge eating disorder: A multicenter study. *International Journal of Eating Disorders, 32(3)*, 309–318. doi: 10.1002/eat.10088

Crow, S.J., Swanson, S.A., Peterson, C.B., Crosby, R.D., Wonderlich, S.A., & Mitchell, J.E. (2012). Latent class analysis of eating disorders: Relationship to mortality. *Journal of Abnormal Psychology, 121(1)*, 225–231. doi: 10.1037/a0024455

Dalle Grave, R., Calugi, S., & Marchesini, G. (2012). Objective and subjective binge eating in underweight eating disorders: Associated features and treatment. *International Journal of Eating Disorders, 45(3)*, 370–376. doi: 10.1002/eat.20943

Davis, C., Levitan, R.D., Kaplan, A.S., Carter, J., Reid, C., Curtis, C., Patte, K., Hwang, R., & Kennedy, J.L. (2008). Reward sensitivity and the D2 dopamine receptor gene: A case-control study of binge eating disorder. *Progress in Neuro-Psychopharmacology and Biological Psychiatry, 32(3)*, 620–628. doi: 10.1016/j.pnpbp.2007.09.024

Dechartes, A., Huas, C., Godart, N., Pousset, M., Pham, A., Divac, S.M., Rouillon, F., & Falissard, B. (2011). Outcomes of empirical eating disorder phenotypes in a clinical female sample: Results from a latent class analysis. *Psychopathology, 44(1)*, 12–20. doi: 10.1159/000315362

Delinsky, S.S., & Wilson, G.T. (2006). Mirror exposure for the treatment of body image disturbance. *International Journal of Eating Disorders, 39(2)*, 108–115. doi: 10.1002/eat.20207

Delinsky, S.S., & Wilson, G.T. (2010). Cognitive behavior therapy with body image exposure for bulimia nervosa: A case example. *Cognitive and Behavioral Practice, 17(3)*, 270–277. doi: 10.1016/j.cbpra.2010.02.004

de Zwaan, M., Mitchell, J.E., Seim, H.C., Specker, S.M., Pyle, R.L., Raymond, N.C., & Crosby, R.B. (1994). Eating related and general psychopathology in obese females with binge eating disorder. *International Journal of Eating Disorders, 15(1)*, 43–52. doi: 10.1002/1098-108X(199401)15:1<43::AID-EAT2260150106>3.0.CO;2-6

Diabetes Prevention Program Research Group. (2004). Achieving weight and activity goals among diabetes prevention program lifestyle participants. *Obesity Research, 12(9)*, 1426–1434. doi: 10.1038/oby.2004.179

Dimeff, L.A., & Linehan, M.M. (2008). Dialectical behavior therapy for substance abusers. *Addiction Science and Clinical Practice, 4(2)*, 39–47. doi: 10.1151/ascp084239

Dimidjian, S., Hollon, S.D., Dobson, K.S., Schmaling, K.B., Kohlenberg, R.J., Addis, M.E., Gallop, R., McGlinchey, J.B., Markley, D.K., Gollan, J.K., Atkins, D.C., Dunner, D.L., & Jacobson, N.S. (2006). Randomized trial of behavioral activation, cognitive therapy, and antidepressant medication in the acute treatment of adults with major depression. *Journal of Consulting and Clinical Psychology, 74(4)*, 658–670. doi: 10.1037/0022-006X.74.4.658

Dunn, B.D., Stefanovitch, I., Evans, D., Oliver, C., Hawkins, A., & Dalgleish, T. (2010). Can you feel the beat? Interoceptive awareness as an interactive function of anxiety- and depression-specific symptom dimensions. *Behaviour Research and Therapy, 48(11)*, 1133–1138. doi: 10.1016/j.brat.2010.07.006

Dzokoto, V. (2010). Different ways of feeling: Emotion and somatic awareness in Ghanaians and Euro-Americans. *Journal of Social, Evolutionary, and Cultural Psychology, 4(2)*, 68–78. doi: 10.1037/h0099299

Eddy, K.T., Dorer, D.J., Franko, D.L., Tahilani, K., Thompson-Brenner, H., & Herzog, D.B. (2008). Diagnostic crossover in anorexia nervosa and bulimia nervosa: Implications for DSM-5. *American Journal of Psychiatry, 165(2)*, 245–250. doi: 10.1176/appi.ajp.2007.07060951

Emborg, C. (1999). Mortality and causes of death in eating disorders in Denmark 1970-1993: A case register study. *International Journal of Eating Disorders, 25(3)*, 243–251. doi: 10.1002/(SICI)1098-108X(199904)25:3<243::AID-EAT1>3.0.CO;2-2

Erskine, J.A.K., & Georgiou, G.J. (2010). Effects of thought suppression on eating behavior in restrained and non-restrained eaters. *Appetite, 54(3)*, 499–503. doi: 10.1016/j.appet.2010.02.001

Fairburn, C.G. (1981). A cognitive behavioural approach to the treatment of eating bulimia. *Psychological Medicine, 11(4)*, 707–711. doi: 10.1017/S0033291700041209

Fairburn, C.G. (1983). Bulimia: Its epidemiology and management. *Psychiatric Annals, 13(12)*, 953–961.

Fairburn, C.G. (2008). *Cognitive behavior therapy and eating disorders*. New York, NY: Guilford.

Fairburn, C.G. (2013). *Overcoming binge eating, 2nd edition: The proven program to learn why you binge and how you can stop*. New York, NY: Guilford Press.

Fairburn, C.G., & Wilson, G.T. (1993). *Binge eating: Nature, assessment, and treatment*. New York, NY: Guilford Press.

Fairburn, C.G., Jones, R., Peveler, R.C., Hope, R.A., & O'Connor, M. (1993). Psychotherapy and bulimia nervosa: Longer-term effects of interpersonal psychotherapy, behavior therapy, and cognitive behavior therapy. *Archives of GeneralPsychiatry,50(6),*419–428.doi:10.1001/archpsyc.1993.01820180009001

Fairburn, C.G., Norman, P.A., Welch, S.L., O'Connor, M.E., Doll, H.E., & Peveler, R.C. (1995). A prospective study of outcome in bulimia nervosa and the long-term effects of three psychological treatments. *Archives of General Psychiatry, 52(4),* 304–312. doi: 10.1001/archpsyc.1995.03950160054010

Fairburn, C. G., Cooper, Z., & Shafran, R. (2003). Cognitive behaviour therapy for eating disorders: A transdiagnostic theory and treatment. *Behaviour Research and Therapy, 41(5),* 509–528. doi: 10.1016/S0005-7967(02)00088-8

Fairburn, C.G., Cooper, Z., Doll, H.A., O'Connor, M.E., Bohn, K., Hawker, D.M., Wales, J.A., & Palmer, R.L. (2009). Transdiagnostic cognitive-behavioral therapy for patients with eating disorders: A two-site trial with 60-week follow-up. *American Journal of Psychiatry, 166(3),* 311–319. doi: 10.1176/appi.ajp.2008.08040608

Fairburn, C.G., Bailey-Straebler, S., Basden, S., Doll, H.A., Jones, R., Murphy, R., O'Connor, M.E., & Cooper, Z. (2015). A transdiagnostic comparison of enhanced cognitive behavior therapy (CBT-E) and interpersonal psychotherapy in the treatment of eating disorders. *Behaviour Research and Therapy, 70,* 64–71. doi: 10.1016/j.brat.2015.04.010

Febbraro, G.A.R., & Clum, G.A. (1998). Meta-analytic investigation of the effectiveness of self-regulatory components in the treatment of adult behavior problems. *Clinical Psychology Review, 18(2),* 143–161. doi: 10.1016/ S0272-7358(97)00008-1

Feldman, G., Hayes, A., Kumar, S., Greeson, J., & Laurenceau, J. (2007). Mindfulness and Emotion Regulation: The Development and Initial Validation of the Cognitive and Affective Mindfulness Scale-Revised (CAMS-R). *Journal of Psychopathology & Behavioral Assessment, 29(3),* 177–190. doi: 10.1007/ s10862-006-9035-8

Foreyt, J.P., & Goodrick, G.K. (1991). Factors common to successful therapy for the obese patient. *Medicine and Science in Sport and Exercise, 23(3),* 292–297. doi: 10.1249/00005768-199103000-00005

Foreyt, J.P., & Poston, II, W.S.C. (1998). The role of the behavioral counselor in obesity treatment. *Journal of the American Dietetic Association, 98(suppl 2),* S27–S30. doi: 10.1016/S0002-8223(98)00707-X

Frank, E. (2007). Interpersonal and social rhythm therapy: A means of improving depression and preventing relapse in bipolar disorder. *Journal of Clinical Psychology, 63(5),* 463–473. doi: 10.1002/jclp.20371

Frank, E., Swartz, H.A., & Kupfer, D.J. (2000). Interpersonal and social rhythm therapy: Managing the chaos of bipolar disorder. *Biological Psychiatry, 48(6),* 593–604. doi: 10.1016/S0006-3223(00)00969-0

Franklin, J.S., Schiele, B., Brozek, J., & Keys, A. (1948). Observations on human behavior in experimental starvation and rehabilitation. *Journal of Clinical Psychology, 4(1),* 28–45. doi: 10.1002/1097-4679(194801)4:1<28::AID-JCLP2270040103>3.0.CO;2-F

Franko, D.L., & Zuroff, D.C. (1992). The Bulimic Automatic Thoughts Test: Initial reliability and validity data. *Journal of Clinical Psychology, 48(4),* 505–509. doi: 10.1002/1097-4679(199207)48:4<505::AID-JCLP2270480411>3.0.CO;2-B

Freiderich, H., Walther, S., Benszus, M., Biller, A., Thomann, P., Zeigermann, S., Katus, T., Brunner, R., Zastrow, A., & Herzog, W. (2012). Grey matter abnormalities within cortico-limbic-striatal circuits in acute and weight-restored anorexia nervosa patients. *NeuroImage, 59(2),* 1106–1113. doi: 10.1016/j.neuroimage.2011.09.042

Garner, D.M., Garfinkel, P.E., Stancer, H.C., & Moldofsky, H. (1976). Body image disturbances in anorexia nervosa and obesity. *Psychosomatic Medicine, 38(5),* 327–336. doi: 10.1097/00006842-197609000-00005

Garner, D.M., Olmsted, M.P., & Polivy, J. (1983). Development and validation of a multidimensional eating disorder inventory for anorexia nervosa and bulimia. *International Journal of Eating Disorders, 2(2),* 15–34. doi: 10.1002/1098-108X(198321)2:215::AID-EAT22600202033.0.CO;2-6

Giedke, H., & Schwarzler, F. (2002). Therapeutic use of sleep deprivation. *Sleep Medicine Reviews, 6(5),* 361–377. doi: 10.1053/smrv.2002.0235

Gillin, J.C., Buchsbaum, M., Wu, J., Clark, C., & Bunney, W. (2001). Sleep deprivation as a model experimental antidepressant treatment: Findings from functional brain imaging. *Depression and Anxiety, 14(1),* 37–49. doi: 10.1002/da.1045

Giuliano, R.J., & Wicha, N.Y.Y. (2010). Why the white bear is still there: Electrophysiological evidence for ironic semantic activation during thought suppression. *Brain Research, 1316,* 62–74. doi: 10.1016/j.brainres.2009.12.041

Gleaves, D.H., Williamson, D.A., & Baker, S.E. (1993). Additive effects of mood and eating forbidden foods upon the perceptions of overeating and bingeing in bulimia nervosa. *Addictive Behaviors, 18(3),* 299–309. doi: 10.1016/0306-4603

Glynn, S.M., & Ruderman, A.J. (1986). The development and validation of an Eating Self-Efficacy Scale. *Cognitive Therapy and Research, 10(4),* 403–420. doi: 10.1007/BF01173294

Goldfield, G.S., Adamo, K.B., Rutherford, J., & Legg, C. (2008). Stress and the relative reinforcing value of food in female binge eaters. *Physiology & Behavior, 93(3),* 579–587. doi: 10.1016/j.physbeh.2007.10.022

Gormally, J., & Rardin, D. (1981). Weight loss and maintenance and changes in diet and exercise for behavioral counseling and nutrition education. *Journal of Counseling Psychology, 28(4),* 295–304. doi: 10.1037/0022-0167.28.4.295

Gormally, J., Black, S., Daston, S., & Rardin, D. (1982). The assessment of binge eating severity among obese persons. *Addictive Behaviors, 7(1),* 47–55. doi: 10.1016/0306-4603(82)90024-7

Halmi, K.A., Agras, W.S., Mitchell, J., Wilson, G.T., Crow, S., Byson, S.W., & Kraemer, H. (2002). Relapse predictors of patients with bulimia nervosa who achieved abstinence through cognitive behavioral therapy. *Archives of General Psychiatry, 59(12),* 1105–1109. doi: 10.1001/archpsyc.59.12.1105

Harnden, J.L., McNally, R.J., & Jimerson, D.C. (1997). Effects of suppressing thoughts about body weight: A comparison of dieters and nondieters. *International Journal of Eating Disorders, 14(3),* 319–329. doi: 10.1002/(SICI)1098-108X(199711)22:3<285::AID-EAT7>3.0.CO;2-J

Hart, S., Abraham, S., Franklin, R.C., & Russell, J. (2011). The reasons why eating disorder patients drink. *European Eating Disorders Review, 19(2),* 121–128. doi: 10.1002/erv.1051

Harvey, A.G., Belanger, L., Talbot, L., Eidelman, P., Beaulieu-Bonneua, S., Fortier-Brochu, E., Ivers, H., Lamy, M., Hein, K., Soehner, A.M., Mérette, C., & Morin, C.M. (2014). Comparative efficacy of behavior therapy, cognitive therapy, and cognitive behavior therapy for chronic insomnia: A randomized controlled trial. *Journal of Consulting and Clinical Psychology, 82(4)*, 670–683. doi: 10.1037/a0036606

Hausenblas, H.A., & Fallon, E.A. (2006). Exercise and body image: A meta-analysis. *Psychology and Health, 21(1)*, 33–47. doi:10.1080/14768320500105270

Heatherton, T.F., & Baumeister, R.F. (1991). Binge eating as an escape from self-awareness. *Psychological Bulletin, 110(1)*, 86–108. doi: 10.1037/0033-2909.110.1.86

Heatherton, T.F., & Polivy, J. (1992). Chronic dieting and eating disorders: A spiral model. In J.H. Crowther, D.L. Tennenbaum, S.E. Hobfoll, & M.A.P. Stephens (Eds.), *The etiology of bulimia nervosa: The individual and family context* (pp. 133–155). Washington D.C.: Hemisphere Publishing Corp.

Hepworth, N.S. (2010). A mindful eating group as an adjunct to individual treatment for eating disorders: A pilot study. *Eating Disorders: The Journal of Treatment and Prevention, 19(1)*, 6–16. doi: 10.1080/10640266.2011.533601

Hickford, C.A., Ward, T., & Bulik, C.M. (1997). Cognitions of restrained and unrestrained eaters under fasting and nonfasting conditions. *Behaviour Research and Therapy, 35(1)*, 71–75. doi: 10.1016/S0005-7967(96)00056-3

Hilbert, A., Tuschen-Caffier, B., & Vogele, C. (2002). Effects of prolonged and repeated body image exposure in binge-eating disorder. *Journal of Psychosomatic Research, 52(3)*, 137–144. doi: 10.1016/S0022-3999(01)00314-2

Hilbert, A., Bishop, M., Stein, R., Tanofsky-Kraff, M., Swenson, A.K., Welch, R.R., & Wilfley, D.E. (2012). Long-term efficacy of psychological treatments for binge eating disorder. *British Journal of Psychiatry, 200(3)*, 232–237. doi: 10.1192/bjp.bp.110.089664

Hoek, H.W. (2006). Incidence, prevalence, and mortality of anorexia nervosa and other eating disorders. *Current Opinion in Psychiatry, 19(4)*, 389–394. doi: 10.1097/01.yco.0000228759.95237.78

Hofmann, S.F., Asnaani, A., Vonk, I.J.J., Sawyer, A.T., & Fang, A. (2012). The efficacy of cognitive behavioral therapy: A review of meta-analyses. *Cognitive Therapy and Research, 36(5)*, 427–440. doi: 10.1007/s10608-012-9476-1

Hohlstein, L.A., Smith, G.T., & Atlas, J.G. (1998). An application of expectancy theory to eating disorders: Development and validation of measures of eating and dieting expectancies. *Psychological Assessment, 10(1)*, 49–58. doi: 10.1037/1040-3590.10.1.49

Hoyer, J., Beesdo, K., Gloster, A.T., Runge, J., Hofler, M., & Becker, E.S. (2009). Worry exposure versus applied relaxation in the treatment of generalized anxiety disorder. *Psychotherapy and Psychosomatics, 78(2)*, 106–115. doi: 10.1159/000201936

Jansen, A., Bollen, D., Tuschen-Caffier, B., Roefs, A., Tanghe, A., & Braet, C. (2008). Mirror exposure reduces body dissatisfaction and anxiety in obese adolescents: A pilot study. *Appetite, 51(1)*, 214–217. doi: 10.1016/j.appet.2008.01.011

Jeffrey, R.W., Vender, M., & Wing, R.R. (1978). Weight loss and behavior change one year after behavioral treatment for obesity. *Journal of Consulting and Clinical Psychology, 46(2)*, 368–369. doi: 10.1037/0022-006X.46.2.368

Jessen, A., Buemann, B., Toubro, S., Skovgaard, M., & Astrup, A. (2005). The appetite suppressant effect of nicotine is enhanced by caffeine. *Diabetes, Obesity, and Metabolism, 7(4)*, 327–333. doi: 10.1111/j.1463-1326.2004.00389.x

Johnson, J.G., Spitzer, R.L., & Williams, J.B. (2001). Health problems, impairment and illnesses associated with bulimia nervosa and binge eating disorder among primary care and obstetric gynaecology patients. *Psychological Medicine, 31(8),* 1455–1466. doi: 10.1017/S0033291701004640

Jorgensen, J. (1992). The epidemiology of eating disorders in Fyn County Denmark, 1977–1986. *Acta Psychiatrica Scandinavica, 85(1),* 30–34. doi: 10.1111/j.1600-0447.1992.tb01438.x

Kerzhnerman, I., & Lowe, M.R. (2002). Correlates of subjective and objective binge eating in binge-purge syndromes. *International Journal of Eating Disorders, 31(2),* 220–228. doi: 10.1002/eat.l0026

Key, A., George, C.L., Beattie, D., Stammers, K., Lacey, H., & Waller, G. (2002). Body image treatment within an inpatient program for anorexia nervosa: The role of mirror exposure in the desensitization process. *International Journal of Eating Disorders, 31(2),* 185–190. doi: 10.1002/eat.10027

Kirkley, B.G., Burge, J.C., & Ammerman, A. (1988). Dietary restraint, binge eating, and dietary patterns. *International Journal of Eating Disorders,* 7(6), 771–778. doi: 10.1002/1098-108X(198811)7:6<771::AID-EAT2260070606>3.0.CO;2-F

Kirschenbaum, D.S., & Wittrock, D.A. (1984). Cognitive-behavioral interventions in sport: A self-regulatory perspective. In J.M. Silva & R.S. Weiberg (Eds.), *Psychological foundations of sport* (pp. 81–90). Champaign, IL, US: Human Kinetics.

Klabunde, M., Acheson, D.T., Boutelle, K.N., Matthews, S.C., & Kaye, W.H. (2013). Interoceptive sensitivity deficits in women recovered from bulimia nervosa. *Eating Behaviors, 14(4),* 488–492. doi: 10.1016/j.eatbeh.2013.08.002

Klajner, F., Herman, C.P., Polivy, J., & Chhanbra, R. (1981). Human obesity, dieting, and anticipatory salivation to food. *Physiology and Behavior, 27(2),* 195–198. doi: 10.1016/0031-9384(81)90256-0

Klein, A.S., Skinner, J.B., & Hawley, K.M. (2012). Adapted group-based dialectical behaviour therapy for binge eating in a practicing clinic: Clinical outcomes and attrition. *European Eating Disorders Review, 20(3),* e148–53. doi: 10.1002/erv.2165

Klein, A.S., Skinner, J.B., & Hawley, K.M. (2013). Targeting binge eating through components of dialectical behavior therapy: Preliminary outcomes for individually supported diary card self-monitoring versus group-based DBT. *Psychotherapy, 50(4),* 543–552. doi: 10.1037/a0033130.

Kristeller, J., Wolever, R.Q., & Sheets, V. (2014). Mindfulness-based eating awareness training for binge eating: A randomized clinical trial. *Mindfulness, 5(3),* 282–297. doi: 10.1007/s12671-012-0179-1

Lamm, C., & Singer, T. (2010). The role of anterior insular cortex in social emotions. *Brain Structure and Function, 214(5-6),* 579–591. doi: 10.1007/s00429-010-0251-3

Lane, B., & Szabo, M. (2013). Uncontrolled, repetitive eating of small amounts of food or 'grazing': Development and evaluation of a new measure of atypical eating. *Behaviour Change, 30(2),* 57–73. doi: 10.1017/bec.2013.6

Laurenceau, J., Barrett, L.F., & Pietromonaco, P.R. (1998). Intimacy as an interpersonal process: The importance of self-disclosure, partner disclosure, and perceived partner responsiveness in interpersonal exchanges. *Journal of Personality and Social Psychology, 74(5),* 1238–1251. doi: 10.1037/0022-3514.74.5.1238

Lavagnino, L., Amianto, F., D'Agata, F., Huang, Z., Mortara, P., Abbate-Daga, G., Marzola, E., Spalatro, A., Fassino, S., & Northoff, G. (2014). Reduced resting-state functional connectivity of the somatosensory cortex predicts psychopathological symptoms in women with bulimia nervosa. *Frontiers in Behavioral Neuroscience, 8(270)*. doi: 10.3389/fnbeh.2014.00270

Leary, M.R., Adams, C.E., & Tate, E.B. (2006). Hypo-egoic self-regulation: Exercising self-control by diminishing the influence of the self. *Journal of Personality, 74(6)*, 1803–1832. doi: 10.1111/j.1467-6494.2006.00429.x

Leermakers, E.A., Auglin, K., & Wing, R.R. (1998). Reducing postpartum weight retention through a correspondence intervention. *International Journal of Obesity, 22(11)*, 1103–1109. doi: 10.1038/sj.ijo.0800734

Le Grange, D., Binford, R., Peterson, C., Crow, S., Crosby, R., Klein, M., Bardone-Cone, A.M., Joiner, T.E., Mitchell, J.E., & Wonderlich, S. (2006). DSM-IV threshold versus subthreshold bulimia nervosa. *International Journal of Eating Disorders, 39(6)*, 462–467. doi: 10.1002/eat.20304

LeGoff, D.B., Leichner, P., & Spigelman, M.N. (1988). Salivary response to olfactory food stimuli in anorexics and bulimics. *Appetite, 11(1)*, 15–25. doi: 10.1016/S0195-6663(88)80018-7

Leon, G.R., Fulkerson, J.A., Perry, C.L., & Early-Zald, M.B. (1995). Prospective analysis of personality and behavioral vulnerabilities and gender influences in the later development of disordered eating. *Journal of Abnormal Psychology, 104(1)*, 140–149. doi: 10.1037/0021-843X.104.1.140

Lilenfeld, L.R.R, Wonderlich, S., Riso, L.P., Crosby, R., & Mitchell, J. (2006). Eating disorders and personality: A methodological and empirical review. *Clinical Psychology Review, 26(3)*, 299–320. doi: 10.1016/j.cpr.2005.10.003

Lin, M., Tai, L.Y., & Fan, S.Y. (2014). Breathing at a rate of 5.5 breaths per minute with equal inhalation-to-exhalation ratio increases heart rate variability. *International Journal of Psychophysiology, 91(3)*, 206–211. doi: 10.1016/j.ijpsycho.2013.12.006

Linehan, M.M. (1993). *Skills training manual for treating borderline personality disorder, 1st edition*. New York, NY: Guilford Press.

Linehan, M.M. (2014a). *DBT skills training handouts and worksheets, 2nd edition*. New York, NY: Guilford Press.

Linehan, M.M. (2014b). *DBT skills training manual, 2nd edition*. New York, NY: Guilford Press.

Lingswiler, V.M., Crowther, J.H., & Stephens, M.A.P. (1989). Affective and cognitive antecedents to eating episodes in bulimia and binge eating. *International Journal of Eating Disorders, 8(5)*, 533–539. doi: 10.1002/1098-108X(198909)8:5<533::AID-EAT2260080505>3.0.CO;2-O

Lock, J., & Le Grange, D. (2012). *Treatment manual for anorexia nervosa: A family-based approach (2nd edition)*. New York, NY: Guilford Press.

Lock, J., Garrett, A., Beenhakker, J., & Reiss, A.L. (2011). Aberrant brain activation during a response inhibition task in adolescent eating disorder subtypes. *American Journal of Psychiatry, 168(1)*, 55–64. doi: 10.1176/appi.ajp.2010.10010056

Loeb, K.L., & Le Grange, D. (2009). Family-based treatment for adolescent eating disorders: Current status, new applications, and future directions. *International Journal of Child and Adolescent Health, 2(2)*, 243–253.

Longmore, R.J., & Worrell, M. (2007). Do we need to challenge thoughts in cognitive behavior therapy? *Clinical Psychology Review, 27(2)*, 173–187. doi: 10.1016/j.cpr.2006.08.001

Lowe, M.R., Butryn, M.L., Didie, E.R., Annunziato, R.A., Thomas, J.G., Crerand, C.E., Ochner, C.N., Coletta, M.C., Bellace, D., Wallaert, M., & Halford, J. (2009). The Power of Food Scale: A new measure of the psychological influence of the food environment. *Appetite, 53(1)*, 114–118. doi: 10.1016/j.appet.2009.05.016

Lynch, T.R., Gray, K.L., Hempel, R.J., Titley, M., Chen, E., & O'Mahen, H.A. (2013). Radically open-dialectical behavior therapy for adult anorexia nervosa: Feasibility and outcomes from an inpatient program. *BMC Psychiatry, 13(7)*, 293. doi: 10.1186/1471-244X-13-293.

Lynch, W.C., Everingham, A., Dubitzky, J., Hartman, M., & Kasser, T. (2000). Does binge eating play a role in the self-regulation of moods? *Integrative Physiological and Behavioral Science, 35(4)*, 298–313. doi: 10.1007/BF02688792

MacBrayer, E.K., Smith, G.T., McCarthy, D.M., Demos, S., & Simmons, J. (2002). The role of family of origin food-related experiences in bulimic symptomatology. *International Journal of Eating Disorders, 30(2)*, 149–160. doi: 10.1002/eat.1067

McCallie, M.S., Blum, C.M., & Hood, C.J. (2006). Progressive muscle relaxation. *Journal of Human Behavior in the Social Environment, 13(6)*, 51–66. doi: 10.1300/J137v13n03_04

McGranahan, D.V. (1940). A critical and experimental study of repression. *Journal of Abnormal and Social Psychology, 35(2)*, 212–225. doi: 10.1037/h0053798

McMain, S., Sayrs, J.H.R., Dimeff, L.A., & Linehan, M.M. (2007). Dialectical behavior therapy for individuals with borderline personality disorder and substance dependence. In A.L. Dimeff & K. Koerner (Eds.), *Dialectical behavior therapy in clinical practice: Applications across disorders and settings* (pp. 145–173). New York, NY: Guilford Press.

Madsen, J., Sallis, J.F., Rupp, J.W., Senn, K.L., Patterson, T.L., Atkins, C.J., & Nader, P.R. (1993). Relationship between self-monitoring of diet and exercise change and subsequent risk factor changes in children and adults. *Patient Education and Counseling, 21(1-2)*, 61–69. doi: 10.1016/0738-3991(93)90060-A

Marcos, Y.Q., Sebastian, M.J.Q., Aubalat, L.P., Ausina, J.B., & Treasure, J. (2013). Peer and family influence in eating disorders: A meta-analysis. *European Psychiatry, 28(4)*, 199–206. doi: 10.1016/j.eurpsy.2012.03.005

Martin, C.K., Williamson, D.A., & Thaw, J.M. (2000). Criterion validity of the multiaxial assessment of eating disorders symptoms. *International Journal of Eating Disorders, 28(3)*, 303–310. doi: 10.1002/1098-108X(200011)28:3<303::AID-EAT7>3.0.CO;2-I

Masheb, R.M., & Grilo, C.M. (2006). Emotional overeating and its associations with eating disorder psychopathology among overweight patients with Binge Eating Disorder. *International Journal of Eating Disorders, 39(2)*, 141–146. doi: 10.1002/eat.20221

Mathes, W.F., Brownley, K.A., Mo, X., & Bulik, C.M. (2009). The biology of binge eating. *Appetite, 52(3)*, 545–554. doi: 10.1016/j.appet.2009.03.005

Matsumoto, R., Kitabayashi, Y., Narumoto, J., Wada, Y., Okamoto, A., Ushijuma, Y., Yokoyama, C., Yamashita, T., Takahashi, H., Yasuno, F., Suhara, T., & Fukui, K. (2006). Regional cerebral blood flow changes associated with interoceptive awareness in the recovery process of anorexia nervosa. *Progress in Neuro-Psychopharmacology and Biological Psychiatry, 30(7)*, 1265–1270. doi: :10.1016/j.pnpbp.2006.03.042

Miklowitz, D.J., Goodwin, G.M., Bauer, M.S., & Geddes, J.R. (2008). Common and specific elements of psychosocial treatments for bipolar disorder: A survey of clinicians participating in randomized trials. *Journal of Psychiatric Practice, 14(2)*, 77–85. doi: 10.1097/01.pra.0000314314.94791.c9

Mitchell, J.E., Halmi, K., Wilson, G.T., Agras, W.S., Kraemer, H., & Crow, S. (2002). A randomized secondary treatment study of women with bulimia nervosa who fail to respond to CBT. *International Journal of Eating Disorders, 32(3)*, 271–281. doi: 10.1002/eat.10092

Mitchell, J.P., Heatherton, T.F., Kelley, W.M., Wyland, C.L., Wegner, D.M., & Macrae, C.N. (2007). Separating sustained from transient aspects of cognitive control during thought suppression. *Psychological Science, 18*, 292–297. doi: 10.1111/j.1467-9280.2007.01891.x

Muhlau, M., Gaser, C., Ilg, R., Conrad, B., Leibl, C., Cebulla, M.H., Backmund, H., Gerlinghoff, M., Lommer, P., Schnebel, A., Wohlschläger, A.M., Zimmer, C., & Nunnemann, S. (2007). Gray matter decrease of the anterior cingulate cortex in anorexia nervosa. *American Journal of Psychiatry, 164(12)*, 1850–1857. doi: 10.1176/appi.ajp.2007.06111861

Murphy, R., Straebler, S., Basden, S., Cooper, Z., & Fairburn, C.G. (2012). Interpersonal psychotherapy for eating disorders. *Clinical Psychology and Psychotherapy, 19(2)*, 150–158. doi: 10.1002/cpp.1780

Murray, G., Suto, M., Hole, R., Hale, S., Amari, E., & Michalak, E.E. (2011). Self-management strategies used by "high functioning" individuals with bipolar disorder: From research to clinical practice. *Clinical Psychology and Psychotherapy, 18(2)*, 95–109. doi: 10.1002/cpp.710

Myers, T.A., & Crowther, J.H. (2008). Is self-objectification related to interoceptive awareness? An examination of potential mediating pathways to disordered eating attitudes. *Psychology of Women Quarterly, 32(2)*, 172–180. doi: 10.1111/j.1471-6402.2008.00421.x

Najmi, S., & Wegner, D.M. (2008). The gravity of unwanted thoughts: Asymmetric priming effects in thought suppression. *Consciousness and Cognition, 17(1)*, 114–124. doi: 10.1016/j.concog.2007.01.006

Nakamura, J., & Csikszentmihalyi, M. (2002). The concept of flow. In *Handbook of positive psychology* (pp. 89–105). New York, NY: Oxford University Press.

Neumarker, K. (2000). Mortality rates and causes of death. *European Eating Disorders Review, 8(2)*, 181–187. doi: 10.1002/(SICI)1099-0968(200003)8:2 <181::AID-ERV336>3.0.CO;2-#

Newman, L.F., Duff, K., & Baumeister, R.F. (1997). A new look at defensive projection: Thought suppression, accessibility, and biased person perception. *Journal of Personality and Social Psychology, 72(5)*, 980–1001. doi: 10.1037/0022-3514.72.5.980

Nielsen, S., Moller-Madsen, S., Isager, T., Jorgensen, J., Pagsberg, K., & Theander, S. (1998). Standardized mortality in eating disorders—A quantitative summary of previously published and new evidence. *Journal of Psychosomatic Research, 44(3/4)*, 413–434. doi: 10.1016/S0022-3999(97)00267-5

O'Neill, S.E., Parra, G.R., & Sher, K.J. (2001). Clinical relevance of heavy drinking during the college years: Cross-sectional and prospective perspectives. *Psychology of Addictive Behaviors, 15(4)*, 350–359. doi: 10.1037//0893-164X.15.4.350

Owens, D., Horrocks, J., & House, A. (2002). Fatal and non-fatal repetition of self-harm. *British Journal of Psychiatry, 181(3),* 193–199. doi: 10.1192/bjp.181.3.193

Page, A.C., Locke, V., & Trio, M. (2005). An online measure of thought suppression. *Journal of Personality and Social Psychology, 88(3),* 421–431. doi: 10.1037/0022-3514.88.3.421

Page, H.A. (1955). The facilitation of experimental extinction by response prevention as a function of the acquisition of a new response. *Journal of Comparative and Physiological Psychology, 48(1),* 14–16. doi: 10.1037/h0042718

Page, H.A., & Hall, J.F. (1953). Experimental extinction as a function of the prevention of a response. *Journal of Comparative and Physiological Psychology, 46(1),* 33–34. doi: 10.1037/h0042718

Pagoto, S., Bodenlos, J.S., Schneider, K.L., Olendzki, B., & Spates, C.R. (2008). Initial investigation of behavioral activation therapy for co-morbid major depressive disorder and obesity. *Psychotherapy: Theory, Research, Practice, and Training, 45(3),* 410–415. doi: 10.1037/a001331

Papini, M.R., Fuchs, P.N., & Torres, C. (2015). Behavioral neuroscience of psychological pain. *Neuroscience and Biobehavioral Reviews, 48,* 53–69. doi: 10.1016/j.neubiorev.2014.11.012

Peat, C.M., & Muehlenkamp, J.J. (2011). Self-objectification, disordered eating, and depression: A test of mediational pathways. *Psychology of Women Quarterly, 35(3),* 441–450. doi: 10.1177/0361684311400389

Peterson, C.B., Crow, S.J., Swanson, S.A., Crosby, R.D., Wonderlich, S.A., Mitchell, J.E., Agras, W.S., & Halmi, K.A. (2011). Examining the stability of DSM-IV and empirically derived eating disorder classification: Implications for DSM-V. *Journal of Consulting and Clinical Psychology, 79(6),* 777–783. doi: 10.1037/a0025941

Pickett, K., Yardley, L., & Kendrick, T. (2012). Physical activity and depression: A multiple mediation analysis. *Mental Health and Physical Activity, 5(2),* 125–134. doi: 10.1016/j.mhpa.2012.10.001

Pierloot, R.A., & Houben, M.E. (1978). Estimation of body dimensions in anorexia nervosa. *Psychological Medicine, 8(2),* 317–324. doi: 10.1017/S0033291700014367

Pinhiero, A.P., Thornton, L.M., Plotonicov, K.H., Tozzi, F., Klump, K.L., Berrettini, W.D., Brandt, H., Crawford, S., Crow, S., Fichter, M.M., Goldman, D., Halmi, K.A., Johnson, C., Kaplan, A.S., Keel, P., LaVia, M., Mitchell, J., Rotondo, A., Strober, M., Treasure, J., Woodside, D.B., Von Holle, A., Hamer, R., Kaye, W.H., & Bulik, C.M. (2007). Patterns of menstruation disturbance in eating disorders. *International Journal of Eating Disorders, 40(5),* 424–434. doi: 10.1002/eat.20388

Pinniger, R., Thorsteinsson, E.B., Brown, R.F., & McKinley, P. (2013). Tango dance can reduce distress and insomnia in people with self-referred affective symptoms. *American Journal of Dance Therapy, 3(1),* 60–77. doi: 10.1007/s10465-012-9141-y

Pisetsky, E.M., Chao, Y.M., Dierker, L.C., May, A.M., & Striegel-Moore, R.H. (2008). Disordered eating and substance use in high-school students: Results from the Youth Risk Behavior Surveillance System. *International Journal of Eating Disorders, 41(5),* 464–470. doi: 10.1002/eat.20520

Plante, T.G., Gores, C., Brecht, C., Carrow, J., Imbs, A., & Willensen, E. (2007). Does exercise environment enhance the psychological benefits of exercise for women? *International Journal of Stress Management, 14(1),* 88–98. doi: 10.1037/1072-5245.14.1.88

Polivy, J. (1976). Perception of calories and regulation of intake in restrained and unrestrained subjects. *Addictive Behaviors, 1(3),* 237–243. doi: 10.1016/0306-4603(76)90016-2

Polivy, J., & Herman, C.P. (1985). Dieting and bingeing: A causal analysis. *American Psychologist, 40(2),* 193–201. doi: 10.1037/0003-066X.40.2.193

Polivy, J., Herman, C.P., Olmsted, M.P., & Jazwinski, C. (1984). Restraint and binge eating. In R.C. Hawkins, W.J. Fremouw, & P.F. Clement (Eds), *The binge-purge syndrome: Diagnosis, treatment, and research* (pp. 104–122). New York, NY: Springer.

Polivy, J., Coleman, J., & Herman, C.P. (2005). The effect of deprivation on food cravings and eating behavior in restrained and unrestrained eaters. *International Journal of Eating Disorders, 38(4),* 301–309. doi: 10.1002/eat.20195

Pollatos, O., Traut-Mattausch, E., Schroeder, H., & Schandry, R. (2007). Interoceptive awareness mediates the relationship between anxiety and the intensity of unpleasant feelings. *Journal of Anxiety Disorders, 21(7),* 931–943. doi: 10.1016/j.janxdis.2006.12.004

Pollatos, O., Kurz, A., Albrecht, J., Schreder, T., Kleemann, A.M., Schopf, V., Kopietz, R., Wiesmann, M., & Schandry, R. (2008). Reduced perception of bodily signals in anorexia nervosa. *Eating Behaviors, 9(4),* 381–388. doi: 10.1016/j.eatbeh.2008.02.001

Pollatos, O., Herbert, B.M., Wankner, S., Dietel, A., Wachsmuth, C., Henningsen, P., & Sack, M. (2011). Autonomic imbalance is associated with reduced facial recognition in somatoform disorders. *Journal of Psychosomatic Research, 71(4),* 232–239. doi: 10.1016/j.jpsychores.2011.03.012

Prakash, S., Ravindra, P.N., Madanmohan, Anilkumar, R., & Balachander, J. (2006). Effect of breathing at six breaths per minute on the frequency of premature ventricular complexes. *International Journal of Cardiology, 111(3),* 450–452. doi: 10.1016/j.ijcard.2005.05.075

Prendergast, M., Podus, D., Finney, J., Greenwell, L., & Roll, J. (2006). Contingency management for treatment of substance use disorders: A meta-analysis. *Addiction, 101(11),* 1546–1560. doi: 10.1111/j.1360-0443.2006.01581.x

Price, K.P. (1974). The application of behavior therapy to the treatment of psychosomatic disorders: Retrospect and prospect. *Psychotherapy: Theory, Research, and Practice, 11(2),* 138–155. doi: 10.1037/h0086329

Proulx, K. (2008). Experiences of women with bulimia nervosa in a mindfulness-based eating disorder treatment group. *Eating Disorders: The Journal of Treatment and Prevention, 16(1),* 52–72. doi: 10.1080/10640260701773496

Putilov, A.A., & Danilenko, K.V. (2005). Antidepressant effects of light therapy and "natural" treatments for winter depression. *Biological Rhythm Research, 36(5),* 423–437. doi: 10.1080/09291010500218506

Rada, P., Avena, N.M., & Hoebel, B.G. (2005). Daily bingeing on sugar repeatedly releases dopamine in the accumbens shell. *Neuroscience, 134(3),* 737–744. doi: 10.1016/j.neuroscience.2005.04.043

Rassin, E. (2005). *Thought suppression.* New York, NY: Elsevier.

Reichborn-Kjennerud, T., Bulik, C.M., Sullivan, P.F., Tambs, K., & Harris, J.R. (2004). Psychiatric and medical symptoms in binge eating in the absence of compensatory behaviors. *Obesity Research, 12(9),* 1445–1454. doi: 10.1038/oby.2004.181

Rezek, P.J., & Leary, M.R. (1991). Perceived control, drive for thinness, and food consumption: Anorexic tendencies as displaced reactance. *Journal of Personality, 59(1),* 129–143. doi: 10.1111/j.1467-6494.1991.tb00771.x

Ricca, V., Mannucci, E., Mezzani, B., di Bernardo, M., Zucchi, T., Paionni, A., Placidi, G.P., Rotella, C.M., & Faravelli, C. (2001). Psychopathological and clinical features of outpatients with eating disorder not otherwise specified. *Eating and Weight Disorders, 6(3),* 157–165. doi: 10.1007/BF03339765

Ritschel, L.A., Lim, N.E, & Stewart, L.M. (2015). Transdiagnostic application of DBT for adolescents and adults. *American Journal of Psychotherapy, 69(2),* 111–128.

Roehrs, T., & Roth, T. (2001). Sleep, sleepiness, and alcohol use. *Alcohol Research and Health, 25(2),* 101–109. doi: 10.1053/smrv.2001.0162

Roehrs, T., & Roth, T. (2008). Caffeine: Sleep and daytime sleepiness. *Sleep Medicine Reviews, 12(2),* 153–162. doi: 10.1016/j.smrv.2007.07.004

Rosen, J.C. (1997). Cognitive behavioral body image therapy. In D.M. Garner, & P. Garfinkel (Eds.), *Handbook of treatment for eating disorders* (pp. 188–204). New York, NY: Guilford Press.

Rosenberg, M. (1979). *Conceiving the self.* New York, NY: Basic Books.

Saunders, R. (1999). Binge eating in gastric bypass patients before surgery. *Obesity Surgery, 9(1),* 72–76. doi: 10.1381/096089299765553845

Saunders, R. (2004). 'Grazing': A high-risk behavior. *Obesity Surgery, 14(1),* 98–102. doi: 10.1381/096089204772787374

Schienle, A., Schafer, A., Hermann, A., & Vaitl, D. (2009). Binge-eating disorder: Reward sensitivity and brain activation to images of food. *Biological Psychiatry, 65(8),* 654–661. doi: 10.1016/j.biopsych.2008.09.028

Sears, R.R. (1943). *Survey of objective studies of psychoanalytic concepts.* New York, NY: Social Science Research Council.

Shackelford, S., Wegner, D.M., & Schneider, D.J. (1987). The effect of reporting technique on thought suppression. Unpublished raw data.

Shafran, R., & Fairburn, C.G. (2002). A new ecologically valid method to assess body size estimation and body size dissatisfaction. *International Journal of Eating Disorders, 32(4),* 458–465. doi: 10.1002/eat.10097

Shiba, Y., Nitta, E., Hirono, C., Sugita, M. & Iwassa, Y. (2002). Evaluation of mastication-induced change in sympatho-vagal balance through spectral analysis of heart rate variability. *Journal of Oral Rehabilitation, 29(10),* 956–960. doi: 10.1046/j.1365-2842.2002.00964.x

Shomaker, L.B., Tanofsky-Kraff, M., Elliott, C., Wolkoff, L.E., Columbo, K.M., Ranzenhofer, L.M., Roza, C.A., Yanovski, S.Z., & Yanovski, J.A. (2010). Salience of loss of control for pediatric binge episodes: Does size really matter? *International Journal of Eating Disorders, 43(8),* 707–716. doi: 10.1002/eat.20767

Sim, L., & Zeman, J. (2004). Emotion awareness and identification skills in adolescent girls with bulimia nervosa. *Journal of Clinical Child and Adolescent Psychology, 33(4),* 760–771. doi: 10.1207/s15374424jccp3304_11

Soetens, B., & Braet, C. (2006). 'The weight of a thought': Food-related thought suppression in obese and normal-weight youngsters. *Appetite, 46(3),* 309–317. doi: 10.1016/j.appet.2006.01.018

Soetens, B., Braet, C., & Moens, E. (2008). Thought suppression in obese and non-obese restrained eaters: Piece of cake or forbidden fruit? *European Eating Disorders Review, 16(1),* 67–76. doi: 10.1002/erv.771

Soetens, B., Braet, C., Van Vlierberghe, L., & Roets, A. (2008). Resisting temptation: Effects of exposure to a forbidden food on eating behaviour. *Appetite, 51(1)*, 202–205. doi: 10.1016/j.appet.2008.01.007

Solomon, R.L., Kamin, L.J., & Wynne, L.C. (1953). Traumatic avoidance learning: The outcomes of several extinction procedures with dogs. *Journal of Abnormal Psychology, 48(2)*, 291–302. doi: 10.1037/h0058943

Somov, P.G. (2008). *Eating the moment*. Oakland, CA, US: New Harbinger Publications, Inc.

Spates, C.R., Pagoto, S., & Kalata, A. (2006). A qualitative and quantitative review of behavioral activation treatment of major depressive disorder. *The Behavior Analyst, 7(4)*, 508–521. doi: 10.1037/h0100089

Spencer, J.A., & Fremouw, W.J. (1979). Binge eating as a function of restraint and weight classification. *Journal of Abnormal Psychology, 88(3)*, 262–267. doi: 10.1037/0021-843X.88.3.262

Sperduto, W.A., Thompson, H.S., & O'Brien, R.M. (1986). The effect of target behavior monitoring on weight loss and completion rate in a behavior modification program for weight reduction. *Addictive Behaviors, 11(3)*, 337–340. doi: 10.1016/0306-4603(86)90060-2

Spiegler, M., & Guevremont, D.C. (2015). *Contemporary Behavior Therapy, 6th Edition*. Boston, MA, US: Wadsworth Publishing.

Spitzer, R.L., Yanovski, S., Wadden, T., Wing, R., Marcus, M.D., Stunkard, A., Mitchell, J., Hasin, D., & Horne, R.L. (1993). Binge eating disorder: Its further validation in a multisite study. *International Journal of Eating Disorders, 13(2)*, 137–153. doi: 10.1002/1098-108x(199303)13:2<137::aid-eat2260130202>3.0.co;2-#

Stein, D.J., Aguilar-Gaxiola, S., Alonso, J., Bruffaerts, R., de Jonge, P., Liu, Z., Caldas-de-Almeida, J.M., O'Neill, S., Viana, M.C., Al-Hamzawi, A.O., Angermeyer, M.C., Benjet, C., de Graaf, R., Ferry, F., Kovess-Masfety, V., Levinson, D., de Girolamo, G., Florescu, S., Hu, C., Kawakami, N., Haro, J.M., Piazza, M., Posada-Villa, J., Wojtyniak, B.J., Xavier, M., Lim, C.C.W., Kessler, R.C., & Scott, K.M. (2014). Associations between mental disorders and subsequent onset of hypertension. *General Hospital Psychiatry, 36(2)*, 142–149. doi: 10.1016/j.genhosppsych.2013.11.002

Stein, R.I., Kenardy, J., Wiseman, C.V., Dounchis, J.Z., Arnow, B.A., & Wilfley, D.E. (2007). What's driving the binge in binge eating disorder?: A prospective examination of precursors and consequences. *International Journal of Eating Disorders, 40(3)*, 195–203. doi: 10.1002/eat.20352

Stewart, S.H., Angelopoulos, M., Baker, J.M., & Boland, F.J. (2000). Relations between dietary restraint and patterns of alcohol use in young adult women. *Psychology of Addictive Behaviors, 14(1)*, 77–82. doi: 10.1037/0893-164X.14.1.77

Stickney, M.I., Miltenberger, R.G., & Wolff, G. (1999). A descriptive analysis of factors contributing to binge eating. *Journal of Behavior Therapy, 30(3)*, 177–189. doi: 10.1016/S0005-7916(99)00019-1

Streeter, C.C., Whitfield, T.H., Owen, L., Rein, R., Karri, S.K., Yakhkind, A., Perlmutter, R., Prescot, A., Renshaw, P.F., Ciraulo, D.A., & Jensen, J.E. (2010). Effects of yoga versus walking on mood, anxiety, and brain GABA levels: A randomized controlled MRS study. *Journal of Alternative and Complementary Medicine, 16(11)*, 1145–1152. doi: 10.1089/acm.2010.0007

Striegel-Moore, R.H., Dohm, F.A., Solomon, E.E., Fairburn, C.G., Pike, K.M., & Wilfley, D.E. (2000). Subthreshold binge eating disorder. *International Journal of Eating Disorders, 27(3)*, 270–278. doi: 10.1002/(SICI)1098-108X(200004) 27:3<270::AID-EAT3>3.0.CO;2-1

Strohle, A. (2009). Physical activity, exercise, depression and anxiety disorders. *Journal of Neural Transmission, 116(6)*, 777–784. doi: 10.1007/s00702-008-0092-x

Stroop, J.R. (1935). Studies of interference in serial verbal reactions. *Journal of Experimental Psychology, 18(6)*, 643–662. doi: 10.1037/h0054651

Swanson, S.A., Crow, S.J., Le Grange, D., Swendsen, J., & Merikangas, K.R. (2011). Prevalence and correlates of eating disorders in adolescents: Results from the national comorbidity survey replication adolescent supplement. *Archives of General Psychiatry, 68(7)*, 714–723. doi: 10.1001/archgenpsychiatry.2011.22

Swanson, S.A., Horton, N.J., Crosby, R.D., Micali, N., Sonneville, K.R., Eddy, K., & Field, A.E. (2014). A latent class analysis to empirically describe eating disorders through developmental stages. *International Journal of Eating Disorders, 47(7)*, 762–772. doi: 10.1002/eat.22308

Swartz, H.A., Frank, E., Frankel, D.R., Novick, D., & Houck, P.R. (2009). Psychotherapy as monotherapy for the treatment of bipolar II depression: A proof of concept study. *Bipolar Disorders, 11(1)*, 89–94. doi:10.1111/j. 1399-5618.2008.00629.x

Swartz, H.A., Levenson, J.C., & Frank, E. (2012). Psychotherapy for bipolar II disorder: The role of Interpersonal and Social Rhythm Therapy. *Professional Psychology: Research and Practice, 43(2)*, 145–153. doi: 10.1037/a0027671

Telch, C.F., Agras, W.S., & Linehan, M.M. (2000). Group dialectical behavior therapy for binge-eating disorder: A preliminary, uncontrolled trial. *Behavior Therapy, 31(3)*, 569–582. doi: 10.1016/S0005-7894(00)80031-3

Telch, C.F., Agras, W.S., & Linehan, M.M. (2001). Dialectical behavior therapy for binge eating disorder. *Journal of Consulting and Clinical Psychology, 69(6)*, 1061–1065. doi: 10.1037/0022-006X.69.6.1061

Thomas, J.J., Vartanian, L.R., & Brownell, K.D. (2009). The relationship between eating disorder not otherwise specified (EDNOS) and officially recognized eating disorders: Meta-analysis and implications for DSM. *Psychological Bulletin, 155(3)*, 407–433. doi: 10.1037/a0015326

Tierney, S. (2006). The dangers and draws of online communication: Pro-anorexia websites and their implications for users, practitioners, and researchers. *Eating Disorders: The Journal of Treatment and Prevention, 14(3)*, 181–190. doi: 10.1080/10640260600638865

Tsai, J.L., Simeonova, D.I., & Watanabe, J.T. (2004). Somatic and social: Chinese Americans talk about emotion. *Personality and Social Psychology Bulletin, 30(9)*, 1226–1238. doi: 10.1177/0146167204264014

Turner, H., & Bryant-Waugh, R. (2004). Eating disorder not otherwise specified (EDNOS): Profiles of clients presenting at a community eating disorder service. *European Eating Disorders Review, 12(1)*, 18–26. doi: 10.1002/erv.552

Tuschen-Caffier, B., Pook, M., & Frank, M. (2001). Evaluation of manual-based cognitive-behavioral therapy for bulimia nervosa in a service setting. *Behaviour Research & Therapy, 39(3)*, 299–308. doi: 10.1016/S0005-7967(00)00004-8

Tylka, T.L., & Hill, M.S. (2004). Objectification theory as it relates to disordered eating among college women. *Sex Roles, 51(11/12)*, 719–730. doi: 10.1007/ s11199-004-0721-2 van Strien, T. (2000). Ice-cream consumption, tendency toward overeating, and personality. *International Journal of Eating Disorders, 28(4)*, 460–464. doi: 10.1002/1098-108X(200012)28:43.0.CO;2-A

van Strien, T., & Ouwens, M.A. (2007). Effects of distress, alexithymia and impulsivity on eating. *Eating Behaviors, 8(2)*, 251–257. doi: 10.1016/j.eatbeh.2006.06.004

van Strien, T., Fritgers, J.E.R., Bergers, G.P.A., & Defares, P.B. (1986). The Dutch Eating Behavior Questionnaire (DEBQ) for assessment of restrained, emotional, and external eating behavior. *International Journal of Eating Disorders, 5(2)*, 295–315. doi: 10.1002/1098-108X(198602)5:2<295::AID-EAT2260050209>3.0.CO;2-T

van Strien, T., Engels, R.C.M.E., van Leeuwe, J., & Snoek, H.M. (2005). The Stice model of overeating: Tests in clinical and non-clinical samples. *Appetite, 45(3)*, 205–213. doi: 10.1016/j.appet.2005.08.004

Veasey, R.C., Gonzalez, J.T., Kennedy, D.O., Haskell, C.F., & Stevenson, E.J. (2013). Breakfast consumption and exercise interact to affect cognitive performance and mood later in the day. A randomized controlled trial. *Appetite, 68*, 38–44. doi: 10.1016/j.appet.2013.04.011

Vitousek, K.B., & Hollon, S.D. (1990). The investigation of schematic content and processing in eating disorders. *Cognitive Therapy and Research, 14(2)*, 191–214. doi: 10.1007/BF01176209

Vocks, S., Wächter, A., Wucherer, M., & Kosfelder, J. (2008). Look at yourself: Can body image therapy affect the cognitive and emotional response to seeing oneself in the mirror in eating disorders? *European Eating Disorders Review, 16(2)*, 147–154. doi: 10.1002/erv.825

Wachtel, E.F. (1976). The multiple meanings of symptoms: A case illustration. *Psychotherapy: Theory, Research, and Practice, 13(3)*, 219–224. doi: 10.1037/h0088344

Waller, G., & Hodgson, S. (1996). Body image distortion in anorexia and bulimia nervosa: The role of perceived and actual control. *Journal of Nervous and Mental Disease, 184(4)*, 213–219. doi: 10.1097/00005053-199604000-00003

Watson, J.B., & Rayner, R. (1920). Conditioned emotional responses. *Journal of Experimental Psychology, 3(1)*, 1–14.

Wechsler, H., & Nelson, T.F. (2001). Binge drinking and the American college student: What's five drinks? *Psychology of Addictive Behaviors, 15(4)*, 287–291. doi: 10.1037//0893-164X.15.4.28

Wechsler, H., Davenport, A., Dowdall, G., Moeykens, B., & Castillo, S. (1994). Health and behavioral consequences of binge drinking in college: A national survey of students at 140 campuses. *Journal of the American Medical Association, 272(21)*, 1672–1677. doi: 10.1001/jama.272.21.1672

Wegner, D.M., & Erber, R.E. (1992). The hyperaccessibility of suppressed thoughts. *Journal of Personality and Social Psychology, 63(6)*, 903–912. doi: 10.1037/0022-3514.63.6.903

Wegner, D.M., & Zanakos, S. (1994). Chronic thought suppression. *Journal of Personality, 62(4)*, 615–640. doi: 10.1111/j.1467-6494.1994.tb00311.x

Wegner, D.M., Schneider, D.J., Carter, S.P., III, & White, T.L. (1987). Paradoxical effects of thought suppression. *Journal of Personality and Social Psychology, 53(5)*, 413–426. doi: 10.1037/0022-3514.53.1.5

Wells, A., & Davies, M.I. (1994). The thought control questionnaire: A measure of individual differences in the control of unwanted thoughts. *Behaviour Research and Therapy, 32(8)*, 871–878. doi: 10.1016/0005-7967(94)90168-6

Wenzlaff, R.M., & Wegner, D.M. (2000). Thought suppression. *Annual Review of Psychology, 51,* 51–91. doi: 10.1146/annurev.psych.51.1.59

Wiebking, C., Duncan, N.W., Tiret, B., Hayes, D.J., Marjanska, M., Doyon, J., Bajbouj, M., & Northoff, G. (2014). GABA in the insula – a predictor of the neural response to interoceptive awareness. *Neuroimage, 86,* 10–18. doi: 10.1016/j.neuroimage.2013.04.042.

Wiebking, C., de Greck, H., Duncan, N.W., Tempelmann, C., Bajbouj, M., & Northoff, G. (2015). Interoception in insula subregions as a possible state marker for depression – an exploratory fMRI study investigating healthy, depressed, and remitted participants. *Frontiers in Behavioral Neuroscience, 9(82).* doi: 10.3389/fnbeh.2015.00082

Wierenga, C., Ely, A., Bischoff-Grethe, A., Bailer, U.F., Simmons, A.N., & Kaye, W.H. (2014). Are extremes of consumption in eating disorders related to an altered balance between reward and inhibition? *Frontiers in Behavioral Neuroscience, 8,* 410. doi: 10.3389/fnbeh.2014.00410

Wildes, J.E., Forbush, K.T., & Markon, K.E. (2013). Characteristics and stability of empirically derived anorexia nervosa subtypes: Towards the identification of homogeneous low-weight eating disorder phenotypes. *Journal of Abnormal Psychology, 122(4),* 1031–1041. doi: 10.1037/a0034676

Wilfley, D.E., Welch, R.R., Stein, R.I., Spurrell, E.B., Cohen, L.R., Saelens, B.E., Dounchis, J.Z., Frank, M.A., Wiseman, C.V., & Matt, G.E. (2002). A randomized comparison of group cognitive-behavioral therapy and group interpersonal psychotherapy for the treatment of overweight individuals with binge-eating disorder. *Archives of General Psychiatry, 59(8),* 713–721. doi: 10.1001/archpsyc.59.8.713

Wilson, G.T. (1999). Cognitive behavior therapy for eating disorders: Progress and problems. *Behaviour Research & Therapy, 37,* S79–S95. doi: 10.1016/S0005-7967(99)00051-0

Wilson, G.T. (2004). Acceptance and change in the treatment of eating disorders: The evolution of manual-based cognitive therapy. In S.C. Hayes, V.M. Follette, & M.M. Linehan (Eds.), *Mindfulness and acceptance: Expanding the cognitive-behavioral tradition* (pp. 243–260). New York, NY: Guilford Press.

Wirz-Justice, A., Benedetti, F., Berger, M., Lam, R.W., Martiny, K., Terman, M., & Wu, J.C. (2005). Chronotherapeutics (light and wake therapy) in affective disorders. *Psychological Medicine, 35(7),* 939–944. doi: 10.1017/S003329170500437X

Wiser, S., & Telch, C.F. (1999). Dialectical behavior therapy for binge eating disorder. *Journal of Clinical Psychology, 55(6),* 765–768. doi: 10.1002/(SICI)1097-4679(199906)55:6<755::AID-JCLP8>3.0.CO;2-R

Wisniewski, L., & Kelly, E. (2003). The application of dialectical behavior therapy to the treatment of eating disorders. *Cognitive and Behavioral Practice, 10(2),* 131–138. doi: 10.1016/S1077-7229(03)80021-4

Wolpe, J. (1958). *Psychotherapy by reciprocal inhibition.* Stanford, CA, US: Stanford University Press.

Wonderlich, S.A., Joiner, T.E. Jr., Keel, P.K., Williamson, D.A., & Crosby, R.D. (2007). Eating disorder diagnoses: Empirical approaches to classification. *American Psychologist, 62(3),* 167–180. doi: 10.1037/0003-066X.62.3.167

Woody, E.Z., Costanzo, P.R., Liefer, H., & Conger, J. (1981). The effect of taste and caloric perceptions on the eating behavior of restrained and unrestrained subjects. *Cognitive Therapy and Research, 5(4),* 381–390. doi: 10.1007/BF01173690

Woolhouse, H., Knowles, A., & Crafti, N. (2012). Adding mindfulness to CBT programs for binge eating: A mixed-methods evaluation. *Eating Disorders: The Journal of Treatment and Prevention, 20(4)*, 321–339. doi: 10.1080/10640266.2012.691791

Wyland, C.L., Kelley, W.M., Macrae, C.N., Gordon, H.L., & Heatherton, T.F. (2003). Neural correlates of thought suppression. *Neuropsychologia, 41(14)*, 1863–1867. doi: 10.1016/j.neuropsychologia.2003.08.001

Zanetti, T., Santonastaso, P., Sgaravatti, E., Degortes, D., & Favaro, A. (2013). Clinical and temperamental correlates of body image disturbance in eating disorders. *European Eating Disorders Review, 21(1)*, 32–37. doi: 10.1002/erv.2190

Zastrow, A., Kaiser, S., Stippich, C., Walther, S., Herzog, W., Tchanturia, K., Belger, A., Weisbrod, M., Treasure, J., & Friederich, H. (2009). Neural correlates of impaired cognitive-behavioral flexibility in anorexia nervosa. *American Journal of Psychiatry, 166(5)*, 608–616. doi: 10.1176/appi.ajp.2008.08050775

Zotter, D.L., & Crowther, J.H. (1991). The role of cognitions in bulimia nervosa. *Cognitive Research and Therapy, 15(5)*, 413–426. doi: 10.1007/BF01173035

Index